BOOK OF REVEAL: HIDDEN SINSATIONS

BOOK OF REVEAL: HIDDEN SINSATIONS

THE CURSE OF HAM & DESCENDANTS OF SUMERIA

By K.L. Crawford
From Our Lie, Life

Copyright © 2024 by K.L. Crawford
All rights reserved. This book or any portion thereof may not be reproduced or used in any manner whatsoever without the express written permission of the publisher except for the use of brief quotations in a book review.

Printed in the United States of America
tri-intelligentsia, 2024

ISBN (Paperback): 979-8-218-41422-1
ISBN (Hardback): 979-8-218-45460-9
ISBN (eBook): 979-8-218-45461-6

Book design by Coverkitchen

www.bookofreveal.com

"That's why I gotta break the curses that were set for me
This is hard work workin', this ain't destiny
My motivation is just lookin' at my family tree
I'm tryna make sure I contribute for the legacy
Once again the clouds are gatherin'
(once again, once agai-again, once)
To release what they held in (once again, once agai-again, once)
Once again the clouds are gatherin'
To release what they held in"

"Talking" - Ye + Ty Dolla Sign

Dedication:
all under the sun (hammah).

θ

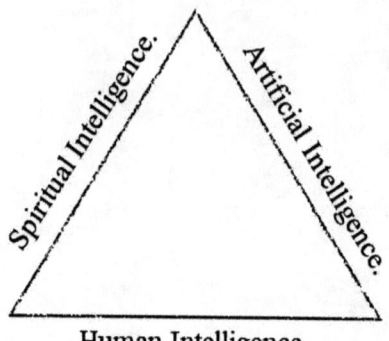

Acknowledgments

Adam D'Angelo (Quora, Poe) ♦ Andre Romell Young
Anthony E. Ray ♦ Anthony George Morris ♦ Antoine Carraby

Billy Carson ♦ Bruce H. Lipton Ph.D. ♦ Byran Van Norden

Cathy Sutton ♦ Chad Meredith Hurley
Christopher Langan ♦ Clifton Daggett Gray
Cornel West ♦ Cydel Charles Young ♦ Cynthia Resser

Damon Dash ♦ Dave Chappelle ♦ Dr. Andrea Myers Achi
Dr. Delbert Blair ♦ Dr. Narco Longo

Edward F. Sandeman ♦ Eric Lynn Wright

Fredrick Allen Hampton Sr.

George Carlin ♦ George Edward Ellis
George Smith ♦ Graham Hancock

Hans G. Guterbock

Irving Finkel ♦ Ivan Van Sertima

James Ivy Richardson II ♦ Jawed Karim ♦ Jibrial Muhammad
Jimmy Donal Wales ♦ Jirka Rysavy (Gaia) ♦ Joseph James Rogan

K.J. Wetherholt ♦ Kaba Hiawatha Kamene
Kendrick Lamar Duckworth ("GOD.", "FEAR.")

Lauryn Noelle Hill ♦ Lawrence "Kris" Parker
Lawrence Mark Sanger ♦ Leo Wiener
Lex Fridman ♦ Lorenzo Jerald Patterson

Malcolm X ✦ Martin Luther King Jr.
Matt LaCroix ✦ Micah "Katt" Williams
Muhammad Ali ✦ Michael Joseph Jackson

Nelson Mandela

O'Shea Jackson Sr.

Paul Mooney ✦ Pharrell Williams
Phylicia Rashad ✦ Prince Rogers Nelson
Professor James Small ✦ Professor Norman Finkelstein

R.H. Charles ✦ Richard Claxton Gregory
Richard Rudd ✦ Robert Edward Grant ✦ Ronald Dalton Jr.

Sadhguru
Scott Wolter (Templar Knight & Forensic Geologist)
Sir Henry Creswicke Rawlinson ✦ Steve Chen

Timothy Hogan (Grandmaster of Knights Templar)[1]

Vladimir Ivanov

Wasalu Muhammad Jaco ✦ Whitney Alyse Webb
Whoopi Goldberg, ✦ William Henry Cosby Jr.

Ye ("HAM", "Moon", "Stars", "Talking", "Never Let You Down", "Jesus Walks", "Heaven and Hell")

al-Battani

---

[1] Gaia, Timothy Hogan, and Scott Wolter. (2024, March 29). Atlantean Secrets revealed by the Knights Templar [Video]. YouTube. 27:27 https://www.youtube.com/watch?v=wLjdgOe-LpA

TABLE OF CONTENTS

PREFACE 21
REVEALING THE HISTORICAL IMPLICATIONS OF
ETHNIC CLEANSING.. 21
SPIRITUALITY IN METADATA, METAPHORS,
METAPHYSICS, AND MATRIARCH... 23

CHAPTER 1
A Broader Review of the Curse
First Sin... 31
INTRODUCTION 31
ETHNIC CLEANSING.. 32
GENOCIDE... 33
ETHNIC CLEANSING V. GENOCIDE 34
CURSE OF HAM 36
COMPOSING THE CURSE 37
TIMING THE CURSE 37
INTERPRETING THE CURSE.. 38
    Literal Application 39

COUNTERING THE CURSE 40
  Hymns 41
CURSED U.S. 44
  Preset for Racism 44
  American Slavery 45
  U.S. Constitution 46
  Slave Patrol 50
  Tulsa Race Massacre 51
  Civil Rights Movement 52
POOR PEOPLE 54
  Sterilization of America 54
  Sterilization Abroad 56

CHAPTER 2
A Review of The Hidden Sins
Second Sin 63
INTRODUCTION 63
COLÓN (COLONIZE) 64
AMERICA 66
  Semitic Derivation 67
HOLY ROMAN EMPIRE 68
UNITED BRETHREN 71
  Powerscourt Conference: U.K. 71
  Scofield Reference Bible 72
RHODES TO APARTHEID 73
EMPIRIC RISE OF ZIONISM 75
CONSCRIPTION: 1917 75
  United Zionism 75
  The "Catastrophe" 77
NIGER-CONGO II: FREE STATE 78
  King Leopold II 78
  Deputation 79

PATTERNS 79
    Zionist Migration 79
    Niger-Congolese Parallels 80

CHAPTER 3
A Biblical And Sumerian Analysis
Third Sin 87
INTRODUCTION 87
NATION CLEANSING, NAMING CONVENTIONS,
AND A NON-CANONICAL BOOK 88
    The World as Known to the Hebrews 89
    Table of Nations 93
    Surname 95
    Father of many Nations 98
    Book of Jubilees 98
MATRIARCH 99
    Paternal v. Maternal 101
    Maternal & Paternal 102
    Intertwined 102
    Notable Matriarchs 103
DELIBERATE DECEPTION 106

CHAPTER 4
A Loss Analysis
Fourth Sin 113
INTRODUCTION 113
LOST TRIBES 113
LOST CITIES 115
LOST ALPHABET 116
LOST LAW 117
LOST ART 118
LOST CULTURE 121

  Africa 121
  America⁺ 121
 LOST SOULS (SOL) 122
  Sun God 122
  Child of Light 124
  Sumerian Trinity 125
  Sumerian Origins 126
  Church in Antioch 129
  Places of Worship 131
  Sumerian-Semitic Parallelisms 133
  Cultural Comparisons 134

CHAPTER 5
An Analysis of Sins
Fifth Sin 145
 INTRODUCTION 145
 SIN 145
  Human Experience 146
  Human Existence 146
  Human Nature 147
  Revelation 12 148
 CONCLUSION 151

APPENDIX 167
AN ONOMASTIC REVIEW OF HAM 167

BIBLIOGRAPHY 215
MAPS & IMAGES 243

PREFACE

REVEALING THE HISTORICAL IMPLICATIONS OF ETHNIC CLEANSING

When critically assessing the potential ramifications of negative portrayals and the historical suppression of a group's identity and heritage, it is imperative to adopt a discerning and insightful lens. If one were to consider the possibility that the Hamites[2] are descendants of the Sumerian sun deity Shamash,[3456] the significant damage

---

[2] Goldenberg, David M. "Was Ham Black?" The Curse of Ham: Race and Slavery in Early Judaism, Christianity, and Islam. (Princeton University Press). p. 144. https://books.google.com/books?id=iTyJ3HiNO-AsC&q=burnt+swarthy+black&pg=PA144#v=snippet&q=burnt%20swarthy%20black&f=false

[3] Woolley, Leonard. 1931. "Shamash." The British Museum. 2000BC-1750BC. https://www.britishmuseum.org/collection/object/W_1931-1010-2

[4] Jacobsen, Thorkild and The Oriental Institute of the University of Chicago. The Sumerian King List. Edited by John A. Wilson and Thomas George Allen. Uploaded by Misty and Lewis Gruber. Assyriological Studies. Fourth. 1939. Reprint, The University of Chicago Press, 1939, pp. 83."Be mindful of Shamash" https://isac.uchicago.edu/sites/default/files/uploads/shared/docs/as11.pdf

[5] Encyclopaedia Judaica. (2007). Sun. Jewish Virtual Library. https://www.jewishvirtuallibrary.org/sun

[6] Gebhard J. Selz, Piotr Michalowski, Paul John Frandsen, Irene J. Winter, Erica Ehrenberg, Clemens Reichel, Reinhard Bernbeck, Michelle Gilbert, David Freidel, Michael Puett, Bruce Lincoln, Greg Woolf, Jerrold S. Cooper, & Kath-

inflicted upon them becomes a more relevant concern. This damage encompasses not only psychological impacts but also factors such as displacement, physical harm, and social marginalization.

The implications of these historical distortions and the alleged secrecy surrounding this knowledge, purportedly preserved through various channels including religious institutions, universities, and other groups warrant careful consideration. This raises important questions about the responsibilities of these institutions in perpetuating, or concealing, certain narratives and the subsequent effects on the affected communities. Exploring the potential harm caused by these dynamics necessitates an interdisciplinary approach encompassing perspectives from history, anthropology, religious studies, sociology, and other relevant fields. By critically analyzing primary sources and engaging in inclusive dialogues, a better understanding of the complexities and consequences of historical misrepresentations can be achieved.

This book's primary focus is the meticulous exploration of historical and contemporary events, serving as a companion piece to biblical, Sumerian, and African history. It aims to provide a comprehensive account of what transpired, including the sequence and interplay of occurrences over time, the underlying mechanisms of these events, the geographical context in which these actions take place, and an inquiry into the agency and identity of the alleged individuals or groups involved. Through its exploration, Book of Reveal: Hidden Sinsations aims to illustrate the profound implications of ethnic cleansing and genocide across different ethnic groups, in particular through the biblical Curse of Ham, shedding light on the enduring impact of these defined atrocities on modern societies.

---

leen D. Morrison. (2008). *Religion and Power: Divine Kingship in the ancient world and beyond*. In N. Brisch (Ed.), The Oriental Institute Seminars: Vol. Number 4. The Oriental Institute, Chicago. https://isac.uchicago.edu/sites/default/files/uploads/shared/docs/ois4.pdf

PREFACE

SPIRITUALITY IN METADATA, METAPHORS, METAPHYSICS, AND MATRIARCH

The examination of naming conventions, as a form of metadata, may reveal invaluable insights into the cultural and religious practices of past civilizations. In the case of Shamash, a sun deity associated with Mesopotamian mythology, scrutinizing onomastic[7] connections may uncover resemblances or shared origins with the biblical figure of Ham. This linguistic analysis serves to identify potential links between the names, thereby shedding light on plausible religious, cultural, or historical interactions when considering Abram's migration from Mesopotamia to Canaan, an extension of the Hamitic region.[8][9]

For instance, John 8 offers valuable context for thematic elements found in the Bible, such as the concept of "light of the world," "son of mankind," "judgment," and "sin" in comparison to Shamash in Sumerian history.[10][11][12] In religious and spiritual practices, the Shamash

---

[7] Zgusta, Ladislav. 2024. "The science of onomastics." Encyclopedia Britannica. March 12, 2024. https://www.britannica.com/topic/name/The-science-of-onomastics

[8] Flow, Christian B., and Rachel B Nolan. 2006. "'Go Forth From Your Country': Negotiation expert plans multi-national retracing of Abraham's path." The Harvard Crimson. November 16, 2006. https://www.thecrimson.com/article/2006/11/16/go-forth-from-your-country-for/

[9] Trimm, C. (2022, March 15). The Destruction of the Canaanites: God, Genocide, and Biblical Interpretation. Amazon. https://www.amazon.com/Destruction-Canaanites-Genocide-Biblical-Interpretation/dp/0802879624

[10] Bible Gateway. John 8. NIV. https://web.mit.edu/jywang/www/cef/Bible/NIV/NIV_Bible/JOHN+8.html

[11] Güterbock, Hans G. "The Composition of Hittite Prayers to the Sun. Journal of the American Oriental Society 78, no. 4 (1958): 237–45, pp. 241, "son of mankind" https://www.jstor.org/stable/595787

[12] Gray, Clifton Daggett. The Šamaš Religious Texts Classified in the British Museum Catalogue as Hymns, Prayers, and Incantations, with Twenty Plates of Texts Hitherto Unpublished, and a Transliteration and Translation of K.3182. 1901. Internet Archive, pp. 13, "light of the world" https://archive.org/details/samasreligiouste00grayrich

Candle[13] in Jewish tradition, is often associated with illumination, enlightenment, and divine presence. Its symbolic representation of light aligns with the metaphorical understanding of light as a source of knowledge, guidance, and spiritual awakening. This symbolism resonates with the biblical theme of the "light of the world," which is often attributed to Christ and his teachings. The concept of being "children of light" is rooted in the biblical imagery of believers being called to embody and reflect the divine light in their lives. This metaphorical understanding emphasizes the pursuit of righteousness, truth, and moral integrity while the Shamash Candle, as a symbol of light, reinforces this metaphorical connection by providing a tangible representation of the spiritual illumination and the call to bearers of light in the world.

Another inference found in the etymology of the term "Jew" reveals its derivation from the name "Judah," indicative of the ancestral linkage that Jews perceive with this particular tribe. Over the course of history, Jews have maintained a collective sense of identity and heritage rooted in their lineage tracing back to Judah. However, within the biblical narrative, a notable occurrence unfolds as Judah engages in relations with Tamar, which results in her assuming the role of the maternal progenitor within the genealogy of the Jewish people. This event assumes exceptional significance due to the subsequent birth of Perez, and the lineage to Christ. It is pertinent to note that this association with the Hamitic Canaanite lineage, as traditionally construed, imparts an additional layer of diverse ancestral elements that have exerted influence on the development of Jewish identity throughout the ages.[14]

---

[13] Becher, M. (n.d.). The Laws of Chanukah. Ohr Somayach. "the shamash" https://ohr.edu/1304

[14] Amit, Yairah. "Tamar, From Victim to Mother of a Dynasty." In *Oxford University Press eBooks*, 294–305, 2013. https://academic.oup.com/book/3782/chapter-abstract/145230184?redirectedFrom=fulltext

Tracing the maternal bloodline entails an exploration of genealogical records and historical texts to delve into the transmission of lineage through maternal descent. This approach can provide valuable information regarding the intermingling of diverse ethnic groups, including the potential movement of individuals between Mesopotamia and regions associated with Ham, such as Africa. By scrutinizing matrilineal connections, scholars can unveil latent narratives and investigate the intergenerational transmission of religious beliefs and practices.[15]

"Thomas Hobbes shared Descrates's radical metaphysical individualism, arguing that there is 'nothing in the world universal but names, for the things named are every one of them individual and singular.'"[16]

---

[15] Paz, Reut Yael: The Stubborn Subversiveness of Judaism's Matrilineal Principle, VerfBlog, 2021/9/29, https://verfassungsblog.de/the-stubborn-subversiveness-of-judaisms-matrilineal-principle/

[16] Bryan W. Van Norden. Foreword by Jay L. Garfield. "Taking Back Philosophy: A Multicultural Manifesto" February 22, 2017. https://cup.columbia.edu/book/taking-back-philosophy/9780231184373

02/20/2021 at 5:33 AM
I thought I was dreaming
but, it didn't feel like a dream
I woke up to a written note on my phone,
thinking I was lucid-dreaming.

A warmth consumed my body, and I heard a voice—it wasn't a booming voice, just a voice. The message was so off-center and vague that it stayed. Thinking something was wrong with me amidst a hardship, that next morning I checked my notes and confirmed what I heard. The voice said, "Don't leave the energy, that turns to sin." Sin is Shamash's father in Sumerian history, which I believe with some certainty, is Ham in the Bible. I came across this a week before Black History Month this year when reviewing biblical names with "ham" as an onomastic data element in an attempt to trace African American lineage that was ethnically cleansed. Out of curiosity, I performed a search for "ham" in the Sumerian King List, and "Be mindful of Shamash" appeared as a result. I was taken aback, literally jumped, and walked away from my computer, when I saw Shamash's father was Nanna, also known as Sin.

hum(an)[17]
hu(man)[18]

---

[17] Bible Gateway. John 1:1-5 (NIV). https://web.mit.edu/jywang/www/cef/Bible/NIV/NIV_Bible/JOHN+1.html
[18] Bible Gateway. Genesis 1:1-3 (NIV). https://web.mit.edu/jywang/www/cef/Bible/NIV/NIV_Bible/GEN+1.html

CHAPTER 1
A Broader Review of the Curse

First Sin

INTRODUCTION

This chapter undertakes a far-reaching examination of the theological and historical underpinnings of "the Curse". It situates this discourse within the broader contexts of ethnic cleansing and genocide, analyzing the nuanced distinctions and common threads between these concepts as they pertain to the biblical text and its interpretations. A deep dive into the origins and evolution of the "Curse of Ham" follows unpacking the complex ways in which this theologically grounded trope has been leveraged to justify horrific acts of oppression and violence against marginalized populations. The construction and timing of this purported "curse" are scrutinized, while also exploring various attempts to challenge and counter its pernicious influence.

The analysis turns to the American context, exposing how this cursory biblical notion has become woven into the very fabric of the United States' foundational documents and institutions—from the Constitution to the racist structures of the slave patrols. The devastating real-world implications are laid bare through an examination of flashpoints such as the Tulsa

Race Massacre. The chapter contextualizes this dark legacy within the broader arc of the Civil Rights Movement, highlighting how communities have resisted and rejected the theological justifications for their subjugation. Throughout, the chapter maintains a critical, scholarly distance while bearing witness to the human toll of these longstanding, theologically grounded systems of oppression.

ETHNIC CLEANSING

Ethnic cleansing, a distressing and morally reprehensible phenomenon, has exerted profound historical ramifications. It entails the deliberate and systematic eradication or expulsion of a specific ethnic, racial, or religious group from a designated geographical area, with the aim of establishing homogeneity or dominance by another group.[19] This brutal act of violence and displacement has inflicted immeasurable suffering and left indelible scars on individuals, communities, and societies. The grim reality of ethnic cleansing often encompasses a range of ruthless tactics, including mass killings, forced displacement, sexual violence, torture, and the deliberate destruction of cultural heritage. It is underpinned by a toxic amalgamation of prejudice, discrimination, and the pursuit of power. Perpetrators frequently justify their actions through ideologies of racial or religious superiority, as well as territorial ambitions. Throughout history, numerous instances of ethnic cleansing have unfolded, from the Holocaust during World War II, the Rwandan genocide in 1994, conflicts in the Balkans, Myanmar,

---

[19] United Nations. (n.d.). Ethnic Cleansing. United Nations Office on Genocide Prevention and the Responsibility to Protect. https://www.un.org/en/genocideprevention/ethnic-cleansing.shtml

Sudan, China with the Uyghurs, Dominican Republic with Dominicans of Haitian descent, and now Gaza.

The ramifications of ethnic cleansing are far-reaching and devastating. The targeted group experiences grievous losses, encompassing both loss of life and the obliteration of their cultural identity. Displaced individuals often face an uncertain future as refugees, grappling with the challenges of seeking safety, shelter, and the means to rebuild shattered lives. The long-term consequences for the social fabric of a society are equally profound, as ethnic divisions deepen, trust erodes, and the potential for future conflicts escalates. From an ethical and legal standpoint, ethnic cleansing is unequivocally condemned. It is classified as a crime against humanity under international law, rendering those responsible for orchestrating or participating in such acts liable to be held accountable for their atrocities. The international community has endeavored to prevent and respond to ethnic cleansing through mechanisms such as international tribunals, peacekeeping operations, and diplomatic negotiations. However, effectively addressing and averting ethnic cleansing present formidable challenges, necessitating unwavering commitment to human rights, justice, and the promotion of inclusive societies. By exploring the historical and contemporary manifestations of ethnic cleansing, it is my aspiration to foster heightened awareness and understanding, ultimately contributing to the prevention of such abominations and the cultivation of peace, tolerance, and reverence for diversity.

GENOCIDE

The term "genocide" holds a distinct legal significance within the framework of international law. It is defined as a specific category of crime under the 1948 United Nations Convention on the Prevention and Punishment of the Crime of Genocide, commonly known as the

Genocide Convention.[20] This convention was adopted by the United Nations General Assembly and has garnered ratification from numerous countries worldwide. According to Article II of the Genocide Convention, genocide involves the commission of certain acts with the intent to destroy, either wholly or partially, a national, ethnical, racial, or religious group. These acts include killing members of the group, inflicting serious bodily or mental harm, imposing conditions of life aimed at the physical destruction of the group, implementing measures to prevent births within the group, and forcibly transferring children of the group to another group.

The Genocide Convention recognizes these acts as criminal offenses, subject to punishment under both domestic and international law. It is important to note that the legal definition of genocide necessitates the specific intent to destroy a protected group and does not apply to all forms of mass violence or human rights abuses. The crime of genocide is widely regarded as one of the most severe offenses against humanity due to its grave and systematic nature holding paramount importance within international human rights and humanitarian law.

ETHNIC CLEANSING V. GENOCIDE

Genocide and ethnic cleansing are distinct but interconnected phenomena within mass violence and human rights abuses.[21] Genocide, by definition, involves intentional acts aimed at the destruction, either wholly or partially, of a national, ethnic, racial, or religious

---

[20] United Nations. (1948). Convention on the Prevention and Punishment of the Crime of Genocide. In United Nations. https://www.un.org/en/genocideprevention/documents/atrocity-crimes/Doc.1_Convention%20on%20the%20Prevention%20and%20Punishment%20of%20the%20Crime%20of%20Genocide.pdf

[21] Lieberman, Benjamin, 'Ethnic Cleansing' versus Genocide?, in Donald Bloxham, and A. Dirk Moses (eds), *The Oxford Handbook of Genocide Studies* (2010; online edn, Oxford Academic, 18 Sept. 2012), https://academic.oup.com/edited-volume/40215/chapter-abstract/344567514

group. The perpetration of genocide requires a specific intent to bring about the demise of the targeted group. In contrast, ethnic cleansing entails the systematic removal, displacement, or expulsion of a particular ethnic, religious, or racial group from a specific geographic area. This process is often executed through various means, including violence, intimidation, or coercion.

The intent behind genocide is to annihilate the protected group, while ethnic cleansing is primarily driven by the goal of creating an ethnically homogeneous region or territory. While genocide encompasses a range of acts such as killings, causing bodily or mental harm, imposing conditions of life conducive to physical destruction, preventing births, and forcibly transferring children, ethnic cleansing involves acts like forced displacement, expulsion, mass killings, rape, torture, destruction of property, and cultural heritage.

From a legal perspective, genocide is recognized as a crime under international law, explicitly defined and prohibited by the Genocide Convention. Perpetrators can be held accountable for this crime, and its commission carries severe penalties. On the other hand, ethnic cleansing is not expressly delineated as a distinct crime under international law. However, the acts associated with ethnic cleansing can constitute other offenses, such as crimes against humanity or war crimes, depending on the circumstances.

In terms of scope, genocide targets a specific national, ethnic, racial, or religious group, irrespective of the population size; however, ethnic cleansing, while also directed at a particular group, may not necessarily seek its complete destruction. Instead, its objectives often revolve around altering the demographic composition of a region or achieving particular political goals.

CURSE OF HAM

Regrettably, throughout history, the Curse of Ham[22] ("the curse") has been distorted and employed as a theological and ideological justification for racial discrimination, slavery, and the subjugation of African peoples. Particularly during the era of transatlantic slavery, proponents of the institution erroneously invoked this narrative to validate the enslavement of Africans, perpetuating notions of racial inferiority and justifying the inhumane treatment and exploitation of enslaved individuals. It is crucial to recognize that biblical scholars and theologians have engaged in extensive debates regarding the proper interpretation of the Curse of Ham.[23] Many argue against viewing it as a divine endorsement of slavery or a hierarchical racial order--but rather as a specific curse directed at Canaan and his descendants within the particular cultural and historical context of ancient Near Eastern societies. They emphasize that the broader principles promoted by the Bible, such as justice, equality, and human dignity, transcend any purported curse.

Nevertheless, the historical impact of the Curse of Ham cannot be understated. It significantly contributed to the development and perpetuation of racist ideologies, particularly during the periods of colonialism and slavery. These ideologies, rooted in notions of racial superiority and inferiority, have had enduring consequences, manifesting in systemic racism, discrimination, and ongoing social inequalities that persist in various forms across the globe.

---

[22] M. Goldenberg, D. (2005, April 7). The Curse of Ham: Race and Slavery in Early Judaism, Christianity, and Islam. Princeton University Press. https://press.princeton.edu/books/paperback/9780691123707/the-curse-of-ham

[23] Bergsma, J. S.; Hahn, S. W. (2005). Noah's Nakedness and the Curse on Canaan (Genesis 9:20–27) (PDF). *Journal of Biblical Literature*. 124 (1): 25–40. https://www.jstor.org/stable/30040989

CHAPTER I

COMPOSING THE CURSE

Traditional Jewish and Christian beliefs ascribe the authorship of Genesis, along with the entirety of the Pentateuch, to Moses. According to this viewpoint, Moses received divine revelation and transcribed the accounts of creation, the flood, and other significant events.

However, contemporary biblical scholarship employs diverse methodologies to examine the authorship of biblical texts. Scholars acknowledge that the composition of Genesis involved a complex process of compilation, editing, and redaction over an extended period of time.[24] The book incorporates various sources and traditions that were interwoven to form the final text which makes determining the specific author or authors of the Curse of Ham narrative within Genesis presents a challenge. The narrative is part of the broader Noah and his sons account, which scholars attribute to distinct sources and traditions subsequently merged together. These sources are commonly identified as the Yahwist (J), Elohist (E), Priestly (P), and Deuteronomist (D) sources.[25] The composite nature of the biblical text, reflecting a rich cultural and literary history of ancient Israel, underscores the intricacy of authorship analysis. Consequently, a consensus regarding precise authorship attributions for individual sections within the book of Genesis has not been universally established.

TIMING THE CURSE

The narrative of the curse is recounted in the book of Genesis, a foundational text within the Hebrew Bible and the Old Testament of

---

[24] The Editors of Encyclopaedia Britannica. (2010, January 13). Redaction criticism | Textual Analysis, Source Criticism, Synoptic Gospels. Encyclopedia Britannica. https://www.britannica.com/topic/redaction-criticism

[25] L. McKenzie, S. (1998, January 1). The Hebrew Bible Today: An Introduction to Critical Issues. Google Books, pp. 9. https://books.google.com/books?id=owwhpmIVgSAC&q=fifth#v=snippet&q=fifth&f=false

the three religions of Abraham—Judaism, Christianity, and Islam.[26] Determining the precise time of its composition poses a challenge due to the complex nature of the biblical text and its development over time. However, scholars generally concur that the book of Genesis, along with the broader Pentateuch (comprising Genesis, Exodus,[27] Leviticus, Numbers, and Deuteronomy), underwent a process of compilation and redaction during the first millennium BCE. The specific passage involving the Curse of Ham is situated in Genesis 9:20-27 which is attributed to the priestly source, denoted as the P source, which represents one of the textual strands interwoven in the composition of the Pentateuch. It is noteworthy to recognize that the Pentateuch is a composite work, reflecting the amalgamation of earlier traditions, oral transmissions, and editorial processes that took place over an extended period. The oral transmission of biblical narratives before its eventual transcription into written form, including those associated with Sumerian history, adds additional complexities to the dating of the Curse of Ham narrative.

INTERPRETING THE CURSE

The biblical perspective on cursing encompasses various aspects that can be examined. The Bible offers guidance regarding the use of language and the significance of words, particularly in relation to cursing others and cursing God.

In terms of cursing[28] others, the biblical teachings advocate for a compassionate and benevolent approach. The New Testament, in

---

[26] Department of History. "The Abrahamic Religions: A Very Short Introduction," December 7, 2023. https://history.wisc.edu/publications/the-abrahamic-religions-a-very-short-introduction/

[27] Christopher Eames. What is the correct time frame for the exodus and conquest of the promised land? Armstrong Institute of Biblical Archeology. https://armstronginstitute.org/350-what-is-the-correct-time-frame-for-the-exodus-and-conquest-of-the-promised-land

[28] curse. (2024). In Merriam-Webster Dictionary. https://www.merriam-webster.

particular, presents the teachings of Christ, who emphasizes the principles of love, forgiveness, and blessing even towards one's enemies. Christ encourages his followers to bless those who curse them and to pray for those who mistreat them, exemplifying an ethic of kindness and non-retaliation. The apostle Paul, in his epistles, echoes this sentiment by urging believers not to repay evil with evil but to bless others instead. The underlying message is one of promoting harmony and reconciliation, rather than perpetuating conflict through cursing or ill will. A key theme that emerges from biblical teachings is the recognition of the power of words. Proverbs 18:21 poignantly states, "The tongue has the power of life and death, and those who love it will eat its fruit."[29] This verse underscores the significant influence words possess, both in shaping interpersonal relationships and impacting personal well-being.

Moreover, the Old Testament contains instances where blessings and curses are associated with obedience or disobedience to divine commands. For instance, in the book of Deuteronomy, blessings are promised to those who faithfully follow God's ways, while curses are pronounced on those who deviate from the path of righteousness. These passages reflect an understanding of the moral consequences that can accompany human actions and words. The underlying message encourages individuals to utilize their words to build up, encourage, and demonstrate love towards others. Simultaneously, it cautions against employing language that is disrespectful, harmful, or dishonoring to God or fellow human beings.

Literal Application

When the Curse of Ham is taken literally, without due consideration of its historical and cultural context, it opens the door to various distortions:

---

[29] com/dictionary/curse
Bible Gateway. Proverbs 18. NIV. https://web.mit.edu/jywang/www/cef/Bible/NIV/NIV_Bible/PROV+18.html

First. A literal understanding of the Curse of Ham may foster the belief in racial determinism, perpetuating the notion that certain races are inherently superior or inferior. This can give rise to harmful stereotypes and discriminatory practices, as individuals from particular racial or ethnic backgrounds may be unjustly stigmatized as cursed or predestined for servitude.

Second. A strict adherence to the literal interpretation may result in the misapplication of the Curse. This misapplication often targets specific racial or ethnic groups, leading to their unjust vilification or mistreatment. Historical instances abound where this narrative has been used to justify the enslavement or oppression of people of African descent, for example.

Third. A literal reading of the Curse of Ham tends to overlook the crucial historical and cultural factors that influenced the biblical narrative. It is essential to place the passage within the broader context of ancient societies, where systems of servitude and hierarchical structures were pervasive. Ignoring these contextual factors can yield a distorted understanding of the intended message of the passage.

Fourth. A literal interpretation often involves selective application, cherry-picking certain aspects of the passage while disregarding others. This selective approach is frequently employed to support personal biases or to justify discriminatory attitudes. Such cherry-picking dismisses the comprehensive message of equality and justice found in other parts of the biblical text.

COUNTERING THE CURSE

In 1958, there was a growing recognition of the imperative to challenge and confront the legacy of the Curse of Ham and its implications.[30] Prominent Christian leader Rev. Dr. Martin Luther King Jr.

---

[30] Branch, Taylor. *At Canaan's Edge: America in the King Years, 1965-68*. https://www.google.com/books/edition/At_Canaan_s_Edge/BNuog1T4XnsC?hl=en&gbpv=1

denounced such attempts as "blasphemy"[31] that contradicts the core principles of the Christian religion.[32] James Burton Coffman, one of the most influential figures among Churches of Christ in the 20th century, similarly argues that the curse should be understood as a prophecy of what would happen rather than a prescription of what should happen. He suggests that the curse alludes to Canaan's historical subjugation under various foreign powers[33]

Hymns

While Martin Luther King Jr. was primarily known for his powerful speeches and civil rights activism, he often drew inspiration from hymns and incorporated them into his sermons and speeches. Hymns played a significant role in the African American church tradition and served as a source of comfort, strength, and hope during the civil rights movement:

"We Shall Overcome."[34] This hymn became an anthem for the civil rights movement. Its lyrics and message of hope and perseverance resonated deeply with Dr. King and other activists. The song, originally a gospel hymn, was adapted and modified during the movement to reflect the struggle for equality and justice.

---

[31] Luther King, M., Jr. (1958, June 3). Paul's Letter to American Christians, Sermon delivered to the Commission on Ecumenical Missions and Relations, United Presbyterian Church, U.S.A. The Martin Luther King, Jr. Research and Education Institute. https://kinginstitute.stanford.edu/king-papers/documents/pauls-letter-american-christians-sermon-delivered-commission-ecumenical

[32] "Church Commissioners for England warmly welcomes Oversight Group's report." 2024. The Church of England. April 3, 2024. https://www.churchofengland.org/media/press-releases/church-commissioners-england-warmly-welcomes-oversight-groups-report

[33] StudyLight.org. "Coffman's Commentaries on the Bible.: Bible Commentaries. Genesis 9.," n.d. https://www.studylight.org/commentaries/eng/bcc/genesis-9.html#verses-25

[34] We shall overcome. (n.d.). The Kennedy Center. https://www.kennedy-center.org/education/resources-for-educators/classroom-resources/media-and-interactives/media/music/story-behind-the-song/the-story-behind-the-song/we-shall-overcome/

"Precious Lord, Take My Hand." Written by Thomas A. Dorsey, was one of Dr. King's favorites. He often referred to it in his speeches and sermons, finding solace and strength in its lyrics. The hymn acknowledges the challenges and hardships of life while seeking God's guidance and comfort. King's last words before his assassination was a request for musician Ben Branch to play it at a service he was due to attend that night. King's exact last words were "Ben, make sure you play 'Take My Hand, Precious Lord' in the meeting tonight. Play it real pretty".[35]

"Lift Every Voice and Sing."[36] Often referred to as the Black National Anthem, this hymn became a symbol of resilience and unity during the civil rights movement. Dr. King frequently invoked its lyrics, which celebrate the struggles and triumphs of African Americans and express a commitment to equality and freedom.

"Amazing Grace."[37] While not specifically associated with the civil rights movement, the hymn "Amazing Grace" is known for its powerful message of redemption and forgiveness. Dr. King referenced this hymn in his speeches to emphasize the importance of love, forgiveness, and reconciliation in the pursuit of justice.

Hymns and spiritual songs played a significant role in helping enslaved individuals cope with the hardships of slavery. Hymns provided emotional solace, spiritual nourishment, and a sense of connection to a higher power. They offered a means of expressing faith, hope, and resilience in the face of oppression. Enslaved individuals often gathered in secret prayer meetings or worship services, where they would sing hymns and spirituals. These gatherings provided a space for communal support, encouragement, and the sharing of expe-

---

[35] McNeil, W. K. "Encyclopedia of American Gospel Music." Routledge & CRC Press, September 29, 2005. https://www.routledge.com/Encyclopedia-of-American-Gospel-Music/McNeil/p/book/9780415875691
[36] NAACP. Lift Every Voice and Sing. February 17, 2023. https://naacp.org/find-resources/history-explained/lift-every-voice-and-sing
[37] Dr. Martin Luther King, Jr. An Amazing Grace. WABC-TV (Television Station. New York, N.Y.). Internet Archive, 1978. https://archive.org/details/drmartinlutherkingjranamazinggrace/drmartinlutherkingjranamazinggrace.mov

riences. Through the act of singing together, they found strength and solace in the collective expression of their faith and shared struggles. Hymns and spiritual songs provided a source of comfort and inspiration, reminding enslaved individuals that their circumstances were not permanent and that they could find solace in their relationship with God. The lyrics often conveyed messages of deliverance, salvation, and the promise of a better life beyond the hardships of slavery. Singing these hymns allowed enslaved individuals to momentarily transcend their physical conditions and find solace in their spiritual connection.

Similarly, Negro spirituals and the Underground Railroad form an interconnected arras within the history of African Americans in the United States during the 18th and 19th centuries. Negro Spirituals, also known as African American spirituals, emerged as a distinct genre of religious songs among enslaved African Americans. Deeply rooted in African musical traditions, these spirituals blended elements of African rhythms, melodies, and religious expressions with Christian themes. Serving as a source of spiritual sustenance, cultural expression, and communication within enslaved communities, Negro spirituals played a significant role in the lives of those enduring the hardships of slavery. The Underground Railroad, on the other hand, was a clandestine network of secret routes and safe houses established during the 19th century. Its purpose was to aid enslaved individuals in their quest for freedom by facilitating their escape from the Southern United States to free states and Canada. It is imperative to note that the Underground Railroad was not an actual railroad; rather, it represented the coordinated efforts of abolitionists, free African Americans, and sympathetic individuals who provided shelter, guidance, and transportation to those seeking liberation from the bonds of slavery.

For instance, the song "Follow the Drinking Gourd"[38] made reference to the Big Dipper constellation, which served as a celestial guide

---

[38] Magazine, B. M. (2023, March 21). "Follow the drinking gourd" lyrics. Classical Music. https://www.classical-music.com/articles/follow-the-drinking-gourd-lyrics

for those traveling northward. By employing these concealed messages, enslaved individuals could communicate with one another and gather information without arousing suspicion from slaveholders or overseers.

CURSED U.S.

Preset for Racism

Professor David M. Whitford, an esteemed scholar in the History of Christianity, conducted a thorough examination of the claim that Puritan theology had an inherent inclination towards racism, thereby playing a central role in the "preset for racism" in America.[39] This claim suggests that the theological beliefs of Puritans, influenced by Calvinist thought, contributed to racial hierarchies by interpreting the Curse of Ham as a justification for racial subordination. To assess the validity of this claim and explore the complex relationship between Calvinist ideas, biblical interpretation, and racial subordination, Whitford employed a multidisciplinary approach, drawing from historical, theological, and cultural perspectives, within which, Whitford discussed the emergence of a "curse matrix"[40] from the ambiguous nature of Genesis 9. Racialists exploited this ambiguity, arguing that the specific group cursed was unimportant, but rather, the generational curse itself could be used to justify actions against black people, such as slavery.

---

[39] Whitford, David M. "A Calvinist Heritage to the 'Curse of Ham': Assessing the Accuracy of a Claim About Racial Subordination." *Church History and Religious Culture 90*, no. 1 (January 1, 2010): 25–45. https://brill.com/view/journals/chrc/90/1/article-p25_2.xml?language=en

[40] David M. Whitford. The Curse of Ham in the Early Modern Era: The Bible and the Justifications for Slavery. St Andrews Studies in Reformation History. Farnham: Ashgate Publishing Limited, 2009. Xiv + 211 Pp. Index. Illus. Bibl. $99.95. ISBN: 978–0–7546–6625–7. Renaissance Quarterly 63, no. 3 (January 1, 2010): 952–54. https://www.cambridge.org/core/journals/renaissance-quarterly/article/abs/david-m-whitford-the-curse-of-ham-in-the-early-modern-era-the-bible-and-the-justifications-for-slavery-st-andrews-studies-in-reformation-history-farnham-ashgate-publishing-limited-2009-xiv-211-pp-index-illus-bibl-9995-isbn-9780754666257/06F8E7DA8DF6A86D3CE685EE540E9931

Pro-slavery intellectuals faced challenges in finding a theological basis for slavery and racism within Christian teachings emphasizing the common descent of all humans from Adam, which suggested equality and equal treatment. The Curse of Ham was used to undermine the notion of a unified human race, as influential thinkers in the Southern United States, like Benjamin Morgan Palmer, claimed that white Europeans descended from Japheth, who was prophesied to cultivate civilization and intellectual prowess. Africans, as descendants of the cursed Ham, were believed to be destined for a life of servitude ruled by base desires.

In the 15th century, Dominican friar Annius of Viterbo invoked the Curse of Ham in his writings to explain the differences between Europeans and Africans. Annius, known for frequently extolling the "superiority of Christians over the Saracens,"[41] asserted that the curse imposed on black people destined them to perpetual subjugation under Arabs and other Muslims. He argued that the enslavement of Africans by heretical Muslims served as evidence of their inherent inferiority. Through writings like Annius's, European authors established a previously unheard-of connection between Ham, Africa, and slavery, which laid the ideological groundwork for justifying the transatlantic slave trade.

American Slavery

During the era of Southern slavery in the United States, the Curse of Ham was among the various grounds used by Christian slave owners to construct an ideological defense of slavery in response to the abolitionist movement. Even prior to the institution of slavery, the Curse of Ham was employed to shift the prevailing Aristotelian belief that phenotypic differences among humans were a result of climatic vari-

---

[41] M. Fredrickson, G. (2015, September 15). Racism: A Short History. Princeton University Press. https://press.princeton.edu/books/paperback/9780691167053/racism

ations, to a racialist perspective that attributed such differences to distinct racial types. This shift often arose from European concerns about avoiding colonization, as settlers feared the high mortality rates associated with disease and warfare in the colonies. Consequently, many Europeans developed the notion that being sent to regions south of the equator "blackened" them, thereby deeming them inferior.

U.S. Constitution

While the Curse of Ham does not appear explicitly within the text of the U.S. Constitution, the widespread misinterpretation and misuse of this narrative had a significant impact on the development of race-based ideologies and policies that shaped certain aspects of the Constitution. During the era of transatlantic slavery, proponents of the institution sought to justify and legitimize their practices through distorted interpretations of biblical texts. One such distortion involved the "Curse of Ham" narrative, which was erroneously employed to provide divine sanction for the enslavement of Africans and the perpetuation of racial hierarchy.[42] These skewed interpretations, alongside other pernicious racist ideologies, shaped the prevailing attitudes towards race and slavery among many of the framers of the U.S. Constitution.

For instance, the Three-Fifths Compromise,[43] contained in Article I, Section 2, Paragraph 3, stipulated that enslaved individuals would be counted as three-fifths of a person for the purposes of determining representation in the House of Representatives. This compromise was a reflection of the prevailing social and political bargains made to address the conflicting interests related to slavery. Additionally,

---

[42] Ham, Paul. 2014. "The 'Curse of Ham': How People of Faith Used a Story in Genesis to Justify Slavery." The Conversation. March 24, 2014. https://theconversation.com/the-curse-of-ham-how-people-of-faith-used-a-story-in-genesis-to-justify-slavery-225212

[43] *The Constitution: How Did it Happen?* (2023, November 28). National Archives. https://www.archives.gov/founding-docs/constitution/how-did-it-happen#:~:text=The%20framers%20compromised%20by%20giving,threatened%20to%20derail%20the%20Union

the Fugitive Slave Clause, found in Article IV, Section 2, Clause 3, mandated the return of escaped slaves to their owners, thereby reinforcing the institution of slavery and denying freedom to those who managed to escape to free states.

As outlined in *The American Yawp*, in the chapter on "The Cotton Revolution:"

> *"As the institution of slavery hardened racism in the South, relationships between missionaries and Native Americans transformed as well. Missionaries of all denominations were among the first to represent themselves as "pillars of white authority." After the Louisiana Purchase in 1803, plantation culture expanded into the Deep South, and mission work became a crucial element of Christian expansion. Frontier mission schools carried a continual flow of Christian influence into Native American communities. Some missionaries learned Indigenous languages, but many more worked to prevent Indigenous children from speaking their native tongues, insisting on English for Christian understanding. By the Indian removals of 1835 and the Trail of Tears in 1838, missionaries in the South preached a pro-slavery theology that emphasized obedience to enslavers, the biblical basis of racial slavery via the curse of Ham, and the "civilizing" paternalism of enslavers."* [44]

In a separate chapter in *The American Yawp* titled "Colliding Cultures," the text further elucidates:

---

[44] Locke, Joseph L., and Ben Wright. 2019. "11. The Cotton Revolution." The American Yawp. January 22, 2019. https://www.americanyawp.com/text/11-the-cotton-revolution/

"Spanish conquerors established the framework for the Atlantic slave trade over a century before the first chained Africans arrived at Jamestown. Even Bartolomé de Las Casas, celebrated for his pleas to save Native Americans from colonial butchery, for a time recommended that Indigenous labor be replaced by importing Africans. Early English settlers from the Caribbean and Atlantic coast of North America mostly imitated European ideas of African inferiority. "Race" followed the expansion of slavery across the Atlantic world. Skin color and race suddenly seemed fixed. **Englishmen equated Africans with categorical blackness and blackness with sin,** *"the handmaid and symbol of baseness." An English essayist in 1695 wrote that "a negro will always be a negro, carry him to Greenland, feed him chalk, feed and manage him never so many ways." More and more Europeans embraced the notions that Europeans and Africans were of distinct races. Others now preached that the Old Testament God cursed Ham, the son of Noah, and doomed Black people to perpetual enslavement."*[45]

In his famous "Cornerstone Speech" delivered in 1861, Alexander Stephens, the Vice President of the Confederate States of America during the American Civil War, outlined the key principles underlying the Confederate government, including its position on slavery. According to the historical record, in this speech Stephens explicitly rejected the principle of racial equality that was present in the U.S. Constitution, stating that the Confederacy was founded on the belief that: (1) "the negro is not equal to the white man;" (2) "slavery—subor-

---

[45] Locke, Joseph L., and Ben Wright. 2019. "2. Colliding Cultures." The American Yawp. January 22, 2019. https://www.americanyawp.com/text/02-colliding-cultures/

dination to the superior race— is his natural and normal condition;" and (3) "The negro by nature, or by the curse against Canaan, is fitted for that condition which he occupies in our system."[46]

The framers of the United States Constitution were confronted with the vexing issue of how to accommodate the institution of slavery, a fundamental point of contention between the Northern and Southern states during the Philadelphia Convention. Ultimately, a series of carefully worded compromises were reached, reflecting the delicate political balances required to secure ratification of the new charter of government. One such compromise was the inclusion of Article I, Section 9, which has become known as the "20-year clause" or the "slave trade clause." This provision explicitly prohibited Congress from outlawing the importation of enslaved Africans prior to the year 1808—a concession granted to the Southern states, who were heavily dependent on the transatlantic slave trade to fuel their plantation economies.

The Act Prohibiting Importation of Slaves, enacted by Congress in 1807, represented a significant milestone in the gradual restriction of the international slave trade. However, it is important to recognize that this legislation was passed within the constitutional parameters set forth a generation earlier. The framers' decision to postpone a potential Congressional ban on the slave trade for two decades was a pragmatic compromise, intended to secure Southern support for the new federal system, highlighting the enduring tensions and complexities inherent in the young nation's approach to the peculiar institution of slavery.

It is relevant to note that the U.S. Constitution has evolved over time, and amendments have been made to rectify the injustices associated with slavery and promote equality. While the legacy of the "Curse of Ham" narrative and its impact on the framers' views can still be seen

---

[46] Locke, Joseph L., and Ben Wright. 2019. "The American Yawp Reader: A Documentary Companion to the American Yawp, Volume I." The American Yawp. https://www.americanyawp.com/reader/wp-content/uploads/The-American-Yawp-Reader-Vol-1-Fall-2020.pdf

in the original provisions of the Constitution, the Thirteenth Amendment, ratified in 1865, abolished slavery, and subsequent amendments, such as the Fourteenth and Fifteenth Amendments, aimed to ensure equal rights and protections for all citizens, irrespective of race.

Slave Patrol

The historical relationship between slave patrols and the development of modern policing in the United States is a subject of inquiry. While it is important to acknowledge that the evolution of law enforcement is a multifaceted process influenced by a range of factors, there are identifiable connections between the two phenomena. Slave patrols emerged during the era of slavery in the Southern states, primarily with the objective of maintaining control over enslaved populations, suppressing potential rebellions, and enforcing the institution of slavery itself. These patrols consisted of armed groups of white men who conducted regular surveillance of plantations, roads, and public spaces, with the specific aim of monitoring and apprehending enslaved individuals attempting to escape or engage in acts of resistance. Following the abolition of slavery after the American Civil War, the Reconstruction period witnessed efforts to establish new systems of law enforcement. The passage of the 13th Amendment in 1865 abolished slavery, yet it included a provision allowing involuntary servitude as punishment for a crime. This provision created a legal framework that facilitated the re-enslavement of African Americans through practices such as convict leasing, which were frequently enforced by local law enforcement agencies.

During the Jim Crow era, which spanned from the late 19th century to the mid-20th century, African Americans faced pervasive racial discrimination and violence. Local law enforcement, including police departments, played a critical role in upholding racial segregation and preserving the racial hierarchy. They were responsible for enforcing racially discriminatory laws, such as Jim Crow laws, and facilitating racial violence and intimidation against African Americans. The development of modern police departments in the United States occurred gradually over time, influenced by a variety of societal factors. Urbanization, industrialization, and the desire for centralized law enforcement control were among the forces that shaped the establishment of formalized police forces tasked with maintaining public order, enforcing laws, and safeguarding communities.

While acknowledging the historical connection between slave patrols and contemporary policing, it is crucial to approach this relationship as part of a broader historical context. The evolution of law enforcement in the United States is a complex subject influenced by socioeconomic, political, and cultural dynamics. Thus, the transition from slave patrols to the police patrol cannot be solely attributed to the slave patrol system, but rather should be examined within the broader historical trajectory of American law enforcement.

Tulsa Race Massacre

The Tulsa Race Massacre, alternatively referred to as the Tulsa Race Riot, took place in 1921 within the Greenwood District of Tulsa, Oklahoma. It constituted a violent and racially motivated assault upon the prosperous African American community of Greenwood, renowned as "Black Wall Street" due to its economic affluence and vibrant cultural milieu. Commencing on May 31, 1921, the massacre ensued subsequent to a baseless accusation made against Dick Rowland, a young Black man, who was alleged to have assaulted a white woman in an elevator. A gathering of white individuals assembled at the courthouse where Rowland was detained, and tensions rapidly escalated. Subsequently, violent acts transpired as the mob targeted and devastated the residences, businesses, and institutions present within the Greenwood District. Throughout the course of the massacre, the white mob, with the assistance of law enforcement personnel and National Guard troops, pillaged and incinerated numerous edifices, including private homes, churches, schools, and medical facilities. Multiple African American residents lost their lives, with a significant number of individuals sustaining injuries or being rendered homeless. Although precise fatality figures remain elusive, estimates range from several dozen to as high as 300.

In the aftermath of the massacre, the Greenwood community was left in ruins, and survivors confronted substantial hardships in their efforts to rebuild their lives and enterprises. For many years, the event was largely suppressed and omitted from historical records, resulting in intergenerational trauma and a dearth of awareness regarding the magnitude of the tragedy. Recent years have witnessed a resurgence of efforts to acknowledge and redress the Tulsa Race Massacre. Endeavors have been undertaken to uncover the complete extent of the events, educate the public, and foster healing and reconciliation. The centennial commemoration in 2021 energized discussions surrounding the tragedy, prompting considerations pertaining to racial justice, reparations, and the imperative of remembering and learning from historical injustices.

Civil Rights Movement

Approximately one life cycle has elapsed since The Civil Rights Movement,[47] a momentous social and political endeavor, unfolded in the United States during the mid-20th century, yet the impact of historical factors associated with the curse continues to resonate in contemporary society. The Civil Rights Movement emerged as a response to deep-rooted racial injustices and systemic discrimination endured by African Americans, particularly in the Southern states. These marginalized communities faced pervasive laws and practices that denied

---

[47] The Civil Rights Movement | The Post War United States, 1945-1968 | U.S. History Primary Source Timeline | Classroom Materials at the Library of Congress | Library of Congress. (n.d.). The Library of Congress. https://www.loc.gov/classroom-materials/united-states-history-primary-source-timeline/post-war-united-states-1945-1968/civil-rights-movement/

them basic civil rights, equal treatment, and opportunities for social and economic advancement.

Taking shape in the 1950s and 1960s, the movement gained remarkable momentum through the tireless efforts of civil rights activists and organizations striving for change. Their multifaceted strategies encompassed nonviolent protests, civil disobedience, legal challenges, grassroots mobilization, and public awareness campaigns. Significant milestones and prominent figures defined the trajectory of the Civil Rights Movement. The landmark Supreme Court ruling of Brown v. Board of Education in 1954 unequivocally declared racial segregation in public schools unconstitutional, overturning the previously established "separate but equal"[48] doctrine of the Plessy v. Ferguson case.

The Montgomery Bus Boycott that ensued from Rosa Parks' courageous act of refusing to yield her bus seat to a white passenger exemplified the power of collective action. Lasting for a year, this boycott in Montgomery, Alabama, led by influential civil rights leaders like Rev. Dr. Martin Luther King Jr., demanded an end to segregated seating on buses. Sit-ins at segregated lunch counters and Freedom Rides challenging racial segregation in interstate transportation captured national attention. These acts of peaceful resistance were meticulously orchestrated to shed light on the injustice of segregation and elicit nonviolent responses from authorities. The transformative March on Washington for Jobs and Freedom in 1963 constituted a seminal event, drawing an estimated 250,000 individuals in a resounding display of solidarity for civil rights and equality. It was on this occasion that Dr. King, Jr. delivered his iconic "I Have a Dream"[49] speech, which resonated deeply and continues to reverberate through history.

---

[48] *Brown v. Board of Education (1954)*. (2024, March 18). National Archives. https://www.archives.gov/milestone-documents/brown-v-board-of-education

[49] National Archives and Records Administration & National Committee on the March on Washington. (n.d.). The March, Part 3 of 3. In *Archival Research Catalog (ARC) Identifier* 2602934. https://www.archives.gov/files/social-media/transcripts/transcript-march-pt3-of-3-2602934.pdf

The legislative achievements of the era cannot be understated. The Civil Rights Act of 1964, a watershed moment, prohibited discrimination based on race, color, religion, sex, or national origin. It dismantled racial segregation in public facilities and bolstered voting rights protections. The subsequent Voting Rights Act of 1965[50] further sought to overcome barriers to African American voting rights, such as literacy tests and poll taxes, by establishing federal oversight of elections in regions with a history of racial discrimination. The Civil Rights Movement stands as a testament to the transformative power of collective action and the indomitable spirit of those who fought for justice.

POOR PEOPLE

Sterilization of America

The forced sterilization of women of color in America between 1907 and 1932 represents a distressing chapter in reproductive injustice.[51] This era witnessed the alarming coercion or involuntary imposition of sterilization procedures upon numerous women hailing from marginalized communities, particularly African American, Native American, and Latina women. These practices were frequently implemented through policies and programs that sought to regulate population growth, curtail the reproductive autonomy of specific groups, or enforce eugenic ideologies. The forced sterilization campaigns specifically targeted women deemed "unfit" or "undesirable" based on racial, ethnic, or socioeconomic considerations. Women often underwent

---

[50] *Voting Rights Act (1965)*. (2022, February 8). National Archives. https://www.archives.gov/milestone-documents/voting-rights-act

[51] Prather, C., Fuller, T. R., Jeffries, W. L., Marshall, K. J., Howell, A. V., Belyue-Umole, A., & King, W. (2018). Racism, African American Women, and their Sexual and Reproductive Health: A Review of historical and contemporary evidence and Implications for Health Equity. *Health Equity*, 2(1), 249–259. https://twu.edu/media/documents/history-government/Autonomy-Revoked--The-Forced-Sterilization-of-Women-of-Color-in-20th-Century-America.pdf

sterilization procedures without their informed consent, sometimes under deceptive circumstances such as during childbirth or while seeking unrelated medical care. In many instances, women were insufficiently informed about the permanent nature of the procedure and its potential ramifications.

Similarly, the establishment of the 1969 Population Control Commission, known formally as the President's Commission on Population Growth and the American Future, bears significance within this historical context. Founded by Zionist John D. Rockefeller III,[52] under the administration of President Richard Nixon, this commission was formed in response to mounting concerns regarding the ramifications of rapid population growth on both national and global scales, encompassing areas such as the environment, resources, and social and economic development.[53]

It is worth acknowledging that the commission's work and recommendations were not immune to scrutiny and controversy. Critics voiced concerns that the emphasis on population control and family planning disproportionately impacted marginalized communities, both domestically and internationally, thereby engendering discussions encompassing reproductive rights and social equity. Disproportionately, it is evident that the African-American population appears as the primary consumer of abortion services. In citing the 2015 Policy Report on The Effects of Abortion on the Black Community,[54] it is revealed that while black women constitute merely 14 percent of the

---

[52] Rosenberg, Y. (2023b, December 18). Why does America support Israel? *The Atlantic.* https://www.theatlantic.com/newsletters/archive/2022/07/biden-israel-lobby-america-walter-mead/676794/

[53] *John D. Rockefeller 3rd, statesman and founder of the Population Council.* (2000, September 1). Population Reference Bureau. https://www.prb.org/resources/john-d-rockefeller-3rd-statesman-and-founder-of-the-population-council/

[54] Daniels, C., Davis, C., Anunkor, I., & Parker, S. (2015). The Effects of Abortion on the Black Community. In Star Parker & Center for Urban Renewal and Education (Eds.), *CURE Document* 202.479.2873. https://www.congress.gov/115/meeting/house/106562/witnesses/HHRG-115-JU10-Wstate-ParkerS-20171101-SD001.pdf

overall childbearing population, they account for a significant 36.2 percent of reported abortions. It is critical to underscore that black women possess the highest abortion ratio nationwide, with a striking figure of 474 abortions per 1,000 live births. These percentages, depicted at such levels, underscore a distressing reality. Over the course of the period from 1973 to 2015, more than 19 million black babies have regrettably met their fate through abortion procedures.

Sterilization Abroad

Parallels can be drawn between the coerced contraception administration to Ethiopian Israeli women and the forced sterilization of women of color in 20th century America, primarily in terms of the infringement upon reproductive autonomy and the disproportionate impact on marginalized communities.[55] Both instances involve the manipulation of power dynamics by those in positions of authority, singling out specific groups based on race or ethnicity, and disregarding the principles of informed consent and bodily integrity.

The recovery of historical links allows us to comprehend the fundamental connection between birth control and broader transnational discussions on race and reproduction, as well as the utilization of sexuality for racial purposes. This association becomes evident when examining the Malthusian writings of Annie Besant, which laid the groundwork for linking birth control to racial concerns. The remarkably similar approaches taken by Marie Stopes and Margaret Sanger in promoting birth control as a eugenic tool further exemplify the entanglement of birth control with eugenic ideologies. The endorsement and support for birth control within prominent British and American eugenics organizations additionally reinforce this relationship. The influential role played by the Racial Hygiene Association,

---

[55] Kaplan, Steven. "Coercion and Control: Ethiopian Israeli Women and Contraception." *International Journal of Ethiopian Studies* 10, no. 1 & 2 (2016): 35–50. https://www.jstor.org/stable/26554851

Australia's largest eugenic organization, cannot be overlooked, as it established the country's inaugural birth control clinic in 1933 and later transformed into the Family Planning Association, highlighting the continued interplay between birth control initiatives and eugenic endeavors.[56] These practices were fueled by deeply entrenched systemic racism, sexism, and eugenicist beliefs that pervaded during that era, violating bodily autonomy, reproductive rights, and human dignity as a tool to ethnically cleanse a marginalized population.

---

[56] Carey, Jane. 2012. "The Racial Imperatives of Sex: Birth Control and Eugenics in Britain, the United States and Australia in the Interwar Years." *Women's History Review* 21 (5): 733–52. https://www.tandfonline.com/doi/abs/10.1080/09612025.2012.658180

"Shallow understanding from people of goodwill is more frustrating than absolute misunderstanding from people of ill will. Lukewarm acceptance is much more bewildering than outright rejection."[57]

**- Rev. Dr. Martin Luther King Jr.,
Letter from the Birmingham Jail**

---

[57] King, M. L. (1963). Letter from Birmingham Jail. In California State University, Chico. https://www.csuchico.edu/iege/_assets/documents/susi-letter-from-birmingham-jail.pdf

CHAPTER 2
A Review of The Hidden Sins

Second Sin

INTRODUCTION

A CENTRAL FOCUS OF THIS CHAPTER IN HISTORY IS THE STRIKING PARALLELS DRAWN BETWEEN THE COLONIZATION OF AMERICA AND THE CONGO FREE STATE UNDER THE BRUTAL PATTERNS OF EXPLOITATION, DISPOSSESSION, AND SUBJUGATION WITNESSED ACROSS THE NIGER-CONGO REGION. THROUGH THIS COMPARATIVE LENS, THE STUDY ELUCIDATES HOW THESE RELIGIOUS AND IDEOLOGICAL SYSTEMS HAVE BEEN INEXTRICABLY LINKED TO THE OPPRESSION AND DISPLACEMENT OF INDIGENOUS PEOPLES THROUGHOUT THE COLONIAL ERA. AT ITS CORE, THIS CHAPTER IS AN EXAMINATION OF HOW THIS RELIGIOUS MOTIF WAS CO-OPTED AND WEAPONIZED BY THE EXPANSIONIST AGENDA OF COLONIAL POWERS. THE ANALYSIS DELVES INTO THE PIVOTAL ROLES OF THE "UNITED BRETHREN MOVEMENT" (THE POWERSCOURT CONFERENCE IN THE U.K. AND THE INFLUENTIAL SCOFIELD REFERENCE BIBLE) IN PROPAGATING THEOLOGICAL INTERPRETATIONS THAT DIRECTLY ENABLED THE RISE OF ZIONISM AND THE IMPLEMENTATION OF CONSCRIPTION POLICIES FROM WORLD WAR I AFTER THE FALL OF THE HOLY ROMAN EMPIRE.

COLÓN (COLONIZE)

Two maritime expeditions embarked from the Port of Palos in Spain on August 3, 1492, sailing down the Rio Tinto. One of these voyages carried the final group of expelled Jews who, rather than renouncing their faith and converting to Christianity, opted to venture into an unknown destiny in a new world. Leading the other ships, namely the Pinta, Niña, and Santa María, was Cristóbal Colón, the Spanish name of Christopher Columbus,[58] a relatively obscure explorer of the time.[59]

Since the late 19th century, historians specializing in Columbus studies have diligently sought to unravel the true genesis of the man who set sail in 1492 with the intent of reaching India but inadvertently discovered a new continent. While some of the narratives surrounding Columbus's association with the expelled Jews may fall into speculation or legend, it has been suggested that he embarked with this group due to a one-day delay in his original departure date set for August 2, 1942. This date marked the commemoration of Tisha B'Av, a day of fasting and mourning for the destruction of the Jewish Temples. According to a 1934 article published by the Jewish Telegraphic Agency (JTA), which highlighted cutting-edge research at the time:

> *"In Spain, it was fatal to admit being a Jew because there was more chance of being favorably accepted in Madrid as a foreigner rather than as a native from Galicia, which at that time was not in the good graces of the ruling provinces of Castile and Aragon."*[60]

---

58   Wishengrad, H. (1934, October 12). Christopher Columbus a Jew? New evidence supports theory. *Jewish Telegraphic Agency.* https://www.jta.org/archive/christopher-columbus-a-jew-new-evidence-supports-theory (not a secure site, scanned article: http://pdfs.jta.org/1934/1934-10-12_2970.pdf)

59   Vincent H. deP. Cassidy. "Columbus and 'The Negro.'" *The Phylon Quarterly* 20, no. 3 (1959): 294–96. https://www.jstor.org/stable/273057

60   Amanda Borschel-Dan. 2018. "Christopher Columbus — the hidden Jew?: With a murky past, theories abound for the origin story of the intrepid explorer — from pirate to crypto-Jew." The Times of Israel. October 8, 2018. https://

A 2012 CNN article titled "Was Columbus secretly a Jew?"[61] further expounds on the subject, asserting that Columbus's voyage was not, as commonly believed, financed by Queen Isabella, but rather by two Jewish Conversos and another prominent Jew. The article cites Louis de Santangel and Gabriel Sanchez, who extended an interest-free loan of 17,000 ducats from their personal funds to support the expedition, along with Don Isaac Abarbanel, a rabbi and Jewish statesman. The JTA article from 1934 contends that this support from members of the Converso community serves as evidence of Columbus's Jewish heritage. The same JTA article states:

> *"The help afforded him by Jewish scientists and financiers of that time can be explained only in the light that he was of the same race," and references the 1892 work "Columbus and his Discovery of America" by Herbert B. Adams, in which Adams posits, "Not jewels, but Jews were the real financial basis for the first expedition of Columbus."*

It is noteworthy that Columbus's initial announcement regarding the discoveries made during his voyage was conveyed to the treasurer of Aragon, Louis de Santangel, who was of Jewish descent. In his Journal of the Third Voyage, documented in the book *Africa and the Discovery of America*,[62] Columbus reveals that before heading to Hispaniola, he was informed by King Juan of Portugal that ships from the coast of Guinea had arrived in the islands of the West with merchandise. As a result, Columbus decided to first visit Guinea "to verify on his way the opinion of King Don Juan" and to investigate reports from the indig-

---

www.timesofisrael.com/christopher-columbus-the-hidden-jew/

61 Garcia, Charles. 2012. "Was Columbus secretly a Jew?" CNN. May 24, 2012. https://www.cnn.com/2012/05/20/opinion/garcia-columbus-jewish/index.html

62 Wiener, Leo. 1928. "Africa and the Discovery of America." Internet Archive. pp. 34. https://archive.org/details/africadiscoveryo0001leow/page/34/mode/2up

enous people of Hispaniola regarding the arrival of "Negro" traders from the south and southeast, who possessed spear points made of a metal called guanin. The significance of this account lies in Columbus's awareness that guanin originated from Guinea and that other merchants or explorers had reached Hispaniola prior to his arrival. This finding supports the etymology of the term caona, related to guanin, originating from the Mande word for "gold," associated with a group of Niger-Congo languages.

AMERICA

In the year 1557, the presence of Canaanites ("sea people"), Amorites, Amalekites,[63] and Moabites were documented in Florida. This assertion finds support in a publication in 1882 titled, "The Red Man and the White Man in North America from its Discovery to the Present Time," which was furnished to Oxford by the Rhodes Trust, an organization associated with the Rhodes Scholarship. Specifically, the section titled "Enslaving of the Natives" references a letter addressed to a King of Spain, providing additional insights into this historical context:

> *"It is lawful that your Majesty, like a good shepherd, appointed by the hand of the Eternal Father, should tend and lead out your sheep, since the Holy Spirit has shown spreading pastures whereon are feeding lost sheep, which have been snatched away by the dragon, the Demon. These pastures are the New World, wherein is comprised Florida, now in possession of the Demon; and here he makes himself adored*

---

[63] Sharon, Jeremy. 2024. "PM's office says it's 'preposterous' to say his invoking Amalek was a genocide call." The Times of Israel. January 16, 2024. https://www.timesofisrael.com/pms-office-says-its-preposterous-to-say-invoking-amalek-was-a-genocide-call/

> *and revered. This is the Land of Promise possessed by idolaters, the Amorite, Amalekite, Moabite, Canaanite. This is the land promised by the Eternal Father to the Faithful, since we are commanded by God in the Holy Scriptures to take it from them, being idolaters, and, by reason of their idolatry and sin, to put them all to the knife, leaving no living thing save maidens and children, their cities robbed and sacked, their walls and houses levelled to the earth."*[64]

These aforementioned groups of people, often associated with the biblical narrative of Canaan and subsequently identified with the land of Israel, were subjected to more than just physical displacement. Their experiences encompassed profound sociocultural and psychological harm, as manifested through a range of injurious mechanisms. Specifically, these mechanisms include demonizing, gaslighting, scapegoating, as described in Leviticus 16,[65] and projecting historical atrocities against this previously displaced group. They were purportedly subjected to a form of "eternal slavery" through the so-called "Curse of Ham".[66] It is essential to consider the prevailing influence of the Roman Empire during the compilation of the Bible, as the biblical text regarding "cursing" serves as a repository of human wisdom and experience, providing a lens through which we can explore aspects of the human condition through casting negative pogroms.

---

[64] Ellis, George Edward. The Red Man and the White Man in North America from Its Discovery to the Present Time. Internet Archive. 1882, pp. 63. https://archive.org/details/redmanwhitemanin00elliuoft/page/62/mode/2up?view=theater

[65] Bible Gateway. Leviticus 16 (NIV), "scapegoat." https://web.mit.edu/jywang/www/cef/Bible/NIV/NIV_Bible/LEV+16.html

[66] Rev. C.I. Scofield, D.D. The Scofield Reference Bible. The Holy Bible. 1917. https://archive.org/details/scofieldreferenc0000revc/page/16/mode/2up?view=theater

Semitic Derivation

The Seminole[67] derivation, Semitic, warrants attention within this discussion. The Seminole people, who trace their origins to indigenous groups of Florida, may have onomastic and cultural connections to the broader Semitic family, as examined in Chapter 3: A Loss Analysis. While the Seminole derivation is distinct from the specific groups associated with the biblical narrative of Canaan, who is the son or extension of Ham, and the land of Israel, the Seminole's Semitic affiliation highlights the interconnectedness and diversity of human history.[68][69] Exploring these connections can provide valuable insights into the cultural influences across different regions and time periods.

HOLY ROMAN EMPIRE

Contrary to its name, the Holy Roman Empire was neither strictly holy nor truly Roman. Jews had lived in Rome for over 2,000 years,[70] longer than in any other European city, and the Holy Roman Empire was composed primarily of Germanic territories, rather than Roman ones.[71][72] The Jewish community in Rome is known to be the oldest

---

[67] Seminole History. Florida Department of State. https://dos.fl.gov/florida-facts/florida-history/seminole-history/#:~:text=The%201770s%20is%20when%20Florida,found%20refuge%20among%20the%20Indians

[68] McKusick, Marshall. "Canaanites in America: A New Scripture in Stone?" The Biblical Archaeologist 42, no. 3 (1979): 137–40. https://www.jstor.org/stable/3209381

[69] Elizabeth Fenton. Old Canaan in a New World. Native Americans and the Lost Tribes of Israel. NYU Press. (2019, July 2). https://nyupress.org/9781479866366/old-canaan-in-a-new-world/

[70] Jacobs, Joseph, and Schulim Ochser. n.d. "Rome." Jewish Encyclopedia. https://jewishencyclopedia.com/articles/12816-rome#1005

[71] Duits, Simon, and Jost De Negker. "Holy Roman Empire." *World History Encyclopedia*, April 2, 2024. https://www.worldhistory.org/Holy_Roman_Empire/

[72] The Hebrew University of Jerusalem Communications. (2022, November 30). Ancient DNA Provides New Insights into Ashkenazi Jewish History: Analysis reveals medieval genetic diversity, illuminates founder event. Harvard Medical School. https://hms.harvard.edu/news/

Jewish community in Europe and also one the oldest continuous Jewish settlements in the world, dating back to 161 BCE. After the Romans invaded Judea in 63 BCE, subsequently becoming a member state of Rome, Jewish prisoners of war were brought to Rome as slaves, Jewish delegates came to Rome on diplomatic missions, and Jewish merchants traveled to Rome seeking business opportunities.[73]

In addition to Rome's longstanding Jewish presence, several other European cities have historically been home to sizable and influential Jewish communities. Amsterdam, for instance, has had a Jewish population since the 16th century, with the community peaking at around 80,000 in the early 20th century. Warsaw, Poland was an even more significant center of Jewish life, with the Jewish population reaching over 350,000 prior to World War II, making it one of the largest Jewish communities in the world at the time. Budapest, Hungary also developed a notable Jewish presence, with over 200,000 Jews living in the city by the early 1900s. Vilnius, Lithuania was known as the "Jerusalem of the North" due to its vibrant Jewish culture and intellectual center, while the Ukrainian port city of Odessa had one of the largest Jewish communities in the Russian Empire, with over 300,000 residents. Even Berlin, Germany, before the Nazi era, had the largest Jewish community in the country, with an estimated 160,000-200,000 Jews living in the city in the 1920s. Therefore, while Rome stands out for its unparalleled longevity as a hub of Jewish life in Europe, several other major European urban centers also emerged as important centers of Jewish population and culture over the centuries.

Due to its early Jewish settlement and Judaism's influence on the Abrahamic faiths, the Holy Roman Empire represents a captivating subject of inquiry. The genesis of the Holy Roman Empire can

---

ancient-dna-provides-new-insights-ashkenazi-jewish-history

[73] The New Jewish Encyclopedia, Heritage: Civilization and the Jews, A History of the Jews, The Jewish Community in Rome, Encyclopedia Judaica, Jewish Communities of the World, Rome Tour.org, et al. n.d. "Virtual Jewish World: Rome, Italy." Jewish Virtual Library. https://www.jewishvirtuallibrary.org/rome-jewish-history-tour

be traced back to the momentous coronation of Charlemagne as Emperor of the Romans by Pope Leo III in the year 800, constituting a loose confederation of territories, which became the foundation for Germany, Italy, Bohemia, modern day Czech Republic, and Burgundy, a Germanic tribe that settled in France. Charlemagne's vast regions of Western Europe marked a resurgence of the concept of a unified Christian empire on the continent. However, following Charlemagne's demise in 814, the empire underwent fragmentation, leading to an era of regionalization and decentralization.

Subsequent centuries witnessed a complex interplay of political, religious, and territorial dynamics within the Holy Roman Empire. Comprising a mosaic of states, including kingdoms, duchies, bishoprics, and free cities, the empire featured a nuanced power structure. The emperor's authority remained circumscribed, with power dispersed among diverse princes and local rulers. Governance within the empire was characterized by a decentralized system, wherein considerable regional autonomy and feudal relations prevailed.

The relationship between the Holy Roman Empire and the Catholic Church assumed paramount significance in defining its identity. The emperor assumed the mantle of the Church's protector and guardian of its interests, with the Pope playing a pivotal role in the coronation of the emperor. Nevertheless, tensions and power struggles between emperors and popes frequently emerged, manifesting in conflicts such as the Investiture Controversy of the 11th and 12th centuries. Enduring for over a millennium, the Holy Roman Empire encountered a plethora of challenges, ranging from external invasions to internal strife due the conflict between the empire's member-states and the rise of powerful nation-states. By the late Middle Ages and the Early Modern period, the empire's influence and import had waned, and it transformed into an amalgamation of fragmented states within the broader European geopolitical landscape.

The formal demise of the Holy Roman Empire transpired in 1806 when Emperor Francis II abdicated in response to Napoleon Bonaparte's ambitious expansionist agenda. This dissolution cleared the way for the emergence of modern nation-states in Central Europe. Despite its historical trajectory and limitations as a political entity, the Holy Roman Empire exerted great influence on the political, religious, and cultural of Europe.

UNITED BRETHREN

Powerscourt Conference: U.K

John Nelson Darby, a significant figure within the original Plymouth Brethren[74] movement, played a pivotal role in the development of modern dispensationalism and was regarded as an influential figure among the fallen Anglicans. Born in Westminster, London, UK, Darby hailed from an Anglo-Irish landowning family with ancestral connections to Leap Castle in King's County, Ireland. He received his education at Trinity College Dublin, a prestigious institution founded by Queen Elizabeth I. During the years 1831 to 1833, Darby actively participated in the Powerscourt Conference, an annual gathering of Bible students organized by Lady Powerscourt, a wealthy widow and devout evangelical writer who was a close friend of Darby's. It was at this conference that Darby publicly espoused his ecclesiological and eschatological views, which included the concept of the pre-tribulation rapture. Of particular significance were his dispensationalist beliefs regarding the fate of the Jewish people and the re-establishment of the Kingdom of Israel, which positioned dispensationalists at the forefront of the Christian Zionist movement.[75] In this pursuit, between 1862

---

[74] Byline Times and The Citizens. "Up To £1.1 Billion in Government PPE Contracts Awarded to Firms Linked to Religious Sect." Byline Times, November 19, 2020. https://bylinetimes.com/2020/11/18/plymouth-exclusive-brethren-ppe-contracts-uk-government/

[75] Marsden, George M. (1982). Fundamentalism and American Culture: The Shaping of Twentieth Century Evangelicalism, 1870-1925. Oxford University Press. p. 46. ISBN 978-0-19-503083-9 https://www.goodreads.com/book/

and 1877, Darby embarked on several missionary journeys to North America, primarily focusing his efforts in New England, Ontario, and the Great Lakes region.

Scofield Reference Bible

Cyrus Scofield, the individual who rose to prominence for popularizing Christian futurism and dispensationalism, was born in 1843 in Clinton Township, Lenawee County, Michigan. His birthplace, nestled near the Great Lakes, symbolized the beginnings of a figure who would shape religious discourse. At the tender age of 17, in 1861, Scofield enlisted as a private in the 7th Tennessee Infantry. Following a month-long stay at Chimborazo Hospital in Richmond, Virginia, Scofield successfully petitioned for discharge. However, his respite proved short-lived as he was once again conscripted into the Confederacy. In an act of desertion, Scofield managed to escape behind Union lines in Bowling Green, Kentucky, ultimately finding safe passage to St. Louis, Missouri, after swearing loyalty to the Union. Through his marriage, Scofield entered the field of law and gained distinction as the youngest-ever appointed US District Attorney. Unfortunately, his tenure was marred by a fraud scandal that unfolded in the same year as his appointment. This setback prompted a significant turning point in Scofield's life, leading to his conversion to evangelical Christianity and subsequent emergence as a leader in the fundamentalist movement. During the early 1890s, Scofield assumed the title of Rev. C. I. Scofield, D.D. However, it is worth noting that there are no surviving records confirming that any academic institution bestowed upon him an honorary Doctor of Divinity degree. In 1909, the Scofield Reference Bible,[76] serving as a seminal work, was published by Oxford Univer-

---

show/911709

[76] Mangum, R. Todd, and Mark S. Sweetnam. 2009. "The Scofield Bible: Its History and Impact on the Evangelical Church." Google Books. December 10, 2009. https://books.google.com/books/about/The_Scofield_Bible.html?id=oRKA1w6TPPcC

sity, marking a notable achievement as the first American book to bear the imprimatur of this esteemed institution. In 1917, coinciding with the publication of the 1917 Tanakh by the Jewish Publication Society of America,[77] the first revisions of the Scofield Study Bible[78] were released, further solidifying Scofield's influence.

RHODES TO APARTHEID

The name Cecil Rhodes continues to reverberate through the halls of academia, evoking a complex and often contradictory legacy. As the celebrated alumnus and benefactor of Oriel College, Oxford, United Kingdom, Rhodes' towering achievements in the realms of business, philanthropy, and colonial expansion have long been the subject of reverence and admiration. In a candid acknowledgment of this complex heritage, the Rhodes Trust[79] issued a statement that sought to redefine the narrative surrounding its renowned scholarship program. "Our reputation as the world's most distinguished academic scholarship," the statement reads, "rests not on the controversial life of our founder but on the enormous contributions our Scholars have made to the world. Today, all of us around the world are called to join the struggle for equality and inclusion of all peoples of diverse backgrounds and identities, to eradicate systemic racism and to confront legacies of slavery, imperialism, and white supremacy."[80]

In their incisive research, scholars Daniel de Kadt and Joachim Wehner shed light on a profoundly troubling aspect of Rhodes'

---

[77] The Holy Scriptures, Tanakh 1917 Edition. The Jewish Publication Society, https://jps.org/books/holy-scriptures-tanakh-1917-edition/
[78] KJV Old Scofield Study Bible - Classic Edition. The KJV Store. https://www.thekjvstore.com/kjv-old-scofield-study-bible-classic-edition/
[79] "Cecil Rhodes and the Rhodes Trust. Saïd Business School," https://www.sbs.ox.ac.uk/about-us/support-us/impact-and-recognition/cecil-rhodes-and-rhodes-trust
[80] Rhodes Trust. "Legacy, Equity & Inclusion." https://www.rhodeshouse.ox.ac.uk/impact-legacy/legacy-equity-inclusion/

legacy—his systematic disenfranchisement of up to 15,000 Black and mixed-race voters in South Africa. Through a series of policy reforms enacted during his tenure as Prime Minister, Rhodes meticulously crafted a legal framework that effectively suppressed the political rights of these marginalized communities, paving the way for the unequal political environment that would eventually give rise to the horrors of apartheid, 50 years prior to white-ruled South Africa's Nationalist Party in 1948.[81] The legal framework, known as the 1892 Cape Franchise and Ballot Act, increased the value of the property of the occupancy qualification and introduced a literacy test. In 1894 he conceived the Glen Grey Act which devised a spatially targeted pattern of landholding for the black population that excluded certain types of property from the occupancy qualification regardless of its value.

The life and legacy of Cecil Rhodes has also been the subject of intense scrutiny, with his connections to the influential Rothschild banking family. At the height of his career, Rhodes founded the diamond company De Beers, which at one point controlled up to 90% of the global diamond supply. It was during this pivotal phase that Rhodes received significant financial backing from the Rothschild family to help fund his acquisition of diamond mining operations in South Africa. The Rothschilds, as one of Rhodes' key financial backers, played a crucial role in the early stages of his meteoric rise to power and influence.

Rhodes' ties to the Rothschild family[82] extended beyond mere financial support, as he also maintained close connections through his involvement in the British South Africa Company. This company,

---

[81] Flowcomm. "Cecil Rhodes Distorted Politics in South Africa Long Before Apartheid." Africa at LSE, July 20, 2023. https://blogs.lse.ac.uk/africaatlse/2023/07/20/cecil-rhodes-distorted-politics-in-south-africa-long-before-apartheid/#:~:text=Cecil%20Rhodes'%20policy%20reforms%20disenfranchised,de%20Kadt%20and%20Joachim%20Wehner

[82] "Nathaniel Mayer (Natty) de Rothschild (1840-1915)." n.d. The Rothschild Archive. https://family.rothschildarchive.org/people/61-nathaniel-mayer-natty-de-rothschild-1840-1915

which held extensive mining rights and political influence in the region, counted the Rothschilds among its major shareholders. This symbiotic relationship between Rhodes and the Rothschild family underscored the intricate web of colonial enterprise and financial power that underpinned Rhodes' expansionist ambitions.[83]

EMPIRIC RISE OF ZIONISM

Odessa, a major port city in Ukraine, emerged as a key center for early Zionist thinkers and activists in the late 19th century. It was here that figures like Leon Pinsker and Ahad Ha'am developed the ideological foundations of modern Zionism, calling for the establishment of a Jewish national homeland in Palestine. The Zionist movement gained significant momentum in Odessa and other parts of Ukraine, which had long been home to thriving Jewish communities. This Ukrainian context, marked by rising anti-Semitism and pogroms, helped spur the growth of Zionist thought and the eventual realization of the Zionist project with the creation of the State of Israel in 1948, underscoring its importance as the birthplace of Zionism in the broader history of Jewish nationalism and the Jewish diaspora in Europe to establish an ethnoreligious state.[84]

CONSCRIPTION: 1917

United Zionism

In 1917, an event of significant historical importance unfolded, characterized by a web of political dynamics and hidden agendas. The Balfour

---

[83] Chapman, S. D. "Rhodes and the City of London: Another View of Imperialism." The Historical Journal 28, no. 3 (1985): 647–66. http://www.jstor.org/stable/2639143

[84] Koss, A. "Zionism in Ukraine: How and why Ukraine was arguably the most important cradle for early Zionists." My Jewish Learning. May 12, 2022. https://www.myjewishlearning.com/article/zionism-in-ukraine/

Declaration[85] stands as a public statement issued by the British Government during the First World War. This declaration, released amidst the turmoil of the global conflict, announced the British Government's support for the establishment of a "national home for the Jewish people" in Palestine—the ramifications of this declaration would reverberate in the form of the 1948 Nakba.[86]

The genesis of the Balfour Declaration can be traced back to the period immediately following the British declaration of war on the Ottoman Empire in November 1914. Recognizing the strategic importance of Palestine, the British War Cabinet initiated discussions regarding the region's future.[87] Within a span of two months, a memorandum, authored by a Zionist Cabinet member named Herbert Samuel, circulated among the Cabinet. This memorandum proposed extending support to Zionist aspirations as a means to secure the backing of Jews in the broader war effort.[88]

Contextualizing this moment within the larger historical landscape is critical. The year 1917 witnessed the conscription of the United States into World War I as the nation aligned itself with the United Kingdom. Notably, this alignment occurred after the United States had achieved independence from its former colonial ruler, the very Kingdom that now sought to secure Jewish support through the Balfour Declaration. The interplay between global conflicts, political maneuvering, and historical legacies underscores the complexity of the events

---

[85] The Zionist Masquerade: The Birth of the Anglo-Zionist Alliance, 1914-1918. 9780230547186. Renton, J., https://www.amazon.com/Zionist-Masquerade-Anglo-Zionist-Alliance-1914-1918/dp/0230547184

[86] League of Arab States. 1948. "Jewish Atrocities in the Holy Land : Memorandum Presented by the Representative of the Arab Higher Commission for Palestine at U.N.O." The Library of Congress. 1948. https://www.loc.gov/item/2017498758/

[87] Mosaic Magazine. "The Forgotten Truth About the Balfour Declaration & Raquo; Mosaic." Mosaic, April 29, 2019. https://mosaicmagazine.com/essay/israel-zionism/2017/06/the-forgotten-truth-about-the-balfour-declaration/

[88] "Balfour Declaration." 1917. The Avalon Project. November 2, 1917. https://avalon.law.yale.edu/20th_century/balfour.asp

surrounding the Balfour Declaration. The consequences of this declaration would unfold over time, ultimately shaping the trajectory of the Palestinian-Israeli conflict and leaving an indelible mark on the history of the region.

The "Catastrophe"

The Nakba, an Arabic term meaning "catastrophe," refers to the tumultuous events that unfolded in 1948 during the establishment of the State of Israel.[89] This watershed moment in Palestinian history had far-reaching ramifications and continues to shape the Israeli-Palestinian conflict. The backdrop of the Nakba can be traced back to the adoption of United Nations General Assembly Resolution 181 in November 1947, which proposed the partition of Palestine into separate Jewish and Arab states. The mounting tensions between Jewish and Arab communities escalated following the end of the British Mandate for Palestine in May 1948, when the State of Israel was declared. The British Mandate for Palestine was an agreement established by the League of Nations in 1920, granting Britain the responsibility to administer and govern the territory of Palestine. The mandate aimed to facilitate the establishment of a Jewish homeland in Palestine.

In response, neighboring Arab states, including Egypt, Jordan, Syria, and Iraq, intervened militarily. The Nakba was characterized by widespread violence, forced displacement, and expulsion of Palestinians. Many Palestinians fled or were forcibly removed from their homes, resulting in a significant refugee crisis. Villages and towns were destroyed or repopulated with Jewish settlers, leading to the loss of land and property for the Palestinian population. The precise number of Palestinian refugees remains a subject of debate, but estimates range

---

[89] Abdullah, Daud Vicary. "A Century of Cultural Genocide in Palestine." In Routledge eBooks, 227–45, 2019. https://www.taylorfrancis.com/chapters/oa-edit/10.4324/9781351214100-10/century-cultural-genocide-palestine-daud-abdullah

between 700,000 and 800,000 individuals who were displaced as a direct consequence of the Nakba.

These displaced Palestinians sought refuge in neighboring Arab countries, where they encountered challenging living conditions and struggled to rebuild their lives. The Nakba holds immense historical and political significance, impacting the Palestinian people and the larger Israeli-Palestinian conflict. It stands as a deeply sensitive and contested issue, with Palestinians asserting their right of return to their ancestral lands and seeking recognition of their historical grievances. The displacement and dispossession experienced during the Nakba have profoundly influenced Palestinian national identity and continue to underpin Palestinian narratives, as well as their demands for justice and self-determination, as 1.9 million out of 2.2 million Palestinians have been displaced from Gaza.[90]

NIGER-CONGO II: FREE STATE

King Leopold II

The Congo Free State, established in the late 19th century under the auspices of King Leopold II of Belgium, represented a private colonial venture that ruthlessly exploited the Congo's abundant natural resources—primarily rubber and ivory—through methods marked by extreme brutality.[91] This regime of exploitation entailed forced labor, widespread violence, and gross human rights abuses. The Niger-Congolese population residing in the region bore the brunt of these cruel

---

[90] UN Women – Headquarters. "'Scared, Exhausted, and Expecting the Worst' – Women in Gaza Describe Humanitarian Crisis. UN Women – Headquarters," January 19, 2024. https://www.unwomen.org/en/news-stories/feature-story/2024/01/scared-exhausted-and-expecting-the-worst-women-in-gaza-describe-humanitarian-crisis

[91] "A Guide to the United States' History of Recognition, Diplomatic, and Consular Relations, by Country, since 1776: The Congo Free State." n.d. Office of the Historian. https://history.state.gov/countries/congo-free-state

practices, enduring the consequences of colonization. These atrocities resulted in an estimated death toll of up to 15 million Niger-Congolese people, marking a deeply disturbing chapter in colonial history.[92]

Deputation

An intriguing intersection unfolds when shifting focus to the son of this brutal king. In a pivotal episode, a Jewish deputation composed of the Chief Rabbi of Belgium, Dr. Joseph Wiener, and representatives of the Jewish consistory, had an audience with the young Belgian monarch. This interaction, published in 1934 by the Jewish Telegraphic Agency titled "Belgian Jews Greet King Leopold III", highlights the historical connections between Belgian royalty and the Jewish population, shedding light on the diverse fabric of intercommunal relations during that era.[93]

PATTERNS

Zionist Migration

The history of Jews in the Democratic Republic of the Congo, specifically around 1907 when the first Jewish immigrants began arriving in the country, hailed primarily from Eastern European countries such as Romania and Poland.[94] Subsequently, over the following years, additional Jewish immigrants arrived from South Africa, further diversi-

---

[92] Johnson, Steven. University of Central Florida. King Leopold II's Exploitation of the Congo From 1885 to 1908 and Its Consequences, https://stars.library.ucf.edu/cgi/viewcontent.cgi?article=2641&context=honorstheses1990-2015

[93] Belgian Jews Greet King Leopold III. (1934, March 20). *Jewish Telegraphic Agency*. https://www.jta.org/archive/belgian-jews-greet-king-leopold-iii (not a secure site, scanned article: http://pdfs.jta.org/1934/1934-03-20_2796.pdf)

[94] World Jewish Congress, International Jewish Cemetery Project, Southern Africa Jewish Genealogy, The Jewish Travelers' Resource Guide, & Encyclopedia Judaica. (n.d.). *Democratic Republic of Congo (ZAIRE) Virtual Jewish History Tour*. Jewish Virtual Library. https://www.jewishvirtuallibrary.org/democratic-republic-of-congo-zaire-virtual-jewish-history-tour

fying the Jewish community in the Congo. Prior to the establishment of the State of Israel in 1948, a period coinciding with the Nakba in Palestine, the Congo served as a home to numerous Zionist organizations in which the Association Sioniste du Congo Belge played a prominent role in advocating for Zionist ideals and organizing within the local Jewish community. This development underscores the presence of Zionist settlements in the Congo during that period, offering a less explored facet of the history of Zionism.

Niger-Congolese Parallels

While recognizing the distinct historical contexts and nuances between American slavery and the Congo Free State, it is essential to observe the common threads of exploitation and oppression endured by the Niger-Congolese people across these parallel historical trajectories. American slavery, a deeply entrenched system of coerced labor in the southern United States spanning several centuries, forcibly enslaved millions of Africans, including those of Niger-Congolese descent. These individuals endured unimaginable hardships, pervasive violence, and the systemic denial of fundamental human rights. The historical association between the Congo Free State and American slavery reveals a shared narrative of exploitation and subjugation with sweeping implications for the Niger-Congolese people, a narrative shared with Christopher Columbus' colonization of the Americas.

"...if we can make the case, which I think--well, I won't say what I think yet; the hearings aren't finished-- but if we can make the case that the threat is real and dire, that a free and democratic Iraq, if it could be accomplished, could have a cleansing impact on that part of the world and make our life easier significantly down the road, which I think could be made in an ideal circumstance--not even an ideal, in a--if we do things right--that it is worth the price."[95] *...in the aftermath of the tragic events on September 11, 2001*

Senator Joseph R. Biden Jr.[96][97]

---

[95] R. Biden, J., Jr. (2002, August 1). Hearings to examine threats, responses, and regional considerations surrounding Iraq. U.S. Government Publishing Office. https://www.govinfo.gov/content/pkg/CHRG-107shrg81697/html/CHRG-107shrg81697.htm

[96] House, W., & R. Biden, J., Jr. (2023, October 18). Remarks by President Biden at Community Engagement to Meet with Israelis Impacted or Involved in the Response to the October 7th Terrorist Attacks | Tel Aviv, Israel. The White House. "You don't have to be a Jew to be a Zionist." https://www.whitehouse.gov/briefing-room/speeches-remarks/2023/10/18/remarks-by-president-biden-at-community-engagement-to-meet-with-israelis-impacted-or-involved-in-the-response-to-the-october-7th-terrorist-attacks-tel-aviv-israel/

[97] Minayev, V. (1953). Zionist Agents of the American Secret Service. In *Central Intelligence Agency*. https://www.cia.gov/readingroom/docs/CIA-RDP78-03362A001600090007-6.pdf

Map Legend

SONS OF JAPHETH (red)

SONS OF HAM (yellow)

SONS OF SHEM (blue)

and EBER (green) with his descendants the Hebrews, Ishmaelites, and Edomites.

Extent of the ancient Assyrian Empire

Map Labels

Gomer, Togarmah, Elishah, Kenaz, Phrygians, Lud(Lydians), Ashkenaz, Ararat, Ur, Mas., Assyrians, Arphaxad, Ash, Haran, Calah, Tarsus, Gozan, Hena, Carchemish, Hamath, Helbon, Athens, Argos, Caphtorim (Crete), MEDITERRANEAN SEA, Rhodes, Kittim (Cyprus), Zidon, Arvad, Phoenicia, Damascus, Babel, Shinar, Casluhim, Sin, Canaan, Amorites, Israel, Nebaioth, Hagar, Dumah, Ishmael, Kedar, Avaris, Memphis (Moph), Goshen, Edom, Midian, Lehabim (Lybians), Phut, Egyptians, Pathrusim, Sinai, Arab, Naphtuhim, RED SEA OR ARABIAN GULF, No Ammon (Thebians), Diklah, Joktan, Syene, Abimael, Sheleph, Nubia, Meroe, Havilah, Hazar, Seba, Uz, Cush, Mesha, Ethiopians

CHAPTER 3
A Biblical And Sumerian Analysis

Third Sin

INTRODUCTION

At the heart of this inquiry lies a deep dive into the complex implication of ethnic cleansing by examining onomastic metadata in relation to Sumerian history and the biblical descendants of Ham, the geographical account from the "World as Known to the Hebrews", and the nuances of the Table of Nations. It then investigates the captivating idea of the "Father of many Nations" and the institution of the Book of Jubilees, illuminating the pivotal yet often overlooked position of ancestral history.

Critically, this chapter delves into the intricate dynamics of maternal lineages by tracing notable matriarchs, illustrating the implications of patriarchal constraints on revealing ancestral history. Equally important, it uncovers the troubling reality of the "Deliberate Deception" – the ways in which certain religious and cultural narratives have been strategically constructed to serve agendas of ancient colonization. Through this rigorous interdisciplinary approach, it aims to shed new light on the complex legacy of these flashpoints in ancient history and their continued reverberations in the modern world.

NATION CLEANSING, NAMING CONVENTIONS, AND A NON-CANONICAL BOOK

This section aims to examine the implications of ethnic cleansing through a review of *The World as Known to the Hebrews,* Table of Nations, and the Book of Jubilees,[98] which are biblical accounts that provide important insights into the origins and interconnections of various ethnic groups. Specifically, it explores the role of Ham, regarded as the progenitor of the African nation, and Canaan, later identified with present-day Israel, as the son or extension of Ham.

In the pursuit of tracking ancestral lineages, scholars have employed diverse methods such as linguistic analysis and DNA examination (i.e. Lemba Tribe DNA relation to the Cohen Modal Haplotype).[99] This section explores a specialized form of linguistic analysis, onomastics. Onomastics stands as a prevalent approach in historical research, utilized for the identification of ethnic minorities within wider populations and for the purpose of prosopography. For instance, Abraham's first son, Ishmael, is succeeded by Isaac and Israel, creating a genealogical chain (Ishmael, Isaac, Israel) that reflects historical developments. Notably, the name "Abraham" incorporates the element "ham" and signifies the father of many nations and Abraham's involvement with Hagar, an Egyptian woman of Hamitic descent, resulted in the birth of Ishmael. Expanding on the theme of Ham and other associated regions, several notable figures emerge: (1) Shamash: The Sumerian sun god of Mesopotamia; (2) Hammurabi:[100] The Amorite-Hamitic

---

[98] The Book of Jubilees. https://www.ccel.org/ccel/c/charles/otpseudepig/files/jubilee/index.htm

[99] Thomas, M. G., Parfitt, T., Weiss, D. A., Skorecki, K., Wilson, J. F., le Roux, M., Bradman, N., & Goldstein, D. B. (2000). Y chromosomes traveling south: the cohen modal haplotype and the origins of the Lemba--the "Black Jews of Southern Africa." American journal of human genetics, 66(2), 674–686. https://www.ncbi.nlm.nih.gov/pmc/articles/PMC1288118/pdf/AJHGv66p674.pdf

[100] Architect of the Capitol. "Hammurabi, Relief Portrait." https://www.aoc.gov/explore-capitol-campus/art/hammurabi-relief-portrait

King of Babylon; (3) Hamul:[101] Son of Perez, whose lineage traces back to Tamar and the Canaanites; (4) Abraham: Descendant of Eber[102] and Azurad, daughter of King Nimrod,[103] representing the Cush-Hamitic lineage and the King of Sumer, Babylon, and other regions; (5) Shammah: Brother of King David and a tribal leader of Edom; and (6) Hamilcar Barca: Father of Hannibal of Carthage, belonging to the Phoenician and Canaanite people, often referred to as the "Sea People."

The World as Known to the Hebrews

It is critical to acknowledge that, as per the Mosaic account, Ham is intimately associated with the continent of Africa.[104] The etymology of the term "Africa" itself is believed to trace its roots to the momentous victory of Roman Scipio Africanus over Hannibal, a pivotal figure who happened to be the son of Hamilcar.[105] This seminal event, transpiring during the ascendancy of the Roman Empire, assumes profound historical import. Understanding this context is instrumental in comprehending subsequent historical developments, including those pertaining to Christ. It is also noteworthy to underline that both Hamilcar and Hannibal were intrinsically linked to the Phoenician and Canaanite peoples. The Mosaic account of *The World as Known to the Hebrews* encompasses the diversity of Hamites in the Afro-Asi-

---

[101] Bible Gateway. Genesis 46. NIV. https://web.mit.edu/jywang/www/cef/Bible/NIV/NIV_Bible/GEN+46.html

[102] Book of Jubilees 8:10. https://www.sefaria.org/Book_of_Jubilees.8.10?lang=bi&with=all&lang2=en

[103] Book of Jubilees 8:11. https://www.sefaria.org/Book_of_Jubilees.8.11?lang=bi&with=all&lang2=en

[104] Lyman Coleman. An Historical Text Book and Atlas of Biblical Geography, pp. 13, https://caleb-cangelosi-437x.squarespace.com/s/Coleman-Lyman-An-Historical-Text-Book-and-Atlas-of-Biblical-Geography.pdf

[105] Africa: Human Geography. "The origin of the name 'Africa' is greatly disputed by scholars" https://education.nationalgeographic.org/resource/africa-human-geography/

atic regions,[106] within which, the events surrounding Hamilcar and Hannibal[107] find their locus in Carthage.

---

[106] Wolff, H. Ekkehard. Afro-Asiatic languages. Encyclopedia Britannica, March 8, 2024. https://www.britannica.com/topic/Afro-Asiatic-languages

[107] Leibovich-Dar, Sara. "The Hannibal Procedure - Haaretz Com." Haaretz. Com, May 20, 2003. https://www.haaretz.com/2003-05-21/ty-article/the-hannibal-procedure/0000017f-dbb8-db22-a17f-ffb9aba40000

TARSHISH

Tarsus

CYPRUS

THE GREAT SEA

Antioch

HAMATHITE

Arad
Archa
ARKITE
Hama

SIDONIANS

CANAAN

Sidon

Damascus

Tyre

ZEMARITE

HIVITE
Gergesa
GIRGASITE

Gibeon
JEBUSITE
Jerusalem
Heshbon

AMORITE

Hebron
HETH

Gaza
PHILISTIM
SINITE

HUSH

CUSH

EPHRAIM

CHAPTER 3

Table of Nations

In accordance with the biblical account provided in the Table of Nations found in Genesis 10, the descendants of Ham are associated with diverse nations and peoples. The Table of Nations serves as a genealogical record, enumerating the progeny of Noah's three sons: Shem, Ham, and Japheth.[108] Within the Table of Nations, the descendants of Ham are identified as Cush (Kush), Misraim (Egypt), Phut, Canaan, Hittites, Girgashites, Hivites, Sinites, Naphtuhites, Jebusites, Arkites, Amorites, and others. These nations and peoples are directly associated with Ham as their progenitor. Cush represents a diverse array of ancient kingdoms situated in the region that encompasses present-day Sudan and Ethiopia. Misraim pertains to the land of Egypt and its inhabitants. Phut likely designates a people residing in North Africa. Canaan encompasses the Canaanite population that occupied the land bearing the same name, which corresponds to modern-day Israel, Palestine, and adjacent regions. The Hittites were a prominent Anatolian civilization that established a formidable empire in what is presently recognized as Turkey.

---

[108] Bible Gateway. Genesis 10 (NIV). "The Hamites" https://www.biblegateway.com/passage/?search=Genesis+10&version=NIV

SUMERIAN ASSOCIATION OR LINGUISTIC RELATION INDICATED IN BOLD

CUSH (KUSH)	MISRAIM (EGYPT)	PHUT	CANAAN[109]
SEBA	LUDITES	-	SIDON
HAVILAH	ANAMITES	-	HITTITES (ANATOLIA)
SABTAH	LEHABITES	-	JEBUSITES (**IJEBU**)
RAAMAH SHEABA DEDAN	NAPHTUHITES	-	AMORITES (HAMMURABI)
SABTEKA	PATHRUSITES	-	GIRGASHITES (**GIRSU**)
NIMROD (**NINGIRSU**)	KASLUHITES	-	HIVITES
-	CAPHTORITES	-	ARKITES
-	-	-	**SIN**ITES (SIN, MT. SINAI)
-	-	-	ARVADITES
-	-	-	ZEMARITES
-	-	-	HAMATHITES

---

[109] Mellish, John. David Rumsey Historical Map Collection. "The Places Recorded in the Five Books of Moses," 1815. https://www.davidrumsey.com/luna/servlet/detail/RUMSEY~8~1~250605~5517137:The-Places-Recorded-in-the-Five-Boo?sort=pub_list_no_initialsort%2Cpub_date%2Cpub_list_no%2Cseries_no&qvq=q:author%3D%22Mellish%2C%2BJohn%22;sort:-pub_list_no_initialsort%2Cpub_date%2Cpub_list_no%2Cseries_no;l-c:RUMSEY~8~1&mi=9&trs=12

CHAPTER 3

Surname

Given the absence of surnames during this period, individuals often incorporated tribal markers associated with Ham into their name as a means of identification and affiliation. This practice allowed for the expression of a deep sense of belonging to a particular tribe or nation, as noted by Hamilcar's name incorporating "ham". This section offers a preliminary exploration of the topic, shedding light on the significance of tribal markers and their implications for understanding historical connections. It serves as a foundation for further research, enabling a more comprehensive analysis of the individuals associated with Ham and the related region. For additional information on the following, please refer to the Appendix: An Onomastic Review of Ham.

HAM (A-J)	ASSOCIATION	HAM (J-Z)	ASSOCIATION
ABRAHAM	ABRAHAMIC FAITHS, MESOPOTAMIA, HAMITIC REGION-CANAAN	JOTHAM	JUDAH
BAAL "LORD" HAMMON	CANAAN	LORU-HAMAH	PROPHET HOSEA AND HIS WIFE GOMER
CHIMHAM	KING JEHOIACHIN, MANASSEH, PROPHET JEREMIAH	MALCHAM	DEITY, BENJAMIN
ELISHAMA	"GOD LISTENS", EPHRAIM, KING DAVID	MISHAM	BENJAMIN
ETHAM	LOCATION	NAHAMANI	JUDAH

GA**HAM**	ABRAHAM, NAHOR	PROPHET MU**HAM**MAD	ISLAM
HAMATH	AMORITE, HITTITES	RA**HAM**	JUDAH
HAMAZI	SUMERIA	SELA-**HAM**-MAHLEKOTH	DIVINE INTERVENTION OR JUDGMENT
HAMILCAR BARCA	CARTHAGINIAN: PHOENICIAN, CANAAN, BARCELONA	**SHAM**A	"ACTIVELY LISTENING TO AND INTERNALIZING GOD'S INSTRUCTIONS"
HAMMATH	NAPHTALI	**SHAM**ASH	SEMITIC SUN GOD, SUMERIAN, MESOPOTAMIA
HAMMEDATHA	KING AHASUERUS PERSIAN EMPIRE AMALEKITES	**SHAM**ASH CANDLE	SHAMASH, HANUKKAH, MENORAH
HAMMELECH	"THE KING", KING DAVID, KING SOLOMON	**SHAM**AYIM	HEAVEN
HAMMOLEKETH	MANASSEH	**SHAM**ER	ASHER
HAMMURABI	AMORITE, KING OF BABYLON	**SHAM**GAR	CANAAN, ANATH-ANCIENT SEMITIC GODDESS
HAMON GOG	LOCATION	**SHAM**HUTH	KING DAVID

HAMOR	HIVITE	**SHAM**IR	ANATH, EPHRAIM, JUDGE IN ISRAEL, FIRST TEMPLE IN JERUSALEM,
HAMUL	JUDAH, PEREZ	**SHAM**MAH	KING DAVID, EDOMITE, ESAU, REUEL
HAMUTAL	KING JEHOIACHIN, KINGDOM OF JUDAH	**SHAM**MAI	MISHNAH
HO**HAM**	AMORITE, KING OF HEBRON	**SHAM**MUA	KING DAVID, PRIESTLY FAMILY OF BILGAI, LEVITE, REUBEN
HOS**HAM**A	JEHOIACHIN, KING OF JUDAH	**SHAM**SHI	ASSYRIAN EMPIRE
HOT**HAM**	KING DAVID, ASHERITE	SHAP**HAM**	GAD, REUBEN, MANASSEH
HUP**HAM**	BENJAMIN	SHO**HAM**	LEVITE
HUS**HAM**	ELECTIVE KING OF THE EDOMITES	SHU**HAM**	DAN
ISHME-**SHAM**ASH	MESOPOTAMIA	SHUP**HAM**	BENJAMIN
IT**HAM**AR	LEVI	SIN-IQI**SHAM**	ANCIENT MESOPOTAMIA

JEHOVAH-S**HAM**-MAH	"THE LORD IS THERE"	T**HAM**AH	LEVITE
JERO**HAM**	PROPHET SAMUEL, DAN, BENJAMIN, JUDAH, PRIEST	ZET**HAM**	LEVITE

Father of many Nations

The name change of the biblical figure Abram to Abraham holds significance within the context of his life journey. As detailed in the Book of Genesis, Abram, who himself incorporated the tribal or national marker of Ham into his name, entered into a covenant with God, wherein he was promised to become the progenitor of numerous nations in his migration to Canaan around the early 2nd millennium BCE. In a momentous act symbolizing the fulfillment of this divine pledge, Abram's name was altered to Abraham, which conveys the meaning "father of a multitude" or "father of many nations".[110] This alteration in nomenclature, with the inclusion of Ham as a tribal or national marker, represents a transformative event in Abraham's identity and purpose, emphasizing his pivotal role as the forefather of a chosen people.

Book of Jubilees

The Book of Jubilees is generally considered to be older than the New Testament, having been composed in the second century BCE. It is an ancient Jewish text that provides additional narratives and details not found in the canonical Old Testament. Alternative traditions, such as

---

[110] Bible Gateway. Genesis 17. NIV. https://web.mit.edu/jywang/www/cef/Bible/NIV/NIV_Bible/GEN+17.html

those found in the non-canonical Book of Jubilees, offer additional narratives and details regarding the events surrounding the Tower of Babel. According to the Book of Jubilees, Nimrod, a figure of prominence associated with kingship and rulership in the land of Shinar (Sumer), is portrayed as the son of Cush and the grandson of Ham, as genealogically delineated. These traditions attribute a significant role to Nimrod during the early post-Flood period, depicting him as a mighty hunter and a powerful king. In the Book of Jubilees, King Nimrod is also identified as the father of Azurad.

MATRIARCH

The maternal bloodline of Abraham, whose blood trace back to Eber and Azurad, is depicted in the provided genealogical chart.[111] This chart offers a comprehensive representation of the familial relationships and connections within this lineage. It emphasizes the importance of tracing both paternal and maternal lines in understanding the broader genealogical history. By incorporating the maternal lineage, the chart highlights the interconnectedness of individuals and the interplay between various family branches. It allows for a deeper understanding of the familial context in which Abraham, a central figure in biblical history, emerged. Tracing Abraham's maternal lineage sheds light on the ancestral and familial influences that shaped his position as the patriarch of the Israelite nation.

---

[111] "Chart of the Genealogy of Abraham: Abraham's Family Tree." n.d. Conforming to Jesus. https://www.conformingtojesus.com/images/webpages/genealogy_of_abraham_1.jpg

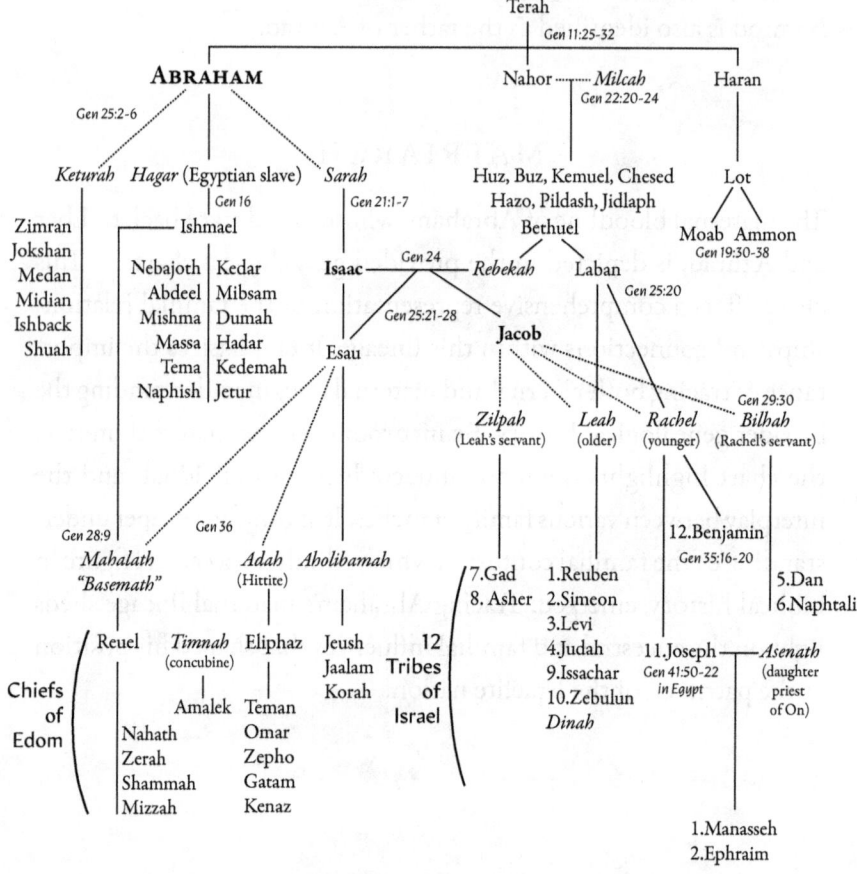

CHAPTER 3

Paternal v. Maternal

The decision to prioritize the paternal bloodline over the maternal bloodline in ancient cultures, including biblical genealogies, can be attributed to several factors. One of the primary reasons is the patriarchal nature of these societies, where the male lineage held greater significance. In such societies, inheritance, property rights, and social status were typically passed down through the male line. Consequently, genealogies focused on tracing the male ancestry to establish legitimacy, inheritance rights, and the continuity of family lines.

However, among the various doctrines asserted within rabbinic Judaism, few are as surprising, and indeed as contentious, as the concept of "matrilineal descent." According to this principle, which is universally accepted among classic commentators, the offspring of a Gentile mother and a Jewish father is considered a Gentile, while the offspring of a Jewish mother and a Gentile father is recognized as Jewish. This precept appears to be inconsistent with other aspects of Jewish law, where paternal ancestry predominantly determines various factors. For instance, it is solely the father who determines a child's status as a priest or Levite, as a member of the tribes of Judah or Benjamin, or as a descendant of the Hasmonean or Davidic dynasty. Genealogy, therefore, is generally determined by the father in nearly all categories except for the most crucial one: whether a child is considered Jewish from the outset. The principle of matrilineal descent seems so incongruous that Yehiel Jacob Weinberg, the eminent German rabbi of the first half of the twentieth century, was compelled to comment: "Why is a child as his mother? The answer is not quite clear."[112]

---

[112] Soloveichik, Meir and Azure. 2013. "Motherhood and Matrilineal Descent." The Tikvah Fund. December 11, 2013. https://tikvahfund.org/library/exploring-matrilineal-descent/

Maternal & Paternal

It is essential to recognize that these practices were rooted in the cultural and societal norms of their time and may not align with contemporary perspectives on gender equality. However, it is worth noting that modern genealogical research and genetic studies have shed light on the significance of both maternal and paternal lineages in comprehending human history and ancestry. Overall, the section provides a detailed and informative representation of the bloodline of Eber and Azurad, as well as their connection to Abraham. It underscores the significance of considering both paternal and maternal lines in unraveling the complex genealogical and historical narratives.

Intertwined

The genealogical chart, as mentioned in the beginning of this section on Matriarch, also provides valuable insights into the lineage of Abraham and their role in the historical context of foreign rulers known as the Hyksos period in Egyptian history.[113][114] It is critical to note that while they were part of the ruling class, their bloodlines were also intertwined with those of slaves, servants, concubines, and beta wives, who likely belonged to the native population of the region.[115]

---

[113] Halpern, Baruch, and רוב דוד. "ויצאי מצרים ויהוסטוריוני הקמראיי / The Exodus and the Israelite Historians." *Eretz-Israel: Archaeological, Historical and Geographical Studies / ארץ-ישראל: מחקרים בידיעת הארץ ועתיקותיה* דכ (1993): 89*-96*. https://www.jstor.org/stable/23624618

[114] Eames, Christopher. n.d. "The Amarna Letters: Proof of Israel's Invasion of Canaan?: The ancient Habiru battled their way through Canaan during the 14th century b.c.e. Who were these people?" Armstrong Institute of Biblical Archaeology. https://armstronginstitute.org/881-the-amarna-letters-proof-of-israels-invasion-of-canaan

[115] Patterns Of Evidence. 2022. "Signs of Israelite Slavery in Egypt - the Exodus." https://www.youtube.com/watch?v=lfQdjdSm2AE

CHAPTER 3

Notable Matriarchs

Hagar and Sarah. Hagar[116] was a Hamitic Egyptian slave or servant who belonged to Sarah, Abraham's wife. Sarah gave Hagar to Abraham as a concubine with the intention of her bearing a child, resulting in Hagar becoming the mother of Ishmael, Abraham's first son, the maternal bloodline associated with Prophet Muhammad.

Zilpah and Bilhah. Zilpah was a servant or handmaid given by Laban to his daughter Leah, Jacob's first wife. In addition to her role as a servant, Zilpah became a secondary wife to Jacob, bearing him two sons, Gad and Asher. Similarly, Bilhah, akin to Zilpah,[117] was another handmaid or servant bestowed by Laban upon Rachel, Jacob's second wife. Like Zilpah, Bilhah also ascended to the status of a wife to Jacob, giving birth to two sons, Dan and Naphtali.

The mention of Naphtali prompts an intriguing connection. The Naphtali tribe, stemming from the progeny of Naphtali, played a momentous role in ancient Israel. Remarkably, a semblance arises between the names "Naphtuhites",[118] "Naphish", and "Naphtali",[119] engendering curiosity. It is prudent, however, to discern the distinction between these appellations. The Naphtuhites, son of Misraim ("Egypt"), delineated in various passages of the Old Testament, constituted a people inhabiting the Hamitic region. They are frequently affiliated with other Canaanite collectives. Moreover, Naphish, as recorded

---

[116] Junior, Nyasha. 2019. "Hagar." Oxford Bibliographies. August 28, 2019. https://www.oxfordbibliographies.com/display/document/obo-9780195393361/obo-9780195393361-0270.xml?rskey=ZRTExz&result=1&q=hagar#firstMatch

[117] Halpern-Amaru, Betsy. "Bilhah and Naphtali in Jubilees: A Note on 4QT-Naphtali." *Dead Sea Discoveries* 6, no. 1 (1999): 1–10. https://www.jstor.org/stable/4193108

[118] Bible Gateway. Genesis 10. NIV. https://web.mit.edu/jywang/www/cef/Bible/NIV/NIV_Bible/GEN+10.html

[119] The Catholic Encyclopedia; an International Work of Reference on the Constitution, Doctrine, Discipline, and History of the Catholic Church. Herbermann, Charles George, 1840-1916. Internet Archive, 1907. "'Naphtali': 'buried in Egypt'." https://archive.org/details/catholicencyclop10herbuoft/page/748/mode/2up?view=theater

in the book of Genesis (Genesis 25:13),[120] is identified as one of the sons of Ishmael—the first son of Abraham and Hagar. This biblical account highlights Naphish's genealogical connection to Ishmael, who himself holds a significant position as the son of the patriarch Abraham and his wife Hagar of Egyptian descent. Conversely, the tribe of Naphtali emerged as one of the twelve tribes of Israel, with its constituents forming an integral part of the Israelite community.

Leah and Rachel. Leah was Jacob's first wife, although he had initially intended to marry her younger sister Rachel. Leah bore Jacob six sons: Reuben, Simeon, Levi, Judah, Issachar, and Zebulun. Her position as Jacob's primary wife and the mother of many of his children is central to the biblical account. She gave birth to two sons, Joseph and Benjamin, both of whom played significant roles in later biblical events.

Mahalath, Adah, and Aholibamah. Mahalath, also known as Basemath, was one of Esau's wives of Hamitic descent. She was the daughter of Ishmael, making her a granddaughter of Abraham. Her marriage to Esau symbolizes the intertwining of the descendants of Abraham and Ishmael. Adah was one of Esau's wives, mentioned as a Hittite. She was one among the women Esau took as wives when he settled in Canaan. Her inclusion represents the intermarriage between Esau and the local Canaanite population. Aholibamah was another wife of Esau, described as a Hivite. She, too, was among the women Esau married while residing in Canaan. Her marriage signifies the mingling of Esau's lineage with the Hivite people.

Timnah. Timnah, as a woman, is mentioned in the book of Genesis within the biblical narrative. According to Genesis 36:12,[121] Timnah is described as a concubine of Eliphaz, the son of Adah and Esau, the twin brother of Jacob. Eliphaz is recognized as one of the prominent figures within the genealogy of the Edomites. Timnah is specifically

---

[120] Bible Gateway. Genesis 25. NIV. https://web.mit.edu/jywang/www/cef/Bible/NIV/NIV_Bible/GEN+25.html

[121] Bible Gateway. Genesis 36. NIV. https://web.mit.edu/jywang/www/cef/Bible/NIV/NIV_Bible/GEN+36.html

listed as one of the mothers of Eliphaz's sons. The most notable of these sons is Amalek, who is significant in biblical history as the progenitor of the Amalekite people. The Amalekites would later emerge as a distinct group, frequently encountered by the Israelites during their journey in the wilderness and subsequent settlement in the Promised Land. The biblical account of Timnah and her association with the lineage of Eliphaz and the Amalekites provides insight into the genealogical connections and historical context of ancient Hamitic peoples in Canaan.

Asenath. Asenath was another Egyptian woman of Hamitic descent who became the wife of Joseph, son of Jacob. She bore Joseph two sons, Manasseh and Ephraim. Asenath's marriage to Joseph solidified his position and influence in Egypt, leading to the preservation of Jacob's family during a time of famine.

Tamar. Tamar's story, detailed in the Book of Genesis, is critical for her actions to secure the continuation of Judah's lineage, commonly associated with the Jewish religion. She was the daughter-in-law of Judah and played a significant role in the ancestral heritage of the Israelite tribe of Judah. It is imperative to note that Tamar is described as a Canaanite woman, and her lineage is traced back to Ham, one of Noah's sons. Following the deaths of her first husband, Er, who was Judah's eldest son, and then Onan, her second husband, Tamar found herself widowed. Despite the challenges she faced, Tamar was determined to secure her right to bear children from the family line of Judah. When Judah was unwilling to allow Tamar, who had been successively Er's and Onan's wife, to be married to Shelah, she resorted to a discreet strategy. Based on biblical account, Tamar disguised herself and, without Judah recognizing her, engaged in an encounter with him. Unaware of her true identity, Judah impregnated her, and later Tamar unveiled her true self and presented the evidence of her pregnancy. This notable occurrence resulted in the birth of twins, Perez and Zerah, which played a significant role in the ancestry leading to King David and, ultimately, Christ.

DELIBERATE DECEPTION

The narrative surrounding the deception involving Rebekah, Jacob, and Esau's birthright within the biblical book of Genesis offers a compelling account of familial dynamics and its consequential implications.[122][123][124] Rebekah, the wife of Isaac and mother to the twin brothers Jacob and Esau, favored Jacob over his elder brother Esau. As Isaac, their father, reached old age and prepared to bestow the birthright upon Esau, Rebekah, driven by her preference for Jacob, devised a sophisticated plan to ensure that the birthright blessings would be redirected to her favored son.

Rebekah orchestrated a scheme that involved Jacob assuming Esau's identity in order to deceive the ailing and visually impaired Isaac. By meticulously dressing Jacob in animal skins to mimic Esau's hairy arms and preparing a savory dish akin to Esau's culinary style, Rebekah sought to convince Isaac that Jacob was, in fact, Esau. Jacob, initially hesitant, ultimately complied with his mother's persuasive strategy. Under the guise of Esau's presence, Jacob presented the prepared meal to Isaac, who, due to his visual impairment, struggled to discern the true identity of his sons. Isaac expressed doubt, noting the peculiar resemblance of Jacob's voice to that of Jacob himself. However, Jacob skillfully invoked divine intervention and attributed his successful hunting expedition to divine favor, thus alleviating Isaac's suspicions.

With Isaac satisfied, Jacob approached his father, allowing Isaac to physically examine him. Isaac, feeling the hairy arms covered in animal skins, was further convinced of Jacob's false identity, thereby

---

[122] Assis, Elie. Identity in Conflict: The Struggle between Esau and Jacob, Edom and Israel. Vol. 19. Penn State University Press, 2016. https://www.jstor.org/stable/10.5325/j.ctv1bxgwxb

[123] Anderson, John E. Jacob and the Divine Trickster, 2011. https://www.jstor.org/stable/10.5325/j.ctv1bxgxcj

[124] Bradford Ashworth Anderson. "Election, Brotherhood and Inheritance: A Canonical Reading of the Esau and Edom Traditions." Thesis. Durham Theses. Durham University, 2010. https://etheses.dur.ac.uk/315/1/Bradford_Anderson.thesis.pdf

bestowing upon him the coveted birthright blessings. These blessings entailed prosperity, dominion over his siblings, and the inheritance of the familial blessings.

Upon learning of Esau's seething anger and his vow to kill Jacob, Rebekah, concerned for Jacob's safety, took decisive action. She urged Jacob to flee to her brother Laban's house until Esau's anger subsided. Recognizing the gravity of the situation, Jacob heeded his mother's counsel and embarked on a journey to Laban's dwelling, effectively separating the brothers for an extended period. The ramifications of this elaborate deception and Rebekah's subsequent decision to send Jacob away were far-reaching in his return, as the Edomites, of Esau's progeny, eventually established themselves as a prominent nation, often engaging in conflicts with the Israelites, who trace their lineage to Jacob, also known as Israel.

The birthright deception played a significant role in shaping the divergent paths taken by the twin brothers. It further contributed to the family's fractured dynamics and the displacement of indigenous populations. This displacement led to a renamed region and forced migration to other lands, including the West Coast of Africa, as indicated by the Kingdom of Juda on the Slave Coast of Africa, in the "Bite of Benin."[125][126][127][128]

---

[125] Bowen, Emanuel. 1747. "A New & Accurate Map of Negroland and the Adjacent Countries..." The Library of Congress. 1747. https://www.loc.gov/resource/g8735.ct010406/?r=-0.457,-0.053,1.898,0.919,0

[126] Eggert, By Nalina. 2018. "Tracing Sickle Cell Back to One Child, 7,300 Years Ago." British Broadcasting Corporation (BBC). March 13, 2018. https://www.bbc.com/news/world-africa-43373247

[127] Bitoungui, Valentina J. Ngo, Gift D. Pule, Neil Hanchard, Jeanne Ngogang, and Ambroise Wonkam. 2015. "Beta-Globin Gene Haplotypes Among Cameroonians and Review of the Global Distribution: Is There a Case for a Single Sickle Mutation Origin in Africa?" *Omics* 19 (3): 171–79. https://www.ncbi.nlm.nih.gov/pmc/articles/PMC4356477/pdf/omi.2014.0134.pdf

[128] Rund, Deborah, Naomi Kornhendler, Oded Shalev, and Ariella Oppenheim. 1990. "The Origin of Sickle Cell Alleles in Israel." Human Genetics 85 (5). https://link.springer.com/article/10.1007/BF00194229

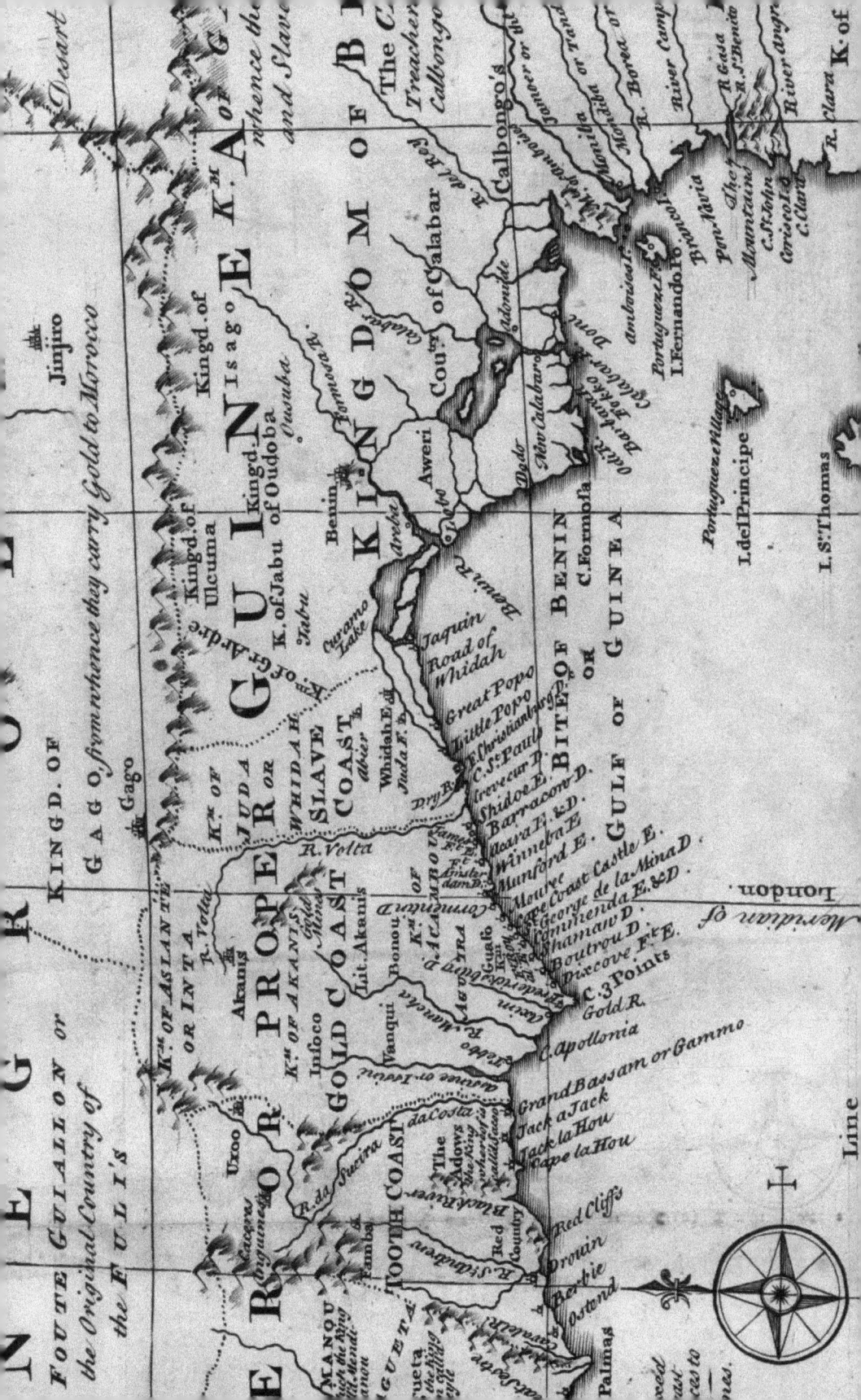

CHAPTER 4
A Loss Analysis

Fourth Sin

INTRODUCTION

THIS SEMINAL CHAPTER DELVES INTO THE TROUBLING PHENOMENON OF ETHNIC CLEANSING THROUGH LOST TRIBES, LOST CITIES, LOST ALPHABET, LOST LAW, LOST ART, AND LOST CULTURE—ALL OF WHICH HAVE THEIR ROOTS FIRMLY PLANTED IN THE ANCIENT CIVILIZATIONS. THIS CHAPTER SHEDS LIGHT ON THE PLIGHT OF HAM THROUGH "LOST SOULS", EXAMINING THEIR INTIMATE RELATIONSHIP WITH THE SEMITIC SUN GOD SHAMASH AND THE CHILD OF LIGHT WITHIN THE HALLOWED CONTEXT OF THE SUMERIAN HISTORY. THE ANALYSIS THEN TRACES THE SIGNIFICANCE OF THE CHURCH IN ANTIOCH AND THE REMARKABLE SUMERIAN-SEMITIC PARALLELISMS THAT HAVE SHAPED PLACES OF WORSHIP OVER THE MILLENNIA.

LOST TRIBES

In examining the genealogical connections and historical contexts outlined in the Matriarch section, we can identify a group of individuals, namely Hagar, Mahalath, Adah, Aholibamah, Asenath, and Tamar, who are associated with Hamitic lineage through their connections to Misraim (Egypt), Hittites, Hivites, and Canaan. Furthermore, it is highly probable that Zilpah, like Bilhah, also share Hamitic ancestry. This inference is based on the name of Naphtali, which could potentially be linked to the Naphtuhites and Naphish, the son of Hagar, who were descendants of Misraim (Egypt). Additionally, the aforementioned section highlights the union of Timnah and Eliphaz, which leads to Hamitic descendants based on the maternal bloodline of Adah and Esau. This observation underscores the significance of maternal lineage in determining the Hamitic heritage of the offspring.

Within the Hebrew language, the term "Edom" bears significant linguistic connotations as it translates to "red". Its etymology finds resonance within the Hebrew Bible, where it is intrinsically linked to the name of its progenitor, Esau, the eldest son of the esteemed Hebrew patriarch Isaac. The narrative accounts within the Hebrew Bible recount Esau's birth, describing him as being "red all over," thus establishing a direct correlation between his "hairy garment" or physical appearance and the appellation "Edom".[129] Delving deeper into the biblical text, the Tanakh elucidates that the Edomites trace their lineage back to Esau, emphasizing his role as their progenitor. It is essential to mention that the matrilineal lineage of the Edomites is attributed to Mahalath, also known as "Basemath," who herself descends from Hagar, the Egyptian (Misraim) handmaiden of Sarah and her husband Abraham. It is also fascinating to observe the resemblance between the names "Edom" and "Edo," as well as "Esau" and "Esan," which provokes curiosity and prompts further exploration of Nigeria and Japan in Haplogroup DE.[130][131] While the term "Edo" is associated with the specific historical and cultural contexts of Edo, Nigeria, and Edo, Japan, it is important to recognize the distinctiveness of each region

---

[129] Bible Gateway. Genesis 25. NIV. https://web.mit.edu/jywang/www/cef/Bible/NIV/NIV_Bible/GEN+25.html

[130] Ighodaro, Peter and Elebute, Ayo. Hypothetical cases for cultural relation between Edo Benin (Nigeria) and Edo Tokyo (Japan). Institution, Smithsonian. https://www.si.edu/object/hypothetical-cases-cultural-relation-between-edo-benin-nigeria-and-edo-tokyo-japan-peter-ighodaro%3Asiris_sil_913792

[131] Haber, Marc et al. "A Rare Deep-Rooting D0 African Y-Chromosomal Haplogroup and Its Implications for the Expansion of Modern Humans Out of Africa." Genetics vol. 212,4 (2019): 1421-1428. https://www.ncbi.nlm.nih.gov/pmc/articles/PMC6707464/pdf/1421.pdf

and the unique contributions they have made to their respective local histories, cultures, and identities. The exploration of these distinct contexts enriches our understanding of the diversity of human civilization across different parts of the world.

Overall, the genealogy and linguistic data present a hypothesis regarding the identification of certain individuals as Hamites based on their connections to specific ancient civilizations and linguistic ties. Further research and analysis would be necessary to corroborate these claims and explore the broader implications for understanding the genealogy and ethnic composition of the associated tribes, and the displacement of those tribes, in particular the tribes associated with the Notable Matriarchs and Patriarchs. These Abrahamic tribes include, but are not limited to, Manasseh, Ephraim, Reuben, Levi, Judah, Dan, Naphtali, Gad, Asher, Benjamin, and the descendants of the Hamitic-women and Esau.[132][133]

LOST CITIES

The narrative of the Tower of Babel, as depicted in the book of Genesis within the Hebrew Bible, presents a story that seeks to address the origins of linguistic diversity and the dispersion of humanity across different regions. According to the account, after the occurrence of a cataclysmic flood, humanity had a unified language and settled in the land of Sumer, where they embarked on an ambitious project to construct a city and a tower reaching the heavens. This endeavor was driven by a desire for renown and a collective aspiration to establish a lasting legacy.

---

[132] Britannica, T. Editors of Encyclopaedia. Ten Lost Tribes of Israel. Encyclopedia Britannica, January 2, 2024. https://www.britannica.com/topic/Ten-Lost-Tribes-of-Israel

[133] Lost Tribes and Promised Lands: The Origins of American Racism: Sanders, Dr Ronald. https://www.amazon.com/Lost-Tribes-Promised-Lands-American/dp/1626542767

In biblical accounts found in the book of Genesis, Nimrod, of Cushite Hamitic descent, is depicted as a significant figure associated with the construction of cities, including Sumer and Babylon, and described as a powerful hunter and influential ruler. According to the biblical narrative, Nimrod played a pivotal role in the development and expansion of these cities, particularly Sumer and Babylon, which subsequently emerged as a prominent political, economic, and cultural hub in ancient Mesopotamia.

LOST ALPHABET

The development of writing systems represents a crucial milestone in human history, facilitating the recording and transmission of information across time and distance. While the earliest known writing systems, such as those of Mesopotamia, Egypt, and possibly India, emerged in the fourth millennium BCE, they were predominantly non-alphabetic, consisting of numerous signs, often numbering over a thousand. It was not until approximately 1800 BCE, as per the consensus among scholars, that the first alphabet came into being.[134] This initial alphabet, commonly referred to as Proto-Canaanite,[135] owes its invention to Semitic-speaking peoples who possessed knowledge of the Egyptian writing system. These individuals adapted certain signs from the Egyptian script to suit their own language, thereby creating the foundation for the first alphabet. It is critical to highlight that the term "Proto-Canaanite" reflects its association with the Canaanites, descendants of Ham, rather than any specific attribution to the

---

[134] Steinmeyer, Nathan. "Oldest Canaanite Sentence Found." Biblical Archaeology Society, June 26, 2023. https://www.biblicalarchaeology.org/daily/biblical-artifacts/inscriptions/oldest_written_canaanite_sentence/

[135] William H. Shea. The 'Izbet Sartah Ostracon. The Biblical Research Institute. Andrews University Seminary Studies, Spring 1990, Vol. 28, No. 1, 59-86 https://digitalcommons.andrews.edu/cgi/viewcontent.cgi?referer=&httpsredir=1&article=1938&context=auss

Phoenicians. Instead, they played a crucial role in adapting and standardizing the alphabet several centuries after its initial invention. As Professor Christopher Rollston, an esteemed scholar in ancient Semitic languages, aptly notes, "The Phoenicians did not invent the alphabet. They adapted and standardized the alphabet several centuries after it was invented."[136] The Phoenicians' contributions in disseminating the alphabet should not be underestimated, as their standardized version became widely adopted. Subsequent to the Phoenicians' efforts, the ancient Israelites embraced the alphabet and developed their own distinct variant, drawing from the standardized Phoenician script. Similarly, the Arameans and Greeks, influenced by the Phoenician adaptation, adopted and modified the Phoenician version to create their own scripts. It is noteworthy to recognize that the fundamental invention of the Proto-Canaanite alphabet occurred only once, around 1800 BCE, coinciding with Abraham's migration from Mesopotamia to Canaan, and all subsequent versions of the alphabet trace their origins back to this initial creation.

LOST LAW

The Code of Hammurabi,[137] a legal compilation attributed to the ancient Babylonian king Hammurabi who reigned from approximately 1792 to 1754 BCE, represents a significant artifact in the study of ancient law and society, which predates the development of Mosaic Law. Inscribed on a stele,[138] this legal code provides us with valuable insights into the legal principles and social norms prevalent in Babylo-

---

[136] Carlpage. "How the First Biblical Writing Links to the Alphabet." Patterns of Evidence, March 28, 2024. https://www.patternsofevidence.com/2019/03/02/first-biblical-writing/

[137] King, L. W. n.d. "Code of Hammurabi." The Avalon Project. https://avalon.law.yale.edu/ancient/hamframe.asp

[138] Musée Du Louvre. "Code De Hammurabi," https://collections.louvre.fr/en/ark:/53355/cl010174436#

nian civilization during that era. At its core, the Code of Hammurabi consists of 282 laws encompassing a wide range of topics, including criminal justice, property rights, trade regulations, and family law. These laws sought to establish a sense of order and justice within Babylonian society, reflecting the king's desire to promote stability and ensure the equitable treatment of his subjects.

Of particular interest is the influence of religious beliefs on the code. Shamash (Šamaš),[139] the sun god and a prominent figure in Babylonian mythology, was regarded as the divine source of justice and wisdom, and his role in the code is evident in the prologue where Hammurabi credits him for the establishment of the laws. The concept of lex talionis, or "an eye for an eye," is a notable aspect of the Code of Hammurabi. This principle, rooted in the notion of proportionate justice, is reflected in the punishments prescribed for various offenses. The code sought to maintain social order and balance by ensuring that the severity of the punishment corresponded to the gravity of the crime committed.

LOST ART

Throughout history, the Roman Empire have amassed collections of African artifacts, often acquired through channels such as colonialism, exploration, and archaeological expeditions. Presented in the following are some notable examples of African artifacts housed in the Rome, France, and United Kingdom:

Rome. The Vatican Museums hold a wide array of art and artifacts, including select pieces from Africa.[140] Their collections encompass early Christian art from North Africa, such as magnificent mosaics and

---

[139] Lawhon, Taylor. "Shamash: The Sun God – Ancient Art," March 12, 2015. https://ancientart.as.ua.edu/shamash-the-sun-god/

[140] Hemingway, Seán, and Colette Hemingway. Africans in Ancient Greek Art. The Met's Heilbrunn Timeline of Art History, January 1, 1AD. https://www.metmuseum.org/toah/hd/afrg/hd_afrg.htm

sculptures. Furthermore, the Vatican Museums exhibit artifacts from ancient Egypt and Nubia, modern-day Sudan. Of particular interest are the Egyptian sarcophagi, papyri, and mummies, which provide intriguing insights into the funerary practices and religious beliefs of ancient African civilizations.

France. French explorers, missionaries, and administrators encountered African cultures and collected objects of artistic and cultural significance. These artifacts were brought back to France, where they became part of museum collections and private holdings. Today, one notable institution housing a significant collection of African artifacts is the Musée du quai Branly - Jacques Chirac in Paris. The museum aims to showcase the artistic excellence and cultural diversity of African civilizations through its extensive collection, which includes sculptures, masks, textiles, and other objects. The presence of African artifacts in France has generated discussions and debates surrounding issues of cultural appropriation, colonial legacy, and the need for repatriation.[141] In recent years, there has been a growing recognition of the need to address the historical circumstances surrounding the acquisition of African artifacts. President Emmanuel Macron's commitment in 2017 to facilitate the return of certain African cultural heritage items acquired during the colonial period without consent has sparked efforts towards repatriation.[142] The focus now lies on fostering dialogue and establishing frameworks for the repatriation of cultural artifacts to their countries of origin. This process involves collaborative partnerships between French and African institutions, aimed at promoting knowledge-sharing, cultural exchange, and a more inclusive approach to the interpretation and display of African cultural heritage.

---

[141] Musée Du Louvre. "Girsu Vase." https://collections.louvre.fr/en/ark:/53355/cl010140094

[142] Campbell, John. "Macron Leads Renewed Calls for Return of Looted African Artifacts." Council on Foreign Relations, November 28, 2018. https://www.cfr.org/blog/macron-leads-renewed-calls-return-looted-african-artifacts

United Kingdom. The British Museum, located in the United Kingdom, boasts an extensive and diverse collection of African artifacts.[143] Among the noteworthy items are the Benin Bronzes, a series of brass sculptures originating from the Kingdom of Benin, present-day Nigeria. These invaluable artworks were unfortunately looted during the punitive expedition of 1897. Additionally, the British Museum houses artifacts from ancient Egypt, which, although geographically situated in Africa, are often examined within the context of ancient Near Eastern civilizations. In the United Kingdom, the Pitt Rivers Museum, located in Oxford, stands as a notable institution housing ethnographic artifacts from diverse cultural backgrounds, including Africa. Among its rich collection are masks, carvings, textiles, and tools, all representing the remarkable cultural diversity found across the African continent. Additionally, the British Library, also situated in the UK, boasts a significant assortment of manuscripts and books from Africa. Within their holdings are ancient Ethiopian manuscripts, Islamic texts originating from West Africa, and a variety of historical documents shedding light on African history, literature, and culture.[144]

> *The artifacts highlighted here represent just a small selection, as numerous African artifacts are dispersed among various museums and collections worldwide.*

---

[143] Gbadamosi, Nosmot. "Stealing Africa: How Britain Looted the Continent's Art." Al Jazeera, October 26, 2021. https://www.aljazeera.com/features/2021/10/12/stealing-africa-how-britain-looted-the-continents-art#:~:text=During%20war%20and%20colonisation%2C%20Western,campaign%20to%20get%20them%20returned

[144] Institute of Ethiopian Studies Collection of Ethiopian Manuscripts [14th Century-21st Century]. Endangered Archives Programme. https://eap.bl.uk/collection/EAP286-1

CHAPTER 4

LOST CULTURE

Africa

The issue of African American lost culture encompasses the multifaceted historical experiences, traditions, and cultural practices that were impacted, disrupted, or lost during the era of slavery and its aftermath in the United States. The forced separation from African homelands, coupled with the oppressive conditions of slavery, had a profound influence on the preservation and transmission of African cultural heritage among enslaved Africans and their descendants. The transatlantic slave trade involved the forcible transportation of millions of Africans to the Americas, resulting in the severing of direct connections to specific African cultures, languages, and traditions. The traumatic disruption of these ties meant that many aspects of African cultural heritage were compromised, as enslaved Africans were subjected to a process of cultural assimilation and forced acculturation, which actively discouraged or suppressed their African customs.

America[+]

The subject of Africans in America before Christopher Columbus (Cristóbal Colón) is a topic that explores the possibility of African presence in the Americas prior to Columbus' renowned voyage in 1492. While the prevailing historical narrative emphasizes Columbus' arrival as the catalyst for European colonization and subsequent contact with the Americas, there exist theories and evidence suggesting that Africans may have already made their way to the continent as revealed in the previous chapters, from quoted letters conveyed to kings in the section on "Enslaving of the Natives." Other historical accounts and oral traditions offer additional glimpses into the possibility of African explorers or traders in the Americas before Columbus. These accounts, often originating from non-Western sources, provide valuable American history insights.

One area of focus is the examination of potential African influences on ancient civilizations, such as the Olmec civilization of Mesoamerica. The Olmecs, flourishing between 1200 BCE and 400 BCE, left behind monumental stone heads bearing features reminiscent of sub-Saharan Africans. While this visual resemblance is intriguing, it is imperative to approach such evidence with caution, as alternative explanations involving cultural and genetic factors exist, as many ancient cultures developed such iconography independently as a way to symbolize various attributes. However, the presence of dark skin tones may indicate a positive connotation, as a sign of reverence, suggesting people of color assisted people with these physical features. Notable examples include the Egyptian goddess Isis with the baby Horus, and the Black Madonna figures found in various religious traditions.[145][146]

Linguistic and cultural parallels between African and Indigenous American peoples also contribute to this discourse. For instance, certain similarities have been identified between specific African and Native American languages, as well as cultural practices such as agricultural techniques and religious rituals, including onomastic data examined in the subsequent section on Sumerian Origins.

LOST SOULS (SOL)

Sun God

The veneration of the sun god Shamash (Šamaš), also known as Utu, constitute a significant facet of ancient Mesopotamian religious traditions. The worship of these deities spans a considerable time, encompassing various historical periods. Within the context of Sumerian

---

[145] Isis and Horus. Late Period–Ptolemaic Period. The Metropolitan Museum of Art. https://www.metmuseum.org/art/collection/search/545969
[146] Michael P. Duricy. Montserrat Black Madonna. University of Dayton, Ohio. (2024, May 17). https://udayton.edu/imri/mary/m/montserrat-black-madonna.php

civilization, which thrived from approximately 4500 BCE to 1900 BCE, Shamash held a position of utmost importance in the Sumerian history. As the solar deity, Shamash was believed to radiate light and warmth upon the earth, ensuring agricultural fertility and the well-being of humanity. The Sumerians regarded Shamash as a discerning judge who administered justice and meted out appropriate retribution. The corpus of Sumerian cuneiform texts[147] reveals the reverence accorded to Shamash, as evidenced by numerous hymns, prayers, and rituals dedicated to his honor.[148]

Ancient Mesopotamian hymns dedicated to Shamash provide valuable insights into the religious beliefs and practices of this civilization. One noteworthy composition is the "Shamash Hymn"[149] or the "Hymn to Shamash,"[150] dating back to the Old Babylonian period (circa 2000-1600 BCE), when the worship of Shamash reached its zenith. This hymn serves to praise and extol the qualities and attributes of Shamash. It highlights his role as the bestower of justice, the protector of the righteous, and the illuminator of the world with his radiant light. The hymn also emphasizes Shamash's divine wisdom and his discernment between truth and falsehood. Worshipers sought his guidance, protection, and assistance in various aspects of life, such

---

[147] Cuneiform Digital Library Initiative. "Shamash Religious Texts Pl. 10 Sm 0728 (P425559)" https://cdli.mpiwg-berlin.mpg.de/artifacts/425559

[148] Gray, Clifton Daggett. The Šamaš Religious Texts Classified in the British Museum Catalogue as Hymns, Prayers, and Incantations, with Twenty Plates of Texts Hitherto Unpublished, and a Transliteration and Translation of K.3182. 1901. Internet Archive. https://archive.org/details/samasreligiouste00grayrich

[149] Mullo-Weir, Cecil J. "Restoration of a Hymn to Shamash." Journal of the Royal Asiatic Society of Great Britain & Ireland 62, no. 1 (1930): 41–42. https://www.cambridge.org/core/journals/journal-of-the-royal-asiatic-society/article/abs/restoration-of-a-hymn-to-shamash/99248AF65E267C80B5C5397F3DB84EEC

[150] Prince, J. Dyneley. "A Political Hymn to Shamash." Journal of the American Oriental Society 33 (1913): 10–15. https://www.jstor.org/stable/592812?searchText=Hymn+to+Shamash&searchUri=%2Faction%2FdoBasicSearch%3FQuery%3DHymn%2Bto%2BShamash%26so%3Drel&ab_segments=0%2Fbasic_search_gsv2%2Fcontrol&refreqid=fastly-default%3Ae2baf7e333c8e4a7b2cde9f18022e056

as maintaining order in society, dispelling darkness, and bestowing prosperity. Shamash also appears in various other religious and mythological texts, often in conjunction with other deities, where narratives explore the interactions between gods and humans. These texts encompass myths, prayers, incantations, and rituals, shedding light on the worship and reverence of Shamash within the broader religious framework of ancient Mesopotamia. These texts offer valuable insights into the religious beliefs and practices surrounding Shamash within the cultural context of Babylonian and Assyrian civilizations.

Child of Light

In the context of ancient Mesopotamian religion and Reallexikon der Assyriologie und Vorderasiatischen Archäologie, Kittum, also known as Niĝgina,[151] held significant religious significance as one of the principal daughters of the sun god Shamash. It is believed that she was venerated in the Ebabbar temples situated in the cities of Sippar and Larsa. Notably, Kittum's veneration extended beyond these major centers, as evidenced by the existence of an old Babylonian local shrine in Badtibira and Rahabu, located in close proximity to Larsa.

During the Neo-Babylonian period, the worship of Kittum in Sippar continued, and her presence is attested through the regular inclusion of her name in animal offerings. These offerings were part of the religious rituals carried out in honor of a range of minor deities associated with Shamash's divine entourage. The sequence of deities in these offerings typically followed the order of Umu, Kittum aka Niĝgina, Mīšaru, and Dajjānu, with Kittum being accorded a noteworthy position within this hierarchy.

Kittum and her worship is primarily derived from surviving textual and archaeological evidence. Ancient cuneiform texts, such as inscrip-

---

[151] Ebeling, Erich; Weidner, Ernst F.: Reallexikon der Assyriologie. Berlin ; [München] [2019]. Reallexikon der Assyriologie und vorderasiatischen Archäologie, https://publikationen.badw.de/en/rla/index#8407

tions and religious documents, provide valuable insights into the religious practices and beliefs of the ancient Mesopotamians. These sources shed light on the role of Kittum as one of the daughters of Shamash and her prominence within the cultic framework of Sippar and Larsa.

Sumerian Trinity

According to Mesopotamian beliefs, Shamash was considered the son of the moon god Nanna (Sin)[152] and his wife Ningal.[153] His twin sister was the goddess Inanna (Ishtar, Queen of Heaven),[154] who played a vital role in Mesopotamian mythology and religion. The concept of a divine family with Sin, Shamash, and Ishtar representing a trinity-like structure can be discerned from the available textual and iconographic evidence. It is pertinent, however, that in this particular trinity, the inclusion of a daughter, Inanna, distinguishes it from the more commonly known Christian conception of the Holy Trinity, which typically consists of the Father, Son, and Holy Spirit. This daughter-inclusive trinity, with Sin (Father), Shamash (Son), and Ishtar (Daughter)[155] as key members, underscores the importance of the female deities within the Mesopotamian religious framework.

Additionally, the dawn goddess Aya[156] (also known as Sherida) was regarded as Shamash's wife. Their union resulted in the birth of various significant deities, including Kittum (Niĝgina).

---

[152] Adam Stone, 'Nanna/Suen/Sin (god)', Ancient Mesopotamian Gods and Goddesses, Oracc and the UK Higher Education Academy, 2019, https://oracc.museum.upenn.edu/amgg/listofdeities/nannasuen/

[153] Kramer, Samuel Noah. "The Sumerians." The University of Chicago Press, 1963. pp. 137, "Ningal" https://isac.uchicago.edu/sites/default/files/uploads/shared/docs/sumerians.pdf

[154] Yağmur Heffron, 'Inana/Ištar (goddess)', Ancient Mesopotamian Gods and Goddesses, Oracc and the UK Higher Education Academy, 2019, https://oracc.museum.upenn.edu/amgg/listofdeities/inanaitar/

[155] Britannica, T. Editors of Encyclopaedia. "Shamash." Encyclopedia Britannica, November 9, 2023. https://www.britannica.com/topic/Shamash

[156] Ruth Horry, 'Šerida/Aya (goddess)', Ancient Mesopotamian Gods and Goddesses, Oracc and the UK Higher Education Academy, 2019, https://oracc.museum.upenn.edu/amgg/listofdeities/aya/

Kittum, personifying truth, a concept of light, as her father, Shamash, was the Mesopotamian-Semitic Sun God.

Sumerian Origins

The identification of possible origins for specific attributes or roles, such as the Sun as the son, Star as Ishtar, Sin as sin (θ), etc., requires careful analysis of available textual and iconographic sources. Similarly, the entities Sin and the Sinites,[157] as well as Shamash and Ham, represent figures from different cultural and religious contexts, namely ancient Mesopotamian mythology and the biblical narrative. Sin and Shamash are deities from ancient Mesopotamian mythology, while the Sinites and Ham are figures within the biblical narrative. Drawing direct connections or equating these entities without careful consideration of their specific cultural backgrounds can lead to oversimplifications or misinterpretations. The Sinites, mentioned in the biblical narrative as descendants of Canaan, present a complex topic for study. The biblical text provides limited information about the Sinites, making it challenging to ascertain their precise identity, historical context, or religious practices.

References to Kush, Phut, Misraim, and Canaan are notably associated with the genealogical lineage of Ham, within the biblical narrative. Shamash is not explicitly identified as Ham in the biblical text, however, it is possible to also explore potential connections or parallels between Shamash and Ham within the framework of comparative analysis to Umu, Kittum aka Niĝgina, Mīšaru, and Dajjānu. This includes a comparative analysis to Sin's Hurrian equivalent Kušuh, also known as Umbu, in relation to Kush (Umu).[158]

---

[157] Sinite. The Institute for Creation Research. https://www.icr.org/books/defenders/276

[158] Schwemer, Daniel. "8 Religion and Power" In Handbook Hittite Empire: Power Structures edited by Stefano de Martino, 355-418. Berlin, Boston: De Gruyter Oldenbourg, 2022. https://www.degruyter.com/document/doi/10.1515/9783110661781-009/html?lang=en

CHAPTER 4

The mention of Kittum, also known as Niĝgina, in ancient Sumerian texts raises important considerations regarding its connection to modern geographical and genealogical derivations, namely Nigeria and Niger. While there may be onomastic similarities, it is critical to approach these connections with caution and consider multiple lines of evidence, such as historical, archaeological, and linguistic data.

A similar approach can be used when observing the intriguing parallels between the following examples based on similarities in the names themselves, vowel placement, as well as the association of tribes, locations, or languages: Sin (Mount Sinai, Sinites),[159] Kengir[160] Aya (Kenya), Girsu[161] (Girgashites),[162] Gudea[163] (Judea),[164] Jebusite[165] (Ijebu),[166] Amazigh[167] (Amazon), Tamar (Tamazight),[168] Barzillai[169]

---

[159] Bible Gateway. Genesis 10 (NIV). "Sinites" https://www.biblegateway.com/passage/?search=Genesis+10&version=NIV

[160] Karel van der Toorn and Pieter Willem van der Horst. Dictionary of Deities and Demons in the Bible. pp. 357, "Kengir." https://books.google.com/books?id=yCkRz5pfxz0C&pg=PA32#v=onepage&q=kengir&f=false

[161] Fletcher Fund. The Metropolitan Museum of Art. Neo-Sumerian. The Metropolitan Museum of Art, 1949. "Mesopotamia, probably from Girsu." https://www.metmuseum.org/art/collection/search/324061

[162] Bible Gateway. Genesis 10 (NIV). "Girgashites" https://www.biblegateway.com/passage/?search=Genesis+10&version=NIV

[163] Statue of Gudea, named "Gudea, the man who built the temple, may his life be long." Neo-Sumerian. The Metropolitan Museum of Art. https://www.metmuseum.org/art/collection/search/329072

[164] Judea. Abarim Publications. The amazing name Judea: meaning and etymology. https://www.abarim-publications.com/Meaning/Judea.html

[165] Niels Peter Lemche. The A to Z of Ancient Israel. Jebus, Jebusites, pp. 161, https://books.google.com/books?id=qzGtpvH_BAwC&q=Siege+of+Jebus+lemche&pg=PA161#v=onepage&q&f=false

[166] Ogunkoya, T. O. "The Early History of Ijebu." Journal of the Historical Society of Nigeria 1, no. 1 (1956): 48–58. http://www.jstor.org/stable/41856613

[167] Minority Rights Group. "Amazigh in Morocco - Minority Rights Group," January 30, 2024. https://minorityrights.org/communities/berber/

[168] Institut Royal de la Culture Amazighe (IRCAM). "Moroccan Tamazight Vernacular Romanization." https://www.loc.gov/catdir/cpso/romanization/tamazight.pdf

[169] Massachusetts Institute of Technology. The Holy Bible: New International Version. 2 Samuel 19, https://web.mit.edu/jywang/www/cef/Bible/NIV/NIV_Bible/2SAM+19.html

(Brazil), Chimham[170] (Chimu),[171] Mīšaru[172] (Misraim), Dajjānu[173] (Canaan), Phoenician (Phoenix), Calah[174] (Calafia, California),[175] Aholibamah (Alabama), Arkites[176] (Arkansas), Sherida (Florida),[177] Semitic (Seminole), Aya (Ayanis, Maya, Mayan),[178][179] Sumer-Dan (Sudan), Sargon (Dogon),[180] Proto-Sam[181] Mali Empire[182] (Somali), Dingir[183] (Dinka), Shamash Ningal Dingir (Shang Di),[184] and Niĝgina (Nigeria, Niger).

---

[170] King James Bible Dictionary. "King James Bible Dictionary - Reference List - Chimham." https://kingjamesbibledictionary.com/Dictionary/Chimham

[171] Britannica, T. Editors of Encyclopaedia. "Chimú." Encyclopedia Britannica, August 30, 2021. https://www.britannica.com/topic/Chimu

[172] Daniel Schwemer. The Storm-Gods of the Ancient Near East: Summary, Synthesis, Recent Studies: Part I., pp. 146, "Mīšaru." https://eprints.soas.ac.uk/7075/1/JANER7%3A2offprint.pdf

[173] Burkhart Kienast. The Oriental Institute of the University of Chicago. Assyriological Studies. Igigui und Anunnakku Nach den Akkadischen Quellen, no. 16, pp. 141, "Dajjānu, 'the judge gods'" https://isac.uchicago.edu/sites/default/files/uploads/shared/docs/as16.pdf

[174] Bible Gateway. Genesis 10 (NIV). "Calah" https://www.biblegateway.com/passage/?search=Genesis+10&version=NIV

[175] Putnam, Ruth. California: The Name. 1917, pp. 306 https://archive.org/details/cu31924008278347/page/n23/mode/2up?view=theater

[176] Bible Gateway. Genesis 10 (NIV). "Arkites" https://www.biblegateway.com/passage/?search=Genesis+10&version=NIV

[177] Florida State Parks. "The Rare Florida Torreya Tree." https://www.floridastateparks.org/learn/rare-florida-torreya-tree

[178] Restall, Matthew. The Black Middle: Africans, Mayas, and Spaniards in Colonial Yucatan. Stanford University Press. https://www.sup.org/books/title/?id=6995

[179] Batmaz, Atilla. "A New Ceremonial Practice at Ayanis Fortress: The Urartian Sacred Tree Ritual on the Eastern Shore of Lake Van." Journal of Near Eastern Studies 72, no. 1 (April 1, 2013): 65–83. https://www.journals.uchicago.edu/doi/abs/10.1086/669099

[180] Chandra Chronicles. Sirius Matters: Alien Contact. November 28, 2000, "Dogon." https://chandra.harvard.edu/chronicle/0400/sirius_part2.html

[181] Ali, Mohamed Nuuh. "A Linguistic Outline of Early Somali History." Ufahamu 12, no. 3, pp. 237-238 (January 1, 1983). https://escholarship.org/uc/item/450167x3

[182] Mali Empire and Djenne Figures. https://africa.si.edu/exhibits/resources/mali/index.htm

[183] Kramer, Samuel Noah. "The Sumerians." The University of Chicago Press, 1963. pp. 114, "dingir" https://isac.uchicago.edu/sites/default/files/uploads/shared/docs/sumerians.pdf

[184] The Editors of Encyclopaedia Britannica. (2009, June 18). Shangdi. Supreme

CHAPTER 4

Church in Antioch

The mention of Simeon being called Niger can be found in the New Testament, specifically in the book of Acts. In Acts 13:1,[185] it` is stated that within the church in Antioch, there were prophets and teachers, including an individual named Simeon, who was referred to as Niger.[186] The term "Niger" derives from the Latin language and translates to "black".[187] Scholars have interpreted this epithet as a descriptor highlighting Simeon's physical appearance or some other distinguishing characteristic. The usage of such descriptive terms in biblical texts often serves to differentiate individuals with common names or to provide additional contextual details. While the exact reasons for Simeon being called Niger are not explicitly stated in the biblical text, scholars have put forth various theories to understand its significance. Some suggest that it may reflect Simeon's ethnicity or serve as an identifier within the diverse community of early Christians in Antioch, as illustrated by the Africa & Byzantium exhibit at The Met Museum:[188]

> *"In 330 CE, the Roman emperor Constantine moved the imperial capital from Rome to a city further east, Byzantion. The emperor's 'New Rome' (modern-day Istanbul) became popularly known as Constantinople. We use the term 'Byzantium' to refer to the eastern*

God, Ancient China, Creator. Encyclopedia Britannica. https://www.britannica.com/topic/Shangdi

[185] Bible Gateway. Acts 13. NIV. https://web.mit.edu/jywang/www/cef/Bible/NIV/NIV_Bible/ACTS+13.html

[186] Janz, and Janz. 2024. "Territories Allotted to the Twelve Tribes of Israel." World History Encyclopedia. June 19, 2024. https://www.worldhistory.org/image/14576/territories-allotted-to-the-twelve-tribes-of-israe/

[187] All The People in the Bible. All the People in the Bible: An A-Z Guide to the Saints, Scoundrels, and Other Characters in Scriptures. "Simeon Niger" https://books.google.com/books?id=j9db9kGwG3MC&pg=PA403#v=onepage&q&f=false

[188] Exhibition Tour—Africa & Byzantium. Met Exhibitions. The Met. December 1, 2023. https://www.youtube.com/watch?v=NHIT9vq6mJU

Roman Empire, which ruled until the fifteenth century. Despite being a vast and historically significant empire that spanned parts of Africa, Europe, and Asia, Byzantium's extensive connections to northern and eastern Africa are not well known. This exhibition explores Africa's position within the Byzantine world's artistic, cultural, economic, and sociopolitical life.

Africa & Byzantium traces three artistic arcs. From the fourth to the seventh century, early Byzantine visual and intellectual culture was shaped by wealthy patrons, artists, and religious leaders in northern Africa. As Islam became a dominant faith of the region in the mid-eighth century, distinctive Christian religious and artistic traditions nevertheless flourished in African kingdoms.[189] After the Byzantine Empire fell in 1453, Ethiopian and Coptic artists in eastern Africa continued to find inspiration in Roman and Byzantine art through the twentieth century. The exhibition design follows these transformations by evoking and gradually abstracting Byzantine architecture in Africa. The vibrant and inspiring art displayed throughout, culminating with a group of contemporary works, brings alive themes of translation, circulation, and memory, raising critical questions about where and when Byzantium 'ends'....

...Christianity has a long history in Africa. According to tradition, the evangelist Saint Mark brought the religion to Egypt in 49 CE and established the

---

[189] Department of Arts of Africa, Oceania, and the Americas and Authors: Department of Arts of Africa, Oceania, and the Americas. "Trade and the Spread of Islam in Africa." The Met's Heilbrunn Timeline of Art History, January 1, 1AD. https://www.metmuseum.org/toah/hd/tsis/hd_tsis.htm

Alexandrian church. North Africa was the birthplace of influential religious leaders such as the father of monasticism, Saint Anthony, who was from Egypt, and Saint Augustine of Hippo, who came from modern-day Algeria. By the fourth century, Christian communities in Egypt were flourishing. The Aksumite Empire, which spanned present-day Ethiopia, Eritrea, and parts of Yemen, formally adopted the religion in about 330. Aksum became a key ally and economic partner of Byzantium.

For hundreds of years, African Christian nations were linked with Byzantium and engaged in religious, commercial, artistic, and even political dialogues across land and sea, resulting in a lively interchange of beliefs and culture. South of Egypt, in Nubia (today part of Sudan), Byzantine missionaries sent by Emperor Justinian and Empress Theodora helped convert local communities in the sixth century. By this time, Nubian royalty were already closely connected to Byzantium. Many of their subjects were fluent in Greek, and they filled their tombs with remarkable artworks that intertwined late Hellenistic and early Byzantine motifs with Nubian forms."[190]

Places of Worship

The White Temple's ziggurat is a remarkable architectural structure that holds significant historical and cultural value within the context

---

[190] The Met. Large Print Exhibition Text Africa and Byzantium, "Christian religious and artistic traditions nevertheless flourished in African kingdoms" https://cdn.sanity.io/files/cctd4ker/production/3753a4bdd69811380de-95a2c209581c8f45958a4.pdf

of ancient Mesopotamia.[191] Situated in the city of Uruk, one of the earliest urban centers in Mesopotamia, the White Temple served as a religious center dedicated to the worship of the sky god Anu.[192] Constructed during the Early Dynastic Period, which spanned approximately from 2900 to 2350 BCE, the White Temple's ziggurat exemplifies the characteristic features of this architectural form. Comprised of a series of stepped terraces, each progressively smaller than the one beneath it, the ziggurat was primarily constructed using sun-dried mud bricks. The exterior of the ziggurat was adorned with a distinctive white plaster or limestone façade, giving rise to its name.

The primary purpose of the ziggurat was to elevate the temple itself, thereby making it more visible and accessible to the heavens. This architectural design reflects the ancient Mesopotamian belief in the connection between the earthly and divine. The ziggurat was seen as a physical manifestation of this connection, serving as a bridge between the human world and gods. Within the White Temple, priests conducted rituals and offered prayers to Anu, who held a prominent position within the Mesopotamian pantheon[193] as the sky god. Anu was revered as a divine mediator between the gods and humanity, symbolizing the link between the celestial and human affairs.

The archaeological exploration of the White Temple site has yielded valuable insights into the religious practices and beliefs of ancient Mesopotamia. Excavations have uncovered artifacts and inscriptions that shed light on the rituals performed within the temple complex and the role of the ziggurat as a focal point of religious activity. The White Temple's ziggurat stands as a testament to the architectural and

---

[191] Uruk: First City of the Ancient World: Crusemann, Nicola, Van Ess, Margarete, Hilgert, Markus, Salje, Beate, Potts, Timothy, pp. 325 https://books.google.com/books?id=muCvDwAAQBAJ&pg=PT327#v=onepage&q&f=false

[192] Kathryn Stevens, 'An/Anu (god)', Ancient Mesopotamian Gods and Goddesses, Oracc and the UK Higher Education Academy, 2019 http://oracc.museum.upenn.edu/amgg/listofdeities/an/

[193] J. Mark, J. (2011, February 25). The Mesopotamian Pantheon. World History Encyclopedia. https://www.worldhistory.org/article/221/the-mesopotamian-pantheon/

religious achievements of ancient Mesopotamia. Its prominent stature and symbolic significance exemplify the cultural importance placed on ziggurats as key structures within the religious and social fabric of ancient Mesopotamian society.

Among the deities associated with these monumental structures was the moon god Sin, also known as Nanna. In the context of ancient Mesopotamian religion, it is worth noting that the ziggurats and the worship of deities like Sin/Nanna and Shamash/Utu predate the events described in the New Testament.[194] However, it is interesting to draw a parallel between the veneration of deities in ancient Mesopotamia and the encounter between Christ and the people in John 8, particularly in relation to the thematic elements of "sin", "son of man", "judge", "judgment", "truth", "above and below", and "light of the world" in the Mesopotamian religious text.[195][196][197]

Sumerian-Semitic Parallelisms

The ascendancy of the Akkadian Empire, under the leadership of Sargon of Akkad, in the 24th century BCE likely played a significant role in the continuation of Shamash's worship, potentially with adap-

---

[194] The Great Ziggurat Was Built as a Place of Worship, Dedicated to the Moon God Nanna in the Sumerian City of Ur in Ancient Mesopotamia. Today, After More Than 4,000 Years, the Ziggurat Is Still Well Preserved in Large Parts as the Only Major Remainder of Ur in Present-day Southern Iraq, https://www.defense.gov/Multimedia/Photos/igphoto/2001116584/

[195] Bible Gateway. John 8. NIV. https://web.mit.edu/jywang/www/cef/Bible/NIV/NIV_Bible/JOHN+8.html

[196] Güterbock, Hans G. "The Composition of Hittite Prayers to the Sun. Journal of the American Oriental Society 78, no. 4 (1958): 237–45, pp. 241, "son of mankind" https://www.jstor.org/stable/595787

[197] Gray, Clifton Daggett. The Šamaš Religious Texts Classified in the British Museum Catalogue as Hymns, Prayers, and Incantations, with Twenty Plates of Texts Hitherto Unpublished, and a Transliteration and Translation of K.3182. 1901. Internet Archive, pp. 13, "light of the world" https://archive.org/details/samasreligiouste00grayrich

tations influenced by Akkadian religious traditions.[198][199] Sargon of Akkad is renowned as one of the earliest and most influential empire builders in history, having conquered southern Mesopotamia, parts of Syria, Anatolia, and Elam (western Iran). His accomplishments extended beyond military conquests, as he established the first Semitic dynasty in the region and is credited with uniting the Semites and Sumerian speakers under one rule.[200]

Cultural Comparisons

The work by Hans G. Guterbock and Clifton Daggett Gray represents a significant contribution to the field, providing invaluable insights into these complexities of ancient Mesopotamian cultures and their relevance to biblical narratives. The inclusion of a full-page exert, unaltered and authentic, serves to substantiate the credibility of the research, offering a compelling visual representation of thematic connections with biblical motifs.

SUMERIAN TEXT	BIBLICAL TEXT	ASSOCIATION
SUN GOD	SUN GOD	SUMERIAN RELIGION, ANCIENT ISRAELITE RELIGION
SON OF MANKIND	SON OF MAN	SHAMASH (SUN GOD), CHRIST
LIGHT OF THE WORLD	LIGHT OF THE WORLD	SHAMASH (SUN GOD), CHRIST

---

[198] Dominique Collon. The British Museum. Statue. "suggestions include Sargon, Naram-Sin and Manishtushu." https://www.britishmuseum.org/collection/object/W_C-281

[199] Dalley, S. Mary. "Sargon." Encyclopedia Britannica, April 5, 2024. https://www.britannica.com/biography/Sargon

[200] The Akkadians. Embassy of the Republic of Iraq in Washington, D.C. https://www.iraqiembassy.us/page/the-akkadians

CHAPTER 4

LORD OF JUDGMENT	JUDGE	SHAMASH (SUN GOD), CHRIST OR ETERNAL FATHER
PERSONIFYING TRUTH	TRUTH	SHAMASH'S DAUGHTER (KITTUM, AKA NIĜGINA)
SIN (MOON GOD)	SIN	SHAMASH'S FATHER, DIVINE TRANSGRESSION
NINURTA	KING NIMROD	SUMERIAN, CUSH (HAMITIC)
ABOVE, BELOW	ABOVE, BELOW	ABODE

TRANSCRIPTION

(49) *kun-a* LÚ.NAM.ULÙ.LU-*aš* IR-KA *Iotanuš luluwai*
(135: *ammuga* [.......] *luluwaiši*)
(50) *nu Ištanui zuwan šeššar šipazakiuwan tiyazi*
(135 probably [*š*]*ip*[*panzakimi*])
(51) *nan ḫantantan* IR-KA *Ištanuš kiššarta ep*

(135: [*nu*]-*mu-za ḫanda*[*ntan* IR-K]A *ḫaššun* [*Ištanuš kiššarta epš*]*i*)

(52) *nu meuš kuiuš Ištanuš turiyan ḫarši*

(53) *nu-šmaš kaša* DUMU.NAM.LÚ.ULÙ-*aš ḫalkin šuḫḫaš*
(54) *nu mewaš-tiš karippandu*
nu kuitman (55) *meyawašteš ḫalkin karippanzi ziga* (56) *Ištanuš hueš*
nu-ta kaša LÚ.NAM.ULÙ.LU IR-KA (57) *uttar memai*
nu uddar-tit ištamaš[*zi*]
(58) *Ištanue šarku ḫaššue*
4 *ḫalḫaltumari ukturi* (59) *ištarna arḫa iyattari kunnaz-tet* (60) *naḫšaranteš ḫuiyanteš*
GÙB-*laz-ma-ta* (61) *we⟨ri⟩temaš ḫuiyanteš*

(A 62-65 fragmentary, omitted in 75)

nu ᵈ*Bunene ku*[*nnaš*](?) ²⁰ ˡᵘˢUKKAL-KA (66) *kunnaz-tit iyatta*
ᵈ*Mišaruš-a-ta* [*ŠA* GÙB ... ?] (67) ˡᵘˢUKKAL-KA GÙB-*laz-tet iyatta*
(68) *nu-kan Ištanuš nepiš*[*za ištarna*(?)] *arḫa pa*[*iši*] (omitted in 75)

The next few lines [21] are too fragmentary for translation. They seem to continue in a similar vein and to connect the hymn proper with the transitional section treated below.

The Babylonian elements in this text are obvious. There are Akkadian prayers that begin with the same address "O Shamash, lord of judgment!" [22] The role of Shamash as judge is well

TRANSLATION

(49) This son of mankind, thy servant, make thou, Istanu, prosperous! (var.: Thou makest me [, the king(?),] prosperous)
then he will (var.: I shall) always offer bread and beer to Istanu,
and thou, Istanu, take him as thy just servant by the hand
(var.: and thou, Istanu, shalt take me, the king, thy just servant, by the hand)!

(52) The Four (draft animals) whom thou, Istanu, hast harnessed,
behold, the son of mankind has heaped up grain for them.
So let thy Four eat!
And while thy Four eat the grain,
live thou, Istanu!
Behold, the son of mankind, thy servant, speaks a word to thee
and listens to thy words.
(58) O Istanu, mighty king!
Thou stridest through the four eternal corners, (while) on your right the Fears are walking and on your left the Terrors are walking.

(After some fragmentary lines, omitted in the variant)

(65) Bunene, thy vizier of [the right (side)?], is walking on thy right,
and Mesharu, thy vizier [of the left (side)?], is walking on thy left,
and (thus) thou, Istanu, passest through the sky (omitted in variant).

known.[23] Shamash is also called king and merciful; he allots the portions, passes through the gates of heaven and illuminates (or in some other way affects) the below and the above. He also has a lapis lazuli beard and is the son of Ningal, the wife of the Moon God, Sin. Of the statement of the Hittite hymn that his father Enlil put the four corners of the world into his hands, the filiation, though not the normal one, can be found in Babylonia, too,[24] whereas the rule over the four corners is not attributed to Shamash but rather to

---

[20] The text has ŠA x[....]x; one expects ŠA Z[AG], but the trace after the break does not fit.
[21] Col. ii 1-8 in *KUB* XXXI 127 + *FHG* 1; the reference to the "gods of heaven" and the "gods of the earth" (lines 1-4) may provide the connection alluded to in the text.
[22] The Nineveh texts K 5900, K 12000, and Rm 601 in C. D. Gray, *The Šamaš Religious Texts* (Chicago, 1901), p. 7 and plates VIII, X, XI.

[23] See, also for the following items, K. Tallqvist, *Akkadische Götterepitheta* (Studia Orientalia VII, Helsinki, 1938), esp. the section on Šamaš, pp. 453-460; Gurney, p. 10 n. 1.
[24] Tallqvist, *op. cit.*, p. 454.

brought unto him a woman taken in adultery; and when they had set her in the midst,

4 They say unto him, Master, this woman was taken in adultery, in the very act.

5 Now ^{o}Moses in the law commanded us, that such should be stoned: but what sayest thou?

6 This they said, tempting him, that they ^{c}might have to accuse him. But Jesus stooped down, and with his finger wrote on the ground, as though he heard them not.

7 So when they continued asking him, he lifted up himself, and said unto them, He that is without ^{e}sin among you, ^{d}let him first cast a stone at her.

8 And again he stooped down, and wrote on the ground.

9 And they which heard it, being convicted by their own conscience, went out one by one, beginning at the eldest, even unto the last: and Jesus was left alone, and the woman standing in the midst.

10 When Jesus had lifted up himself, and saw none but the woman, he said unto her, Woman, where are those thine accusers? hath no man ^{c}condemned thee?

11 She said, No man, Lord. And Jesus said unto her, Neither do I condemn thee: go, and ^{j}sin no more.

Discourse after the feast: Jesus the light of the world. (Cf. John 1. 9.)

12 Then spake Jesus again unto them, saying, ^{t}I am the light of the ^{h}world: he that followeth me shall not walk in darkness, but shall have the light of ^{l}life.

13 The Pharisees therefore said unto him, Thou bearest record of thyself; thy record is not true.

14 Jesus answered and said unto them, ^{j}Though I bear record of myself, yet my record is true: for I know whence I came, and whither I go; but ye cannot tell whence I come, and whither I go.

15 Ye judge after the ^{h}flesh; I judge no man.

16 And yet if I judge, my judgment is true: for I am not alone, but I and the Father that sent me.

17 It is also ^{l}written in your law, that the testimony of two men is true.

18 I am one that bear witness of myself, and the Father that sent me beareth witness of me.

A.D. 32.

a Lev.20.10; Deut.22.22.
b John 18.31.
c Sin. Rom. 3.23, note.
d Mt.7.1,5.
e Lk.12.14.
f John 5.14.
g Isa.9.2; Mal.4.2; 2 Tim.1.10.
h kosmos (Mt.4.8) = mankind.
i Life (eternal). John 10. 10.28. (Mt.7. 14; Rev.22. 19.)
j Cf.John 5. 31.
k Flesh. Rom.7.5-25. (John 1.13; Jude 23.)
l Deut.19.15.
m John 17.25.
n John 14.7,9.
o kosmos = world-system. John 12.25, 31. (John 7.7; Rev.13.3.)
p Death (the second). vs. 21,24; Rev. 2.11. (John 8.21,24; Rev.21.8.)
q Faith. John 10.26. (Gen. 3.20; Heb. 11.39.)
r kosmos (Mt.4.8) = mankind.
s Mt.8.20, note.
t Deut.18.15, 18,19.
u Rom.8.15,17.

19 Then said they unto him, Where is thy Father? Jesus answered, ^{m}Ye neither know me, nor my Father: ^{n}if ye had known me, ye should have known my Father also.

20 These words spake Jesus in the treasury, as he taught in the temple: and no man laid hands on him; for his hour was not yet come.

21 Then said Jesus again unto them, I go my way, and ye shall seek me, and shall die in your ^{c}sins: whither I go, ye cannot come.

22 Then said the Jews, Will he kill himself? because he saith, Whither I go, ye cannot come.

23 And he said unto them, Ye are from beneath; I am from above: ye are of this world; I am not of this ^{o}world.

24 I said therefore unto you, that ye shall ^{p}die in your ^{c}sins: for if ye ^{q}believe not that I am he, ye shall die in your sins.

25 Then said they unto him, Who art thou? And Jesus saith unto them, Even the same that I said unto you from the beginning.

26 I have many things to say and to judge of you: but he that sent me is true; and I speak to the ^{r}world those things which I have heard of him.

27 They understood not that he spake to them of the Father.

28 Then said Jesus unto them, When ye have lifted up the ^{s}Son of man, then shall ye know that I am he, and that ^{u}I do nothing of myself; but as my Father hath taught me, I speak these things.

29 And he that sent me is with me: the Father hath not left me alone; for I do always those things that please him.

30 As he spake these words, many believed on him.

31 Then said Jesus to those Jews which believed on him, If ye continue in my word, then are ye my disciples indeed;

32 And ye shall know the truth, and the truth shall make you free.

33 They answered him, We be Abraham's seed, and were never in bondage to any man: how sayest thou, Ye shall be made free?

34 Jesus answered them, Verily, verily, I say unto you, Whosoever committeth ^{c}sin is the servant of sin.

35 And the servant abideth not in the house for ever: but the Son ^{u}abideth ever.

RECONSTRUCTED TEXT.

TRANSLATION.

COLUMN I.

1. O thou who makest to shine [. . . . .] the heavens,
2. Who bringest destruction upon [. . . . .] above and below.
3. O Šamaš, thou who makest to shine [. . . . .] the heavens,
4. Who bringest destruction upon [. . . . .] above and below.
5. Casting down (?) like a drag-net [. . . . .] thy brilliance,
6. To the mighty mountains [. . . . .] the sea.
7. At thy appearance rejoice the [. . . . .],
8. The whole [. . . . .] of the Igigi shout joyfully to thee.
9. A perpetual mystery is the teaching of thy [. . . . .],
10. In the brightness of thy light their walk [. . . . .].
11. Thy splendor reaches [. . . . .],
12. The four regions like fire [. . . . .].
13. Wide open is the gate of all [. . . . .],
14. As for all the Igigi, their free-will offerings [. . . . .].
15. O Šamaš, at thy rising are bowed down the [. . . . .],
16. [. . . . .] Šamaš [. . . . .].
17. Thou who makest to shine, who openest the darkness, who [. . .],
18. Who makest to quiver the   (?)   of light, the planting of corn [. . . . .].
19. The mighty mountains are pregnant with thy glory,
20. Thy brilliancy fills and overwhelms the countries.
21. Thou approachest the mountains, thou gazest upon the earth,
22. At the ends of the earth, in the midst of the heavens thou art suspended.
23. The people of the countries, all of them, thou protectest,
24. What Ea, the king, the prince, has created, of all that thou art protector.
25. Thou shepherdest all created life together,
26. Thou art leader of the things above and below.
27. Thou marchest across the heavens regularly,
28. To   (?)   the earth thou comest day by day.
29. The flood, the sea, the mountains, the earth, the heavens,
30. Like a [. . . . . .] regularly thou traversest day by day.
31. The things below, belonging to Ea (?), Azaggid, and the Anunnaki, thou protectest,
32. The things above, belonging to the inhabited world, all of them thou directest.
33. Shepherd of what is below, leader of what is above,
34. Director of the light of the world art thou, O Šamaš.

Dictionary of deities and demons in the Bible : (DDD) / Karel van der Toorn . . . ed. —

GOD (I)

clear, however, that the gods do not wholly coincide with 'their' phenomena. By means of the sign for 'god' (dingir, *ilu*) immediately preceding a term to mark it as a divine name, it was possible to distinguish between the sun as a natural phemenon and the Sun as a god (T. JACOBSEN, The Graven Image, *Ancient Israelite Religion* [ed. P. D. Miller, Jr. *et al.*; Philadelphia 1987] 15-32, esp. 18 and n. 7).

Most Mesopotamian gods, in addition to being associated with certain natural or cultural phenomena, were each linked with a city. Each community had its own temple, in which its particular god or goddess was worshipped. An (later Anu) was the god of Uruk, Enlil of Nippur, and Enki (→Ea) of Eridu. For reasons that are still elusive, nearly every city had a different patron deity; duplications are rare. This remarkable distribution of the gods over the various cities can hardly be accidental; it looks like the implementation of an early agreement and would thus seem to attest to the one time existence of a Sumerian league (for this 'Kengir League' see JACOBSEN 1970:139-141). The association of gods with cities gave Mesopotamian theology a political dimension: since a god's glory reflects on his city, city theologians endeavoured to promote their god to a superior position in the divine hierarchy. The career of Marduk, consolidated in *Enuma elish*, illustrates how gods could rise in rank as their cities rose in importance: listed as number 294 in a mid-third millennium catalogue of gods (MANDER 1986:29), Marduk had become 'king of the gods of heaven and earth' by the end of the second millennium (LAMBERT 1964; 1984).

In what has been described as the 'city theology' of the Mesopotamians, the observable monotheistic tendencies have a political flavour as well. As the one city-state extended its sphere of influence, turning others into its satellites, its god reduced those of the others to subordinate deities. The redefinition of their mutual relations could lead to the absorption of the lesser deity by the greater god: the former might live on as a name or an aspect of the latter. In this process, the god triumphant might add a number of new traits to his 'biography': thus Marduk of Babylon became the son of Ea (Sumerian Enki) by the identification with Asalluhi of Kuar subsequent to the entry of the latter village into the orbit of Babylon. The merging of deities sometimes took remarkable forms. The most arresting examples are, once more, from the Marduk theology. Thus a small god list, conceived in the style of the classical ones, interprets a number of important gods as facets of Marduk: Ninurta (→Nimrod) is "Marduk of the pickaxe", →Nergal is "Marduk of battle", Enlil is "Marduk of lordship and consultations", and Shamash is "Marduk of justice" (LAMBERT 1975). Is this monotheism? Considering the fact that similar statements were made about gods other than Marduk it was a local form of monotheism at best. Since, moreover, the existence of other gods was not denied, but rather integrated into an overarching design, this monotheism should be qualified as inclusive.

Because there is no Mesopotamian treatise on the nature of the gods, the characteristics that make gods stand apart from other beings, and mark them off as divine, must be culled from a variety of disparate sources. Fundamental for the Mesopotamian conception of the gods is their anthropomorphism: gods have human form, male or female, and are moved by reasons and sentiments similar to those of humans. Their divinity lies in the fact that they are in a sense superhuman. They surpass humans in size, beauty, knowledge, happiness, longevity—briefly: in all things that were positively valued. When a god appears in a dream, the sleeper typically sees "a young man of gigantic size, with splendid limbs, and clad in new garments" (*Ludlul* III 9-10). Size, beauty, power and vitality combine to constitute the *melammu* which the gods exude. This *melammu* is conceived of materially as an invisible raiment endowing the gods with a terrifying lustre. Every being endowed with *melammu* is a god or like a god (*Ee* I 138; II 24; III 28). Since humans

§ 2.1. Affiliation of K. and places of worship. K., like N., was considered to be the principal daughter of Šamaš. She was probably worshipped in the Ebabbar temples of Sippar and Larsa. An OB local shrine (É ᵈKi-it-tim) is attested in Badtibira and Raḫabu in the vicinity of Larsa (AbB 2, 30: 6–8; cf. A. R. George, House Most High no. 1340). In NB Sippar K. occurs regularly in animal offerings, among other minor deities belonging to Šamaš's circle in the sequence: Ūmu, K., Mīšaru, Dajānu (A. C. V. M. Bongenaar, The Neo-Babbar Temple at Sippar [1997] 231). In NA Aššur, K. is occasionally attested in the Tākultu ritual (ᵈZI), alongside Mīšarri and Belšarri (Frankena, Tākultu 98 no. 115), and is also included in the 'Addressbook', shipped in the temples of Sin-Šamaš, ibid no. 28). K. and Mīšaru are frequently referred to as the "attendants of Ekur (zāz) Ekur; cf. Frankena, ibid. 25 i 2

§ 2.2. K. in Akkadian texts. K. attested in prayers and incantations dressed to Šamaš, as well as in of legal nature, invoking Šamaš as divine witnesses

*alternating from
light to dark in our
creative remains lie
the life within life*

CHAPTER 5
An Analysis of Sins

Fifth Sin

INTRODUCTION

In conclusion, this chapter undertakes a comprehensive examination of the multifaceted concepts of Sin on Human Experience, Human Existence, and Human Nature, delving deep into the symbolic history and prophecy contained within the esoteric Book of Revelation, Chapter 12.

SIN

The Spectrum of Sin is a concept that draws upon the mathematical trigonometric function of sine and its symbolic representation as sin (θ). However, it extends beyond mathematics to incorporate theological and cosmological elements rooted in biblical cosmology. The Sumerians, renowned for their sophisticated understanding of mathematics, made noteworthy contributions to the field, developing advanced techniques for arithmetic, geometry, and algebra. These mathematical foundations laid the groundwork for subsequent civilizations, including the exploration of fractals and the theory of 369 as expressed in the framework of their numbering system.[201][202]

In mathematics, the sine function is defined as the ratio of the side of a triangle opposite a given angle (θ) divided by the length of the

---

[201] Swanson, Mark. *The Babylonian Number System*. Educational, 2021. https://www.nku.edu/~longa/classes/2014fall/mat115/mat115-006/images/babylonian/BabylonianNumbers.pdf

[202] Hodgkin, Luke. *A History of Mathematics*. Oxford University Press, 2005. https://uruk-warka.dk/news/2020-MATH/A_History_of_Mathematics_From_Mesopotamia_to_Modernity_by_Luke_Hodgkin.pdf

hypotenuse. The symbol sin (θ) represents this trigonometric function, with theta (θ) denoting the 8th letter in the Greek alphabet. The choice of sin (θ) and theta is symbolic, as the number 8 represents infinity (∞), underscoring its related significance to Human Experience, Human Existence, and Human Nature.

Human Experience

Sine waves, a fundamental concept in physics, are symmetrical oscillations that alternate between positive and negative values.[203] They are frequently employed to represent the direction or polarity of a wave's displacement or amplitude. A positive wave pertains to a wave in which the displacement or amplitude oscillates above the equilibrium or zero position. Conversely, a negative wave describes a wave in which the displacement or amplitude fluctuates below the equilibrium or zero position. Within this context, the terms "positive" and "negative" do not connote positive or negative values with regard to numerical quantities. Instead, they denote the direction or position of the wave in relation to an equilibrium position, as positive+ or negative- sin, while also representing the cyclical nature of history and human events.

Human Existence

Expanding beyond mathematical concepts, sin (θ) is also a conceptualized symbol for the firmament,[204] which encompasses three components within biblical cosmology. First, shamayim, or the "heavens", which is regarded as the dwelling place of God and other heavenly beings according to biblical accounts. Second, midheaven, referred to as the "earth", represents the dimension inhabited by the living. Third,

---

[203] Hayes, Adam. "Sine Wave: Definition, What It's Used for, Example, and Causes." Investopedia, January 4, 2022. https://www.investopedia.com/terms/s/sine-wave.asp

[204] The Wabash Center. A Common Cosmology of the Ancient World also known as the Three-Story Universe. https://www.wabashcenter.wabash.edu/syllabi/g/gier/306/commoncosmos.htm

sheol, commonly known as the "grave", signifies the shared resting place of humanity after death. These three components, shamayim, midheaven, and sheol, can be seen as variable derivatives of sin (θ), positioned both above and below its mathematical representation. The use of sin (θ) as a metaphorical metaphysic-framework allows for the exploration of theological and cosmological concepts related to the divine, human existence, and mortality.

Human Nature

The notion that all individuals possess both light (Sin) and dark (sin) aspects within themselves is a concept that has been explored within various philosophical, psychological, and spiritual frameworks. This perspective acknowledges the inherent complexity of human nature and the coexistence of positive and negative qualities within each individual.

Psychoanalyst Carl Jung found himself intrigued by the coexistence of contrasting elements within the human psyche, leading him to explore these dynamics through the utilization of the I Ching, also known as the Book of Changes—a classic Chinese text associated with Sinology.[205] Jung's conceptualization of the persona, which is the social mask we present to the world, and the shadow, representing the unconscious aspects of our personality, sheds light on the multifaceted nature of the human mind. The shadow encompasses both positive and negative qualities, including traits that may be socially undesirable or morally challenging.

Similarly, within spirituality and religion, the recognition of duality within individuals is a recurring theme. This duality often manifests as the interplay between good and evil, light and darkness, or the divine and the egoic self. Acknowledging the existence of these opposing forces within oneself is often seen as a catalyst for self-awareness,

---

[205] Chinese Philosophy of Change (Yijing) (Stanford Encyclopedia of Philosophy), September 18, 2023. https://plato.stanford.edu/entries/chinese-change/

personal growth, and spiritual development. Furthermore, the idea that all individuals possess both light and dark aspects aligns with the human experience of moral ambiguity and ethical decision-making. It recognizes that individuals are capable of expressing kindness, compassion, and virtuous behavior, while simultaneously having the potential for selfishness, aggression, and morally questionable actions.

Revelation 12

One particular reference that pertains to light and darkness is found in the biblical Book of Revelation, specifically in Revelation 12.[206] This chapter depicts a battle between the forces of good and evil, utilizing vivid imagery and symbolic language. The imagery of light and darkness in Revelation 12 conveys deeper metaphorical meanings related to spiritual warfare, cosmic conflict, and the ultimate triumph of righteousness. Revelation 12 is also a poetic composition that utilizes astronomical motifs to convey theological messages:

> *"A great and wondrous sign appeared in heaven:*
> *a woman clothed with the sun, with the moon*
> *under her feet and a crown of twelve stars on*
> *her head. She was pregnant and cried out*
> *in pain as she was about to give birth."*

The passage describes a vision in which a woman, clothed with the Sun, the Moon beneath her feet, and a crown of twelve Stars, appears in the Heavens. This evocative imagery suggests a symbolic representation of the Virgin Mary, traditionally associated with the birth of Christ in Christian theology. The poetic nature of this passage invites multiple layers of interpretation. Some scholars have proposed a connection between the woman described in Revelation 12 and the astronomi-

---

[206] Bible Gateway. Revelation 12. NIV. https://web.mit.edu/jywang/www/cef/Bible/NIV/NIV_Bible/REV+12.html

cal constellation Virgo, which aligns with the imagery of the woman clothed with the Sun. By examining the positioning of celestial bodies, particularly on September 11, 3 BCE,[207] proponents of this interpretation suggest that it symbolically points to the birth of Christ, corresponding with the Ethiopian New Year and September 11, 2001.

The intertwining narratives of the birth of Christ and the massacre of the innocents, as chronicled in the Gospel of Matthew, offer an exploration of contrasting themes and moral implications. According to this biblical account, the birth of Christ in Bethlehem prompted the visitation of wise men from the East, who sought the newly born king. Their arrival stirred trepidation in, King Herod, who perceived this as a potential threat to his reign and sought to eliminate any challengers. In a calculated act of cruelty, Herod ordered the execution of all male infants in Bethlehem and its environs who were two years old or younger, an event infamously known as the Massacre of the Innocents. This abhorrent act was driven by Herod's desire to consolidate his power and eradicate any perceived rivals to his throne. The juxtaposition of the birth of Christ and the massacre of the innocents serves as a powerful literary device, underscoring the stark contrast between the hope and promise and the depths of human depravity and tyranny.

> *"Then another sign appeared in heaven: an enormous red dragon with seven heads and ten horns and seven crowns on his heads. His tail swept a third of the stars out of the sky and flung them to the earth. The dragon stood in front of the woman who was about to give birth, so that he might devour her child the moment it was born."*

---

[207] September 11th, the Day Jesus Christ Was Born: Ray, Tony. https://www.amazon.com/September-11th-Jesus-Christ-Born/dp/1466232382

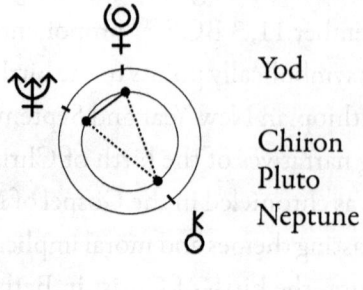

208 Keevan Lavell Crawford. Astro-chart. Natal Chart. Patterns, September 22, 1982, Paramount, CA, 15:17. https://astro-charts.com/chart/7a944f1cf/

CHAPTER 5

CONCLUSION

The Curse of Ham narrative has undeniably played a significant role in contributing to the development and perpetuation of racism throughout history. The misinterpretation of this biblical narrative have been employed to justify and reinforce racial discrimination, particularly against individuals of African descent. During the era of transatlantic slavery, proponents of the Curse of Ham interpretation utilized it as a theological foundation for the enslavement and subjugation of Africans. They argued that the curse placed upon Ham and his progeny served as divine validation for the belief in racial inferiority, positioning Africans as predestined for servitude and relegating them to a subordinate status. This distorted understanding of the Curse of Ham narrative contributed to the establishment of racial hierarchies, with people of African descent deemed inherently inferior and fated to lives of servitude. It provided a religious and moral justification for the systemic oppression and dehumanization of African individuals. Even after the abolition of slavery, the legacy of the Curse of Ham narrative continued to exert influence, perpetuating stereotypes and prejudices, shaping societal attitudes toward race, and reinforcing racial inequities.

The Curse of Ham also raises the broader issue of historical injustices related to genocide, ethnic cleansing, and colonization of promising lands, rich in cultivated resources and religious culture. Several noteworthy analyses contribute to this complex issue: (1) the Shamash candle, a significant element in Jewish traditions, derives its name from Shamash, the Sumerian Mesopotamian sun god often revered as the "light of the world" and "son of mankind." This connection highlights the ancient cultural influences that have shaped religious practices and traditions across different civilizations; (2) Sargon of Akkad established the first Semitic dynasty in the region in the 24th to 23rd centuries BCE, uniting Semites and Sumerian speakers under one rule. This is reflected in the thematic elements found in Sumerian and Abrahamic religious text; (3) according to the Book of Jubilees 8:10-11, Abraham, a prominent figure in Abrahamic faiths, has a matrilineal connection to the Hamitic Cushites through Azurad, the daughter of King Nimrod. King Nimrod played a pivotal role in the construction of prominent regions in Mesopotamia such as Babylon and Sumer. These historical connections underscore the intricate interplay between diverse ethnic and cultural groups, challenging simplistic narratives of racial hierarchy and emphasizing the shared heritage among different peoples; (4) the biblical narrative recognizes Tamar, a Hamite Canaanite, as a maternal figure within the Jewish lineage. This recognition indicates the significance of Hamitic ancestry within the Jewish tradition, further emphasized by the Orthodox Judaism and Conservative Judaism law of Halakha; (5) onomastic data related to "Ham" includes the term "Hammelech" (or "Hamelech") meaning "the king," which is associated with figures such as King David (Star of David), King Solomon, and others. This linguistic connection highlights the enduring influence of Hamitic ancestry within Jewish royalty and leadership; (6) letters and journals contain references to the presence of both African and Semitic peoples in the Americas as early as 1492 and 1557, mentioning Canaanites, Amalekites, Amorites, and other Niger-Congolese peoples. These historical records offer additional insights into the diverse and intertwined nature of human migrations and cultural interactions throughout history; and (7) inherited haplotype "BEN" (Benin), traced back 7,300 years B.P., connecting Hamitic populations in ancient Israel and parts of the Mesopotamia with those in West Africa. This genetic evidence, combined with linguistic data, cultural traditions, artifacts, and historical maps—such as the depiction of "Kingdom of Juda" on the West

African coast—provides further documentation of the interconnected nature of human history across regions.[209] [210] [211] [212]

---

[209] Bitoungui, Valentina J. Ngo, Gift D. Pule, Neil Hanchard, Jeanne Ngogang, and Ambroise Wonkam. 2015. "Beta-Globin Gene Haplotypes Among Cameroonians and Review of the Global Distribution: Is There a Case for a Single Sickle Mutation Origin in Africa?" Omics 19 (3): 171–79. https://www.ncbi.nlm.nih.gov/pmc/articles/PMC4356477/pdf/omi.2014.0134.pdf

[210] Rund, Deborah, Naomi Kornhendler, Oded Shalev, and Ariella Oppenheim. 1990. "The Origin of Sickle Cell Alleles in Israel." Human Genetics 85 (5). https://www.researchgate.net/profile/Ariella-Oppenheim/publication/21177689_The_origin_of_sickle_cell_gene_in_Israel/links/5eecb4c-d458515814a6ad500/The-origin-of-sickle-cell-gene-in-Israel.pdf

[211] Jasim, Sabah Abboud and Oriental Institute Publications. 2021. "Tell Abada: Ubaid Village in Central Mesopotamia." The University of Chicago. 2021. 6,000 to 5,000 BCE. https://isac.uchicago.edu/sites/default/files/uploads/shared/docs/Publications/OIP/oip147.pdf

[212] Carter, Robert A. and Philip, Graham. 2010. *Beyond the Ubaid*. The Oriental Institute, Chicago. https://isac.uchicago.edu/sites/default/files/uploads/shared/docs/saoc63.pdf

TABLE 4. GLOBAL β-S HAPLOTYPE DISTRIBUTION FROM PREVIOUSLY REPORTED DATA

Continents	Countries	β-S Haplotypes						
		Arab-Indian N* (%)	Bantu/Car N (%)	Benin N (%)	Cameroon N (%)	Senegal N (%)	Atypical N (%)	References
Africa	Algeria	0 (0.0)	0 (0.0)	20 (100.0)	0 (0.0)	0 (0.0)	0 (0.0)	Pagnier et al., 1984
	Angola	0 (0.0)	42 (95.5)	2 (4.5)	0 (0.0)	0 (0.0)	0 (0.0)	Lavinha et al,. 1992
	Cameroon	3 (0.3)	5 (0.5)	799 (73.8)	207 (19.1)	2 (0.2)	66 (6.1)	The present data
	Congo	0 (0.0)	211 (91.0)	0 (0.0)	0 (0.0)	0 (0.0)	21 (9.1)	Mouele et al., 1999
	Egypt	0 (0.0)	0 (0.0)	28 (100.0)	0 (0.0)	0 (0.0)	0 (0.0)	El-Hazemi et al., 1999
	Guinea	0 (0.0)	9 (22.5)	0 (0.0)	31 (77.5)	0 (0.0)	0 (0.0)	Sow et al., 1995
	Kenya	0 (0.0)	109 (98.2)	2 (1.8)	0 (0.0)	0 (0.0)	0 (0.0)	Ojwang et al., 1987
	Madagascar	0 (0.0)	32 (91.4)	0 (0.0)	0 (0.0)	1 (2.9)	2 (5.7)	Hewitt et al., 1996
	Mauritania	5 (5.6)	4 (4.4)	8 (8.9)	0 (0.0)	70 (77.8)	3 (3.3)	Veten et al., 2012
	Nigeria	0 (0.0)	6 (1.0)	624 (93.2)	23 (3.4)	0 (0.0)	16 (2.4)	Adekile et al., 1992
	Senegal	0 (0.0)	0 (0.0)	0 (0.0)	0 (0.0)	90 (100.0)	0 (0.0)	Currat et al,. 2002
	Sudan	0 (0.0)	4 (2.8)	42 (29.4)	50 (35.0)	26 (18.2)	21 (14.6)	Elderdery et al., 2012
	Tanzania	0 (0.0)	41 (100.0)	0 (0.0)	0 (0.0)	0 (0.0)	0 (0.0)	Oner et al., 1992
	Tunisia	0 (,0)	9 (2.7)	201 (60.5)	0 (0.0)	0 (0.0)	122 (36.7)	Imen et al,. 2011
	Uganda	0 (0.0)	207 (99.5)	0 (0.0)	0 (0.0)	1 (0.5)	0 (0.0)	Ndugwa et al., 2012
Asia	India	128 (91.4)	0 (0.0)	0 (0.0)	0 (0.0)	0 (0.0)	12 (8.6)	Mukherjee et al., 2004
	Bahrain	33 (89.2)	2 (5.4)	1 (2.7)	0 (0.0)	0 (0.0)	1 (2.7)	Al-Arrayed,1995
	Iran	87 (53.7)	5 (3.1)	19 (11.7)	4 (2.5)	6 (3.7)	41 (25.3)	Rahimi et al., 2003
	Iraq	16 (12.5)	10 (7.8)	89 (69.5)	0 (0.0)	0 (0.0)	13 (10.2)	Al-Allawi et al., 2012
	Jordan	4 (20.0)	0 (0.0)	16 (80.0)	0 (0.0)	0 (0.0)	0 (0.0)	El-Hazemi et al., 1999
	Kuwait	101 (80.8)	7 (5.6)	14 (11.2)	0 (0.0)	0 (0.0)	3 (2.4)	Adekile, 2001
	Lebanon	10 (10.0)	15 (15.0)	73 (73.0)	0 (0.0)	0 (0.0)	2 (2.0)	Inati et al., 2003
	Oman	31 (26.5)	25 (21.4)	61 (52.1)	0 (0.0)	0 (0.0)	0 (0.0)	Daar et al,. 2000
	Palestine (wb)#	0 (0.0)	6 (5.1)	104 (88.1)	0 (0.0)	0 (0.0)	8 (6.8)	Samarah et al., 2009
	Saudi-arabia (se)^	2 (1.6)	0 (0.0)	122 (98.4)	0 (0.0)	0 (0.0)	0 (0.0)	El-Hazemi et al., 1999
	Syria	6 (33.3)	0 (0.0)	12 (66.7)	0 (0.0)	0 (0.0)	0 (0.0)	El-Hazemi et al., 1999
	United Arab Emirates	49 (52.0)	24 (26.0)	21 (22.0)	0 (0.0)	0 (0.0)	0 (0.0)	El-Kalla & Baysal, 1998
North America	Canada	0 (0.0)	7 (11.5)	30 (49.2)	8 (13.1)	8 (13.1)	8 (13.1)	Oner et al., 1992
	Cuba	0 (0.0)	81 (40.9)	101 (51.0)	0 (0.0)	16 (8.1)	0 (0.0)	Muniz et al., 1995
	Jamaica	0 (0.0)	37 (8.3)	339(76.0)	0 (0.0)	23 (5.2)	47 (10.5)	Ndugwa et al., 2012
	Mexico	0 (0.0)	26 (78.8)	6 (18.2)	0 (0.0)	0 (0.0)	1 (3.0)	Magana et al., 2002
	Trinidad	9 (3.2)	49 (17.3)	175 (61.8)	10 (3.5)	24 (8.5)	16 (5.7)	Jones-Lecointe et al., 2008
	USA$	12 (0.8)	129 (21.6)	503 (58.9)	38 (6.1)	76 (8.0)	48 (4.6)	Crawford et al., 2002
South America	Uruguay	0 (0.0)	6 (60.0)	2 (20.0)	0 (0.0)	0 (0.0)	2 (20.0)	Luz et al., 2006
	Brazil	1 (0.4)	104 (41.6)	138 (55.2)	3 (1.2)	1 (0.4)	3 (1.2)	Adorno et al., 2008
	Colombia	1 (0.4)	68 (29.7)	76 (33.2)	10 (4.4)	10 (4.4)	64 (27.9)	Fong et al., 2013
	Suriname	0 (0.0)	23 (29.9)	41 (53.2)	2 (2.6)	2 (2.6)	9 (11.7)	Oner et al, 1992
	Venezuela	0 (0.0)	57 (32.2)	90 (50.8)	4 (2.3)	25 (14.1)	1 (0.6)	Arends et al., 2000
Europe	Portugal	0 (0.0)	14 (42.4)	12 (36.4)	0 (0.0)	7 (21.2)	0 (0.0)	Lavinha et al., 1992
	Italy	0 (0.0)	0 (0.0)	64 (100.0)	0 (0.0)	0 (0.0)	0 (0.0)	Schiliro et al., 1992
	Turkey	1 (0.5)	0 (0.0)	206 (96.3)	0 (0.0)	0 (0.0)	7 (3.3)	Oner et al., 1992
	Greece	0 (0.0)	0 (0.0)	13 (92.9)	0 (0.0)	1 (7.1)	0 (0.0)	Oner et al., 1992

*N, number of chromosomes; #WB, West Bank; ^SE, South Eastern; $USA, combined African-American and Hispanic data.

2007), together with next-generation sequencing, should provide definitive answers to this long-standing question.

It is then perhaps provocative and ambitious, but not unreasonable, to hypothesize that, there could be a single origin of the sickle cell mutation, in the region of East Africa/Sudan, with additional haplotypes generated by diverse structural mechanisms, and the spread to the rest of the continent through traditional migratory patterns. Recently, both phylogenetic and network analysis indicate that east Africans possess more ancestral mitochondrial lineages in comparison to various continental populations placing them at the foot of the human evolutionary tree. Interestingly, the two most ancestral mitochondrial sequences in the NJ tree figure refer to Nubian individuals in Sudan (Elhassan et al., 2014). Moreover, a compound associated with a lithic Middle Stone Age industry was discovered in Dhofar Oman and regarded as evidence of human migration out of Africa through an Arabian route (Rose et al., 2011).

Therefore, the shared rs7482144 SNP in both the Senegal and Indian-Arab haplotypes invites the question of whether

Table 1. Haplotypes of the sickle chromosomes in Israel by ethnicity and location

Patient	Genotype	Ethnicity	Location	Haplotype
A. R.	S/S	Arab-Moslem	Nablus	Benin
A. Z.	A/S	Arab-Moslem	Nablus	Benin
Aw. U.	S/S	Arab-Moslem	Nazareth	Benin
H. L.	S/S	Arab-Moslem	Nablus	Benin
Ha. Y.	S/Thal	Arab-Moslem	Jaffa	Benin
He. H.	S/S	Arab-Moslem	Gaza	Benin
M. E.	S/Thal	Arab-Moslem	Um El Fachem	Benin
R. U.	A/S	Jewish	Gilgal[a]	Benin
Sa. U.	S/S	Arab-Moslem	Jerusalem	Benin
Si. F.	S/S	Arab-Christian	Bethlehem	CAR[b]

[a] Family originated in Iraq and Bukhara
[b] Also referred to as Bantu haplotype

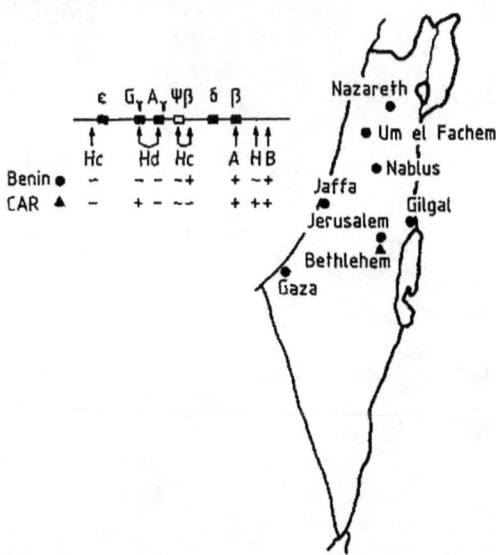

Fig. 2. Geographical distribution of the sickle allele in Israel. The various haplotypes are characterized by patterns of polymorphic restriction sites along the β-globin gene cluster, as designated (Antonarakis et al. 1984; Pagnier et al. 1984). *Hc* HincII, *Hd* HindIII, *A* AvaII, *H* HpaI, *B* BamHI. The CAR haplotype is also referred to as the Bantu haplotype

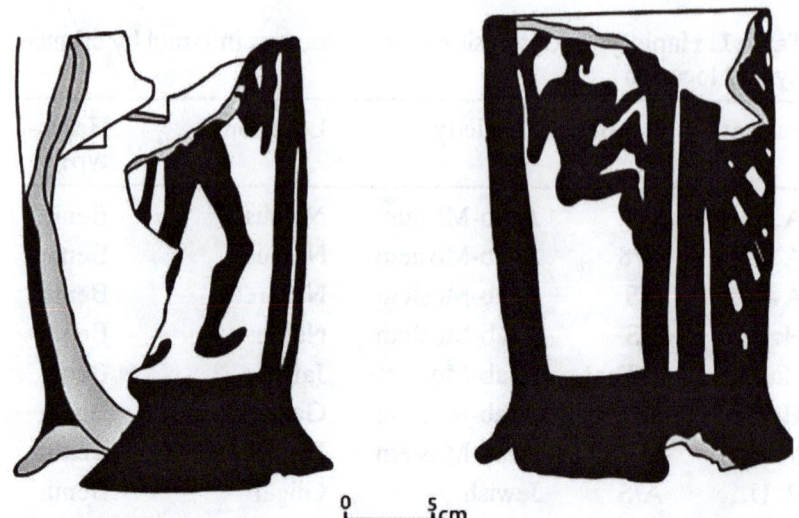

FIGURE 365. Ubaid 3 pottery, beaker from level II, Tell Abada.

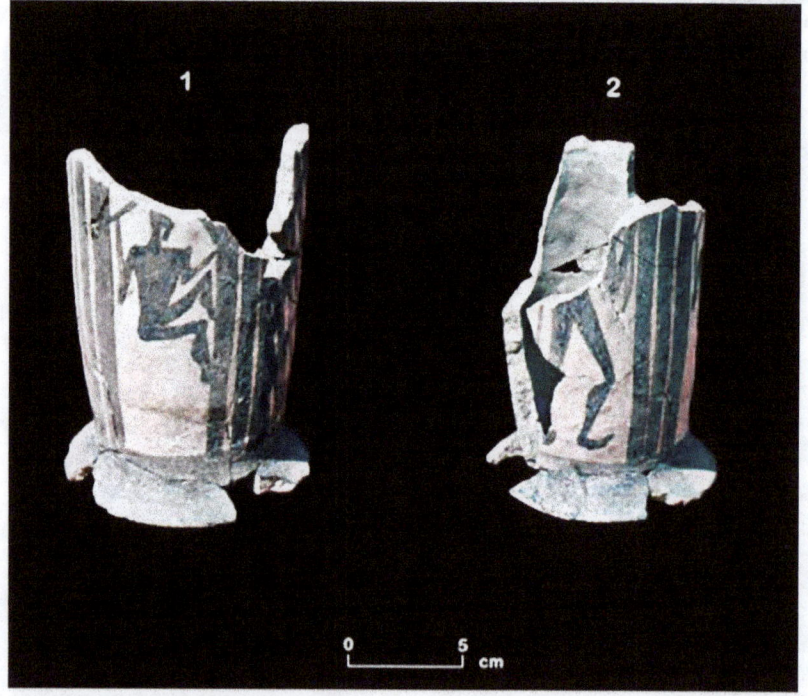

FIGURE 366. Ubaid 3 pottery, a unique beaker from level II, Tell Abada.

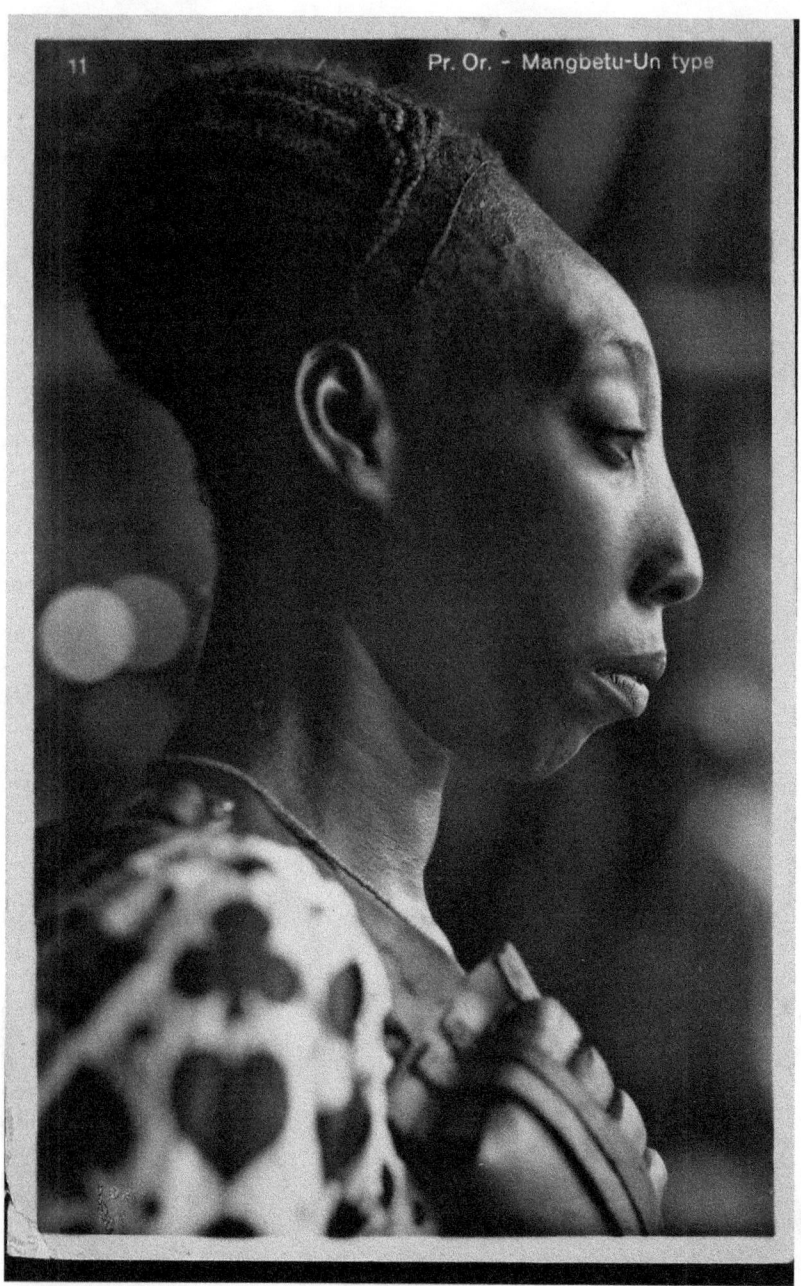

UBAID HEADSHAPING: NEGOTIATIONS OF IDENTITY THROUGH PHYSICAL APPEARANCE? 127

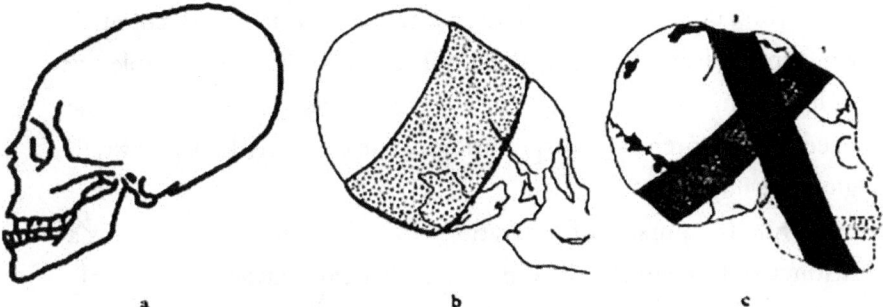

Figure 9.2. (*a*) Circumferential-type headshaping (cranium 117b from Byblos, redrawn after Özbek 1974); (*b*) one-band-type circumferential headshaping (from Değirmentepe, after Özbek 2001: fig. 4b); (*c*) two-band-type circumferential headshaping (after Özbek 1974); the image shows the location of sequentially introduced bands (1 precedes 2; see Lorentz 2008c). Not to any scale

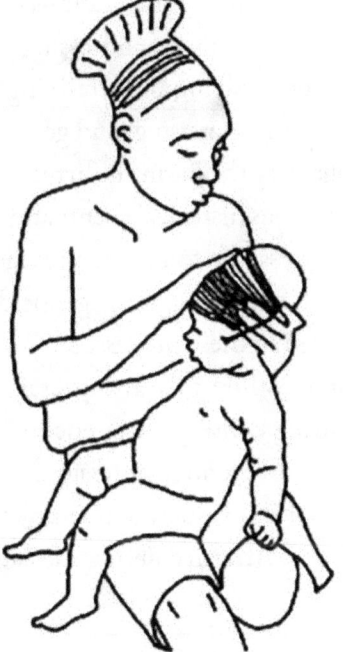

Figure 9.1. Mangbetu woman readjusting the headshaping bandages of an infant (redrawn after Cotlow 1966)

Collectively, these aspects contribute to a nuanced understanding of the historical and cultural dimensions surrounding the Curse of Ham and its broader implications in the context of racism, slavery, colonialism, ethnic cleansing, and genocide. They underscore the complexity of human history, challenge simplistic narratives, and emphasize the need for comprehensive exploration of the enduring legacies of religious heritage.

While the pursuit of reparations for Jewish individuals holds a distinctive place in the discourse on historical injustices, it not only addresses the specific circumstances surrounding Jewish suffering but also provides a model for addressing such injustices and fostering conversations about reparations for other marginalized groups.[213] It is crucial to recognize that each historical context and each group affected by injustice requires careful consideration and tailored approaches to reparations. The pursuit of Jewish reparations offers valuable lessons and insights into the complexities of addressing historical wrongs and the importance of acknowledging and rectifying the consequences of systemic oppression, ethnic cleansing, and genocide.

Attempting to quantify the harms inflicted upon individuals and communities across various historical events and systems is a complex undertaking. Nevertheless, the following provides a summary of the impacts associated with ethnic cleansing, genocide, colonization, and the mechanisms utilized in these processes.

The Curse of Ham. While this interpretation has been widely discredited, its enduring consequences encompassed dehumanization, discrimination, and systemic oppression. Ascertaining an exact numerical estimation of individuals harmed by this belief is elusive; however, it is evident that African communities suffered profound and

---

[213] Zusammenfassung Abkommen Zwischen Der Bundesrepublik Deutschland Und Dem Staate Israel [Wiedergutmachungsabkommen], 10. September 1952 / Bayerische Staatsbibliothek (BSB, München). Bayerische Staatsbibliothek 1997-2009. https://www.1000dokumente.de/index.html?c=dokument_de&dokument=0016_lux&object=abstract&st=&l=de

far-reaching effects throughout history tracing its roots back to 2,000 years, to the writing of the book of Genesis.

The Transatlantic Slavery. American slavery, spanning several centuries, inflicted immeasurable suffering upon millions of enslaved Africans and their descendants. The transatlantic slave trade forcibly transported an estimated 12.5 million Africans to the Americas,[214] with many perishing during the treacherous journey. Enslaved individuals endured physical abuse, family separations, forced labor, and the denial of basic human rights for hundreds of years. While precise quantification of those impacted by American slavery remains challenging, the impacts on successive generations are undeniable.

The Poor People's Choice. Disproportionately, it is evident that the African-American population appears as the primary consumer of abortion services. In citing the 2015 Policy Report on The Effects of Abortion on the Black Community, it is revealed that while black women constitute merely 14 percent of the overall childbearing population, they account for a significant 36.2 percent of reported abortions. Furthermore, it is critical to underscore that black women possess the highest abortion ratio nationwide, with a striking figure of 474 abortions per 1,000 live births. These percentages, depicted at such levels, underscore a distressing and sobering reality. Over the course of the period from 1973 to 2015, more than 19 million black babies have regrettably met their fate through abortion procedures.

The Rhodes to Apartheid. During his time as Prime Minister, Cecil Rhodes enacted a series of policy reforms that crafted a legal framework effectively suppressing the political rights of marginalized communities in South Africa. This laid the groundwork for the unequal political environment that would eventually give rise to the horrors of apartheid and the white-minority rule of the Nationalist Party starting in 1948. The long-term impacts of these policies were far-reaching, including

---

[214] Gilder Lehrman Institute of American History. Historical Context. Facts About the Slave Trade and Slavery. https://www.gilderlehrman.org/history-resources/teacher-resources/historical-context-facts-about-slave-trade-and-slavery

Nelson Mandela being placed on the Terrorist Watch List due to his anti-apartheid activism.[215]

The Congo Free State. Under the rule of King Leopold II of Belgium in the Congo Free State from 1885 to 1908, the indigenous population endured immense suffering. While the exact death toll is debated, estimates suggest that as many as 15 million Congolese people lost their lives due to forced labor, violence, and other forms of abuse during Leopold II's brutal reign. These atrocities, committed in the pursuit of rubber extraction and colonial expansion, had a devastating and long-lasting impact on the Congolese people and the region as a whole.

The Genocide in Palestine. The Israeli-Palestinian conflict has engendered substantial harm and suffering for both Israelis and Palestinians. Since the establishment of the state of Israel in 1948, the conflict has resulted in significant casualties and displacement. During the 1948 Arab-Israeli war, approximately 700,000 Palestinians were displaced or forced to flee their homes. Many sought refuge in neighboring countries, while others were internally displaced within Palestine. It is worth noting that the Israeli-Palestinian conflict has evolved over time, and subsequent conflicts and periods of violence have resulted in further casualties and displacement. Considering the Israeli-Palestinian conflict and its impact on the Gaza Strip, it is distressing to note that out of the 2.2 million inhabitants in Gaza, a staggering figure of over 1.9 million individuals has suffered displacement, as of February 2024. In fact, roughly half of the population consists of women and children who are particularly vulnerable and susceptible to the multifaceted consequences of the Israeli-Palestinian conflict. This vulnerability creates an environment that can contribute to the growth of the resistance group symbolized by: Hamas.

---

[215] Senator Sheldon Whitehouse. 2008. "Kerry, Corker, Whitehouse Announce Nelson Mandela Will Be Removed From Terror Watch Lists - Senator Sheldon Whitehouse." July 15, 2008. https://www.whitehouse.senate.gov/news/release/kerry-corker-whitehouse-announce-nelson-mandela-will-be-removed-from-terror-watch-lists/

CHAPTER 5

"But then let's look at the facts: Early back in 2003, the Hebrew university sociologist Baruch Kimmerling, he was a distinguished sociologist, now when I say back in 2003, bear in mind that the blockade, the intensity of the blockade, was notched up in 2006 after the elections that brought Hamas to power. So, when Kimmerling was speaking, it was before the intensity of the blockade had set in, and he described Gaza as, and now I'm quoting him, "the world's largest concentration camp ever."[216]

Blacklisted Academic Professor Norman Finkelstein on Gaza
Primary fields of research are the politics of the Holocaust and the Israeli–Palestinian conflict

---

[216] Jeremy Scahill. "Blacklisted Academic Norman Finkelstein on Gaza, "The World's Largest Concentration Camp"" The Intercept, May 21, 2018. https://theintercept.com/2018/05/20/norman-finkelstein-gaza-iran-israel-jerusalem-embassy/

JUSTICE-JUDGMENT

DIVINE LAW

TRUTH

LOVE

☉

FH

"All power to all people.
We say white power to white people.
White power to white people.
Brown power to brown people.
Brown power to brown people.
Yellow power to yellow people.
Yellow power to yellow people.
Black power to black people.
Black power to black people.
X power to those we left out.
X power to those we left out."

APPENDIX

AN ONOMASTIC REVIEW OF HAM

Onomastics can be helpful in data mining, with applications such as named-entity recognition, or recognition of the origin of names. It is a popular approach in historical research, where it can be used to identify ethnic minorities within wider populations and for the purpose of prosopography.[217] Names that include the element "ham" hold particular interest due to their potential historical and cultural implications. In this context, the intermixing of names like Ham and Shem raises intriguing possibilities, suggesting the existence of an inclusive naming convention denoted by the term "Sham". Alternatively, "Shamash" could serve as a composite term encompassing "Ham" in both Sumer and Ashur, thus reflecting the intertwining of these two distinct cultural and linguistic entities, resembling a formulaic nature, or syntax.

The exploration of naming conventions as a means of understanding historical and cultural dynamics is an intriguing avenue. Names have long served as markers of identity, lineage, and cultural affiliation. They can provide insights into historical migrations, ethnic inter-

---

[217] "Onomastics | EPFL Graph Search," n.d. https://graphsearch.epfl.ch/en/concept/145171

actions, and the transmission of cultural and linguistic traits across different populations.

The inclusion of the term "ham" within names raises questions about its potential origin and meaning. "Ham" is a biblical name associated with one of Noah's sons, and it has been linked to various interpretations and etymological theories. Some suggest that it may be connected to the notion of "warmth" or "hot," while others propose links to geographical regions or ethnic groups. It is important to note that the presence of "ham" in an individual's name does not inherently imply a direct ancestral connection to Ham, the son of Noah mentioned in the Hebrew Bible, and should not be misconstrued as an exclusive indicator of genealogical descent from Ham.

∞

ABRAHAM. The figure of Abraham, as depicted in various historical and religious texts, holds significant importance in the narratives of multiple cultures and belief systems. The name "Abraham" itself carries symbolic weight, as it translates to "father of many nations". It represents a significant aspect of Abraham's character and his role in the development of diverse ethnic and cultural groups. The concept of being a progenitor evokes the idea of ancestral lineage, the passing down of traditions, and the formation of distinct nations or peoples. Eber and Azurad, mentioned in relation to Abraham, are figures associated with genealogical lines and ancestral connections. Their inclusion in Abraham's lineage accentuates the narrative's emphasis on tracing back his origins and establishing ancestral ties to King Nimrod. According to the Book of Jubilees, King Nimrod was a powerful and influential ruler who held sway over the Mesopotamian region in the time of the biblical patriarch Abraham and sought to undermine the divine calling of Abraham and obstruct the emergence of monotheistic faith.

Abraham, known as the patriarch of these traditions, plays a central role in the religious and cultural heritage of the Abrahamic faiths—

Christianity, Islam, and Judaism. According to the biblical account, Abraham was originally from Ur of the Chaldeans (in present-day Iraq) and was chosen by God to become the father of a great nation. Abraham's story unfolds as he embarks on a journey of faith and obedience.

∞

BAAL HAMMON.[218] The topic of Baal Hammon ("Lord Hammon") represents an intriguing facet of ancient Phoenician and Carthaginian religious beliefs and practices. Baal Hammon, an amalgamation of the term "Baal," a Canaanite deity associated with fertility and weather, and "Hammon," a local Phoenician or Carthaginian epithet, held a significant position within the religious pantheon of Carthage, a prominent city-state and cultural center in the ancient Mediterranean. Carthage, situated in present-day Tunisia, played a pivotal role in the diffusion of Phoenician culture and exerted considerable influence in trade and politics during its heyday. Baal Hammon was venerated as the principal deity of the Carthaginian religious system, occupying a central position in the rituals and ceremonies of the city-state.

The worship of Baal Hammon primarily revolved around fertility and agricultural abundance, as is characteristic of many ancient Near Eastern cultures. Devotees sought the favor and protection of Baal Hammon to ensure prosperous harvests and the overall welfare of the community. It is worth noting that Baal Hammon was also associated with weather phenomena, such as rain and storms, which were vital for agricultural success in the region. As a weather god, Baal Hammon was associated with the powers of fertility and agricultural abundance, akin to the Greek deity Zeus.

Due to the scarcity of surviving written records from the Phoenician and Carthaginian civilizations, our understanding of Baal Hammon primarily relies on archaeological findings, references in

---

[218] Turfa, Jean Macintosh. "Fragments of Carthage Rediscovered." Expedition Magazine 63, no. 1 (February, 2021): -. Accessed April 26, 2024. https://www.penn.museum/sites/expedition/fragments-of-carthage-rediscovered/

the writings of foreign civilizations, and subsequent interpretations by Greek and Roman authors. These sources provide valuable insights into the religious beliefs, rituals, and iconography attributed to Baal Hammon, although they require careful analysis and contextual assessment. Scholars continue to engage in discourse and research to unravel the multifaceted nature of Baal Hammon's worship and its significance within the broader religious landscape of the ancient Mediterranean.[219]

∞

CHIMHAM. Chimham is a biblical figure mentioned in the Old Testament, specifically in the book of Jeremiah. He is associated with an incident involving the prophet Jeremiah and the exiled king of Judah, Jehoiachin. According to the biblical account, Jehoiachin was taken captive by the Babylonians during their conquest of Jerusalem in 597 BCE. However, in a gesture of favor, the Babylonian king, Nebuchadnezzar, released Jehoiachin from prison and granted him a place of honor in Babylon. In Jeremiah 41,[220] we learn that after the fall of Jerusalem, a man named Ishmael, who belonged to the royal family of Judah, assassinated Gedaliah, the governor appointed by the Babylonians. Following this act, Ishmael took some captives, including Chimham, and fled towards the land of the Ammonites.

Chimham is also mentioned in the biblical text as a notable figure associated with Barzillai the Gileadite, a supporter of King David during his exile. According to the account, Barzillai, who hailed from the tribe of Manasseh, extended his support to David during a period of political turmoil. In recognition of Barzillai's loyalty and assistance, David invited him to reside in the royal court for the remainder of his

---

[219] Kennedy, Maev. "Carthaginians Sacrificed Own Children, Archaeologists Say." The Guardian, February 14, 2018. https://www.theguardian.com/science/2014/jan/21/carthaginians-sacrificed-own-children-study

[220] Massachusetts Institute of Technology. The Holy Bible: New International Version. Jeremiah 41, https://web.mit.edu/jywang/www/cef/Bible/NIV/NIV_Bible/JER+41.html

life. However, Barzillai declined the king's offer and instead sent his son, Chimham, in his place.

∞

ELISHAMA. The name Elishama, originating from Hebrew etymology, holds significance within its linguistic composition. Rooted in Hebrew, "Elishama" is a compound term comprised of "Eli" and "shama". The first element, "Eli," emanates from the Hebrew word (El), which connotes "God" or "mighty". It is a frequently employed component in Hebrew names, symbolizing a connection to the divine authority and power. The second element, "shama," can be traced back to the Hebrew verb (shama), signifying "to hear" or "to listen". It carries connotations of attentiveness, obedience, and responsiveness.

Combining these linguistic constituents, the name Elishama can be construed to convey meanings such as "God has heard" or "God listens". It implies an association between the bearer of the name and a sense of divine attentiveness or receptiveness.

The name Elishama finds its place in history as it appears across diverse historical and biblical contexts. As previously indicated, Elishama appears with frequency in the Old Testament, and with each occurrence, it designates a distinct individual. These individuals are mentioned within genealogical records, historical accounts, and even occupy leadership roles within their respective tribes.

Among the notable figures bearing the name Elishama, we encounter a leader named Elishama, son of Ammihud, who emerged from the tribe of Ephraim during the era of Moses (Numbers 1:10).[221] This Elishama assumed a position of prominence, exemplifying the influence and authority vested in leaders within the tribe of Ephraim during that period.

---

[221] Massachusetts Institute of Technology. The Holy Bible: New International Version. Numbers 1, https://web.mit.edu/jywang/www/cef/Bible/NIV/NIV_Bible/NUM+1.html

Additionally, Elishama enters the narrative in a different capacity as the father of Ishmael, the biblical text does not provide an extensive portrayal of this particular Elishama, his mention within the lineage of King David implies a position of familial importance and ancestral heritage.

∞

ETHAM. Etham, mentioned in the book of Exodus, is a significant location associated with the Israelite exodus from Egypt under the leadership of Moses. The biblical narrative describes Etham as a place where the Israelites encamped after crossing the Red Sea and departing from the region of Elim.

The biblical text provides limited details about Etham, offering only a brief mention of its name and its position within the broader journey of the Israelites. According to the account, the Israelites traveled from Elim to Etham, passing through the "wilderness of Shur," which is believed to refer to a desert region located in the northeastern part of Egypt's Sinai Peninsula.

∞

GAHAM. Gaham, a figure mentioned in the book of Genesis, is part of the genealogical record associated with the lineage of Nahor, the brother of Abraham. According to Genesis 22:24,[222] Gaham is listed as one of the sons of Nahor and his wife Reumah. Reumah, one of Nahor's wives, gave birth to four sons, namely Tebah, Gaham, Tahash, and Maakah. The biblical account primarily includes the mention of Gaham and his siblings within the genealogical framework, establishing the lineage and familial connections of the descendants of Nahor.

∞

---

[222] Massachusetts Institute of Technology. The Holy Bible: New International Version. Genesis 22, https://web.mit.edu/jywang/www/cef/Bible/NIV/NIV_Bible/GEN+22.html

HAMATH. Hamath, also referred to as Hamath-Zobah or Hamath of the Hittites, appears as an ancient city of historical and biblical significance. Situated in what is now modern-day Syria, near the Orontes River, Hamath boasts a lengthy and noteworthy history dating back to the Bronze Age. During the second millennium BCE, Hamath served as a prominent city-state within the Amorite kingdom of Yamhad. Subsequently, it fell under the dominion of the Hittite Empire, becoming an influential center of Hittite influence in the region. References to the city of Hamath can be found in a variety of ancient texts, including Egyptian inscriptions and the Hebrew Bible. Particularly within biblical accounts, Hamath frequently serves as a geographic marker or reference point denoting the northern extent of Israelite territory. Its mention often occurs alongside other significant cities and regions of the ancient Near East, such as Damascus, Tyre, and Aram.

Archaeological investigations conducted in modern times have yielded valuable insights into the historical and cultural of Hamath. Excavations at the ancient site have revealed remnants of imposing architectural structures, including temples, palaces, and defensive fortifications, attesting to its political and religious prominence in antiquity. Throughout the Iron Age, Hamath continued to flourish and exert influence in regional politics. It fell under the dominion of the Assyrian Empire in the 9th century BCE and subsequently experienced successive conquests by various powers, including the Neo-Babylonians, Persians, and Seleucids. In contemporary times, the ancient site of Hamath, known as Tell Hama, can be found in present-day Hama, Syria.

A historical account where Hamath, represented by its ruler King Tou, plays a significant role in diplomatic relations with King David. This event is chronicled in 2 Samuel 8:9-10,[223] a biblical narrative. According to the biblical passage, Tou, the king of Hamath, receives

---

[223] Massachusetts Institute of Technology. The Holy Bible: New International Version. 2 Samuel 8, https://web.mit.edu/jywang/www/cef/Bible/NIV/NIV_Bible/2SAM+8.html

news of King David's decisive victory over Hadadezer, the king of Zobah. In response to this military triumph, Tou dispatches his son Joram, also known as Hadoram, to personally convey greetings and congratulations to King David. The purpose of this mission is to acknowledge David's successful campaign against Hadadezer, with whom Tou had been at odds. As a sign of goodwill and esteem, Joram presents King David with a selection of valuable items crafted from gold, silver, and bronze.

∞

HAMAZI. Hamazi, also known as Khamazi in Sumerian, is believed to have been an ancient kingdom or city-state that gained prominence during the Early Dynastic period.

∞

HAMILCAR BARCA. Hamilcar Barca, a prominent Carthaginian general and statesman, played a pivotal role in the First Punic War, and his strategic acumen and military achievements laid the foundation for Carthaginian power in the Mediterranean. Born circa 275 BCE, Hamilcar belonged to the illustrious Barcid family, which wielded significant influence within the Carthaginian political landscape.

Hamilcar Barca commenced his military career amidst the tumultuous backdrop of the First Punic War (264-241 BCE), a conflict between Carthage and Rome over supremacy in Sicily. Serving as a commander in various engagements, Hamilcar demonstrated exceptional leadership qualities and exhibited a remarkable grasp of strategic maneuvers. Of particular note is his role in the post-war negotiations with Rome, wherein he orchestrated a diplomatic settlement that secured favorable terms for Carthage.

Following the First Punic War, Hamilcar Barca redirected his attention towards expanding Carthaginian dominion in Iberia (modern-day Spain). Recognizing the immense potential of Iberia as a resource-rich region capable of compensating for the loss of Sicily, Hamilcar, along with his son Hannibal and other Carthaginian forces, undertook a series of military campaigns in the region. Through these endeavors, they gradually established Carthaginian hegemony, employing innovative tactics and forging diplomatic alliances with indigenous tribes.

Hamilcar's exploits in Iberia garnered him a reputation as a skilled tactician and an inspirational leader. His utilization of unconventional strategies, coupled with diplomatic overtures, solidified Carthaginian control over the region. As a result, Carthage reaped substantial economic benefits from Iberia, enabling the rebuilding of military forces and replenishment of the treasury. While Hamilcar Barca remained engrossed in Iberian affairs, he never lost sight of the ultimate objective—avenging Carthage's defeat in the First Punic War and challenging Rome's burgeoning supremacy. Instilling in his son Hannibal an unwavering loyalty to Carthage and an ardent desire to confront Rome, Hamilcar's untimely demise on the battlefield in 228 BCE did not deter Hannibal's pursuit of his father's aspirations. On the contrary, it stoked the flames of Hannibal's determination to wage war against Rome, ultimately giving rise to the momentous Second Punic War (218-201 BCE). Hamilcar Barca's enduring legacy is predominantly characterized by his strategic vision, ability to inspire unwavering devotion among his troops, and his instrumental role in establishing the Carthaginian Empire in Iberia. His military triumphs, coupled with the subsequent achievements of his son Hannibal in the Second Punic War, solidified the Barcid family's reputation as formidable adversaries to Rome and indelibly imprinted their mark on ancient history.

∞

HANNIBAL OF CARTHAGE. A renowned military commander of antiquity, known for his exceptional strategic prowess during the Second Punic War (218-201 BCE) against the burgeoning Roman Republic. Born in 247 BCE into the esteemed Barcid family, which held significant political and military influence in Carthage, Hannibal emerged as one of the most celebrated figures of ancient history. Under the tutelage of his father, Hamilcar Barca, Hannibal imbibed a loyalty to Carthage and an unwavering determination to confront Rome. Displaying remarkable military acumen and leadership qualities from a tender age, Hannibal assumed command of Carthaginian forces in Spain, embarking on a daring campaign to challenge Roman hegemony.

Among Hannibal's most iconic feats was his audacious crossing of the treacherous Alps in 218 BCE. Leading his army, including a contingent of war elephants, from the Iberian Peninsula into Italy, he caught the Romans off-guard, inflicting significant losses upon them. Hannibal's tactical brilliance, coupled with his ability to inspire unwavering loyalty among his troops, enabled him to secure remarkable victories, most notably the Battle of Cannae in 216 BCE, where his forces decisively vanquished a vastly larger Roman army.

Notwithstanding Hannibal's remarkable military successes, his campaign ultimately encountered setbacks due to a dearth of reinforcements from Carthage and the Roman Republic's adaptive strategies. As Rome steadily gained the upper hand, Carthage found itself besieged on multiple fronts. In 202 BCE, Hannibal was recalled to defend Carthage itself, but despite his valiant efforts, he could not reverse the tide of the war. The conflict culminated in Carthage's defeat in 201 BCE. Hannibal's enduring legacy extends beyond military exploits. His strategic brilliance and innovative tactics continue to captivate the minds of military historians and strategists. Moreover, his adeptness in forging alliances with diverse Mediterranean peoples and maintaining the unwavering loyalty of his troops exemplify his diplomatic acumen and leadership qualities. Despite his ultimate defeat, Hannibal's bold and tireless pursuit of victory against a formidable adversary has secured his place as an object of perennial fascination and admiration throughout history.

∞

HAMMATH. Hammath, alternatively spelled Hammath or Hammath Tiberias, appears within the Hebrew Bible's narrative as one of the fortified cities allocated to the tribe of Naphtali during the territorial division of the Promised Land. Joshua 19:35[224] enumerates its presence in the context of the apportionment of land among the Israelite tribes. The precise identification of Hammath remains an area of debate, as the biblical account does not provide explicit geographical markers. Some scholars contend that Hammath may correspond to Hamat Gader, a site situated in the Yarmouk River valley near the modern borders of Israel, Jordan, and Syria. Renowned for its hot springs, Hamat Gader has been continuously inhabited since ancient times.

Other scholars propose that Hammath could be equated with Hammat Tiberias, located in the proximity of the southern extremity of the Sea of Galilee, in the vicinity of the contemporary city of Tiberias. Hammat Tiberias gained repute in antiquity due to its thermal baths, attracting visitors in search of the curative properties associated with its hot springs.

∞

HAMMEDATHA. Hammedatha, as encountered in the Book of Esther within the Hebrew Bible, assumes a notable role in the narrative as Haman, the primary antagonist. Described as Hammedatha the Agagite, Haman occupies a position of prominence as a high-ranking official in the Persian Empire during the reign of King Ahasuerus, traditionally identified as Xerxes I. The designation "Agagite" ascribed to Haman suggests a lineage entwined with the Amalekites, a people historically engaged in conflict with the Israelites. The name Hammedatha appears in Esther 3:1,[225] wherein Haman is introduced as "Haman son of Hammedatha the Agagite".

---

[224] Massachusetts Institute of Technology. The Holy Bible: New International Version. Joshua 19, https://web.mit.edu/jywang/www/cef/Bible/NIV/NIV_Bible/JOSH+19.html

[225] Massachusetts Institute of Technology. The Holy Bible: New International

Haman's central role within the Book of Esther revolves around his malevolent scheme to annihilate the Jewish population residing within the Persian Empire. Persuading King Ahasuerus to issue a decree calling for the extermination of the Jews, Haman endeavors to bring about their demise. However, through the intervention of Queen Esther and her cousin Mordecai, who themselves belong to the Jewish community, the plot is ultimately thwarted, leading to the execution of Haman and his sons. The inclusion of the name Hammedatha in the Book of Esther serves the purpose of delineating Haman's lineage and providing additional insights into his background. It underscores the historical and ethnic dimensions of the conflict depicted in the narrative, as well as the significance of Haman's ancestry in relation to the Jewish people.

The portrayal of Haman has elicited various interpretations throughout history and across different cultural contexts. Some perceive him as a symbol of unrestrained power, hubris, and anti-Semitism, while others view him as an emblematic figure cautioning against the perils of hatred and intolerance.

In terms of etymology, the name "Hammedatha" is widely interpreted to have Persian origins. It is posited that the name conveys the meaning of "given by the moon" or "moon-given," aligning with the cultural milieu of the Persian Empire, where celestial bodies, including the moon, held significant symbolic import.

∞

HAMMELECH. The term "Hammelech," derived from Hebrew, holds the meaning of "the king" in English. Within biblical and Jewish literature, it assumes a significant role as a title or epithet utilized to underscore the ultimate sovereignty and kingship of God over all creation. The notion of God as the King constitutes a foundational

---

Version. Esther 3, https://web.mit.edu/jywang/www/cef/Bible/NIV/NIV_Bible/ESTH+3.html

element within Jewish theological tenets and finds frequent expression in prayers, psalms, and liturgical texts. It encapsulates the belief that God stands as the supreme ruler and authority, governing the universe with justice and wisdom.

Beyond its theological import, "Hammelech" may also be employed to designate earthly kings or rulers. Throughout the biblical narratives, numerous monarchs are referenced with this title, including notable figures such as King David and King Solomon. The utilization of "Hammelech" concisely conveys the regal status and authority associated with these rulers, emphasizing their dominion and leadership over their respective region.

∞

HAMMOLEKETH. In the genealogical records of the Old Testament, specifically in 1 Chronicles 7:16,[226] we encounter the mention of Hammoleketh, who appears as the sister of Gilead. This verse presents Hammoleketh as the daughter of Maacah and Machir, and the granddaughter of Manasseh. It states that she bore three sons: Ishhod, Abiezer, and Mahlah.

Although the biblical text does not provide extensive details regarding Hammoleketh herself, her inclusion in the genealogy highlights her position within the ancestral line of Manasseh, one of the tribes of Israel. As a sister of Gilead, she plays a role in the lineage of this prominent family.

∞

HAMMURABI. Hammurabi, the notable sovereign of ancient Babylon, ascended to power around 1792 BCE and held the throne until approximately 1750 BCE. His enduring renown stems primarily from his codification of laws, famously known as the "Code of Hammu-

---

[226] Massachusetts Institute of Technology. The Holy Bible: New International Version. 1 Chronicles 7, https://web.mit.edu/jywang/www/cef/Bible/NIV/NIV_Bible/1CHRON+7.html

rabi". This legal compendium stands as one of the earliest recorded legal systems in human history, offering invaluable insights into the socio-economic fabric and cultural milieu of ancient Babylonian society.

The Code of Hammurabi encompasses a comprehensive corpus of 282 laws, addressing a broad range of subjects spanning family law, property rights, contractual obligations, trade practices, labor regulations, and criminal justice. The legal code exhibits a foundational principle of "lex talionis," signifying the concept of "an eye for an eye," wherein penalties for transgressions are proportionate to the nature of the offense committed. Furthermore, it accommodates distinct provisions catering to different social strata, thereby fostering a sense of justice and order within Babylonian society.

Beyond his jurisprudential reforms, Hammurabi's reign witnessed substantial territorial expansion and the elevation of Babylon as a preeminent political and cultural hub in the Mesopotamian region. Noteworthy infrastructural endeavors, including the construction of canals and edifices, sought to enhance the economic and agricultural circumstances prevailing within his kingdom. Hammurabi's rule left an indelible imprint on the ancient Near East, with his legal code exerting a profound influence on subsequent legal systems across the region. His accomplishments in governance and administration provided a model for future Babylonian monarchs, solidifying Babylon's prominence. Thus, Hammurabi's sagacity as a benevolent and equitable ruler endures through the relevance of his code, positioning him as an eminent figure in antiquity.

∞

HAMON GOG. The term "Hamon Gog" finds its origin in the biblical book of Ezekiel, specifically in Ezekiel 39:11.[227] Within this passage,

---

[227] Massachusetts Institute of Technology. The Holy Bible: New International Version. Ezekiel 39, https://web.mit.edu/jywang/www/cef/Bible/NIV/NIV_Bible/EZEK+39.html

it denotes a valley designated as the burial place for the multitude of Gog, along with his forces. Etymologically, "Hamon Gog" can be deconstructed as a combination of two constituent elements: "hamon," signifying a "multitude" or "horde," and "Gog," a figure prominently featured in the preceding chapters of Ezekiel. Gog, depicted as a leader who assembles a coalition of nations for a future attack on Israel, serves as a central character within the prophetic narrative.

The biblical account in Ezekiel outlines that subsequent to the defeat of Gog and his forces, a specific valley, known as "Hamon Gog," will be designated as their final resting place. This burial site serves a twofold purpose: as a tangible reminder of the judgment and downfall of Gog's multitude, and as a symbol of divine retribution for their hostile actions.

∞

HAMOR. Hamor is a notable figure in the biblical narrative as depicted in the book of Genesis. Specifically, his prominence arises within the context of the account featuring Jacob and his sons, with particular reference to an incident involving his daughter Dinah. In the biblical narrative found in Genesis 34,[228] Hamor assumes the role of a leader or prince of the city of Shechem. As the story unfolds, his son Shechem becomes enamored with Dinah, prompting him to approach Jacob and his sons with a proposal for her hand in marriage. Undertaking the role of mediator, Hamor advocates for the union, extolling the potential benefits that could arise from the intermarriage of their respective families and the establishment of social and economic ties. Hamor's significance within the narrative primarily lies in his function as an intermediary and representative of the city of Shechem. His objective centers around securing a matrimonial alliance between his family and that of Jacob, emphasizing the potential advantages that such a union

---

[228] Massachusetts Institute of Technology. The Holy Bible: New International Version. Genesis 34, https://web.mit.edu/jywang/www/cef/Bible/NIV/NIV_Bible/GEN+34.html

could offer. Regrettably, his efforts ultimately culminate in a tragic turn of events, as Dinah's brothers employ deceit against the men of Shechem, exacting retribution upon them.

∞

HAMUL. Hamul is a biblical figure whose name appears in the genealogical records found in the book of Genesis. Specifically, he is listed as one of the sons of Pharez, who himself is the son of Tamar and Judah, a significant matriarch in the Canaanite Hamite tradition and a significant patriarch within the Israelite tradition, respectively.

The mention of Hamul occurs within the context of a comprehensive enumeration in Genesis 46:12,[229] wherein the descendants of Jacob who migrated to Egypt are documented. As part of this genealogical record, Hamul is identified as one of the offspring of Pharez, who was born to Judah and Tamar. It is worth noting that the tribe of Judah holds particular importance within the Israelite tribal structure, as it became one of the dominant and influential tribes in ancient Israel.

∞

HAMUTAL. Hamutal is a name that appears in the biblical narrative, particularly within the context of the Old Testament. It is associated with two distinct individuals, each mentioned in different circumstances.

First. Hamutal, a prominent figure in the biblical narrative, appears as one of the queens of the Kingdom of Judah. The scriptural account identifies her as the daughter of Jeremiah of Libnah and the wife of King Josiah, a revered ruler of Judah during the 7th century BCE. Josiah is celebrated for his efforts to instigate religious reforms and restore the worship of Yahweh in the kingdom. By virtue of her marriage to Josiah, Hamutal assumed the esteemed position of queen consort,

---

[229] Massachusetts Institute of Technology. The Holy Bible: New International Version. Genesis 46, https://web.mit.edu/jywang/www/cef/Bible/NIV/NIV_Bible/GEN+46.html

conferring upon her both symbolic and political influence within the royal court of Judah. As a pivotal figure in the ruling establishment, she likely played a significant role in shaping the political and social dynamics of the kingdom.

Moreover, Hamutal's maternal role holds particular importance in the dynastic lineage of Judah. She bore two sons, Jehoahaz and Zedekiah, who both ascended to the throne of Judah. Jehoahaz, also known as Shallum, held a brief reign before being deposed by the Egyptian pharaoh, while Zedekiah became the final king of Judah prior to the Babylonian exile. While the scriptural account provides valuable insights into Hamutal's familial connections and her position within the royal household, regrettably, it remains deficient in furnishing detailed information regarding her personal history, individual attributes, and specific contributions to the political and cultural milieu of the Kingdom of Judah.

Second. Within the same book of 2 Kings, a separate Hamutal is referenced as the mother of King Jehoiachin, who ascended to the throne subsequent to Josiah's reign. Jehoiachin's rule was characterized by political tumult and the eventual Babylonian exile. Hamutal's role within the narrative primarily lies in her status as the mother of a monarch and her membership in the royal lineage of Judah.

∞

HOHAM. Hoham, as mentioned in the biblical narrative, specifically in the Old Testament book of Joshua, comes to the forefront as a significant figure during the Israelite conquest of the Promised Land. Hoham is identified as the king of Hebron and is mentioned as one of the five Amorite kings who formed a coalition to resist the incursion of the Israelites, led by Joshua. The biblical account, found in Joshua 10:3-5,[230] elucidates the unification of Hoham with four other kings, including

---

[230] Massachusetts Institute of Technology. The Holy Bible: New International Version. Joshua 10, https://web.mit.edu/jywang/www/cef/Bible/NIV/NIV_Bible/JOSH+10.html

Adoni-Zedek of Jerusalem, Piram of Jarmuth, Japhia of Lachish, and Debir of Eglon. Together, these kings joined forces to confront the advancing Israelite army. The narrative in Joshua 10:16-27 details the ensuing confrontation between Hoham and Joshua. It chronicles the decisive victory of the Israelites over the coalition of Amorite kings. Pursuing the retreating kings, Joshua implores the divine intervention of the Lord to extend daylight, ensuring the comprehensive defeat of their adversaries. According to the text, the Lord grants Joshua's request, and the Israelites achieve a resounding triumph, resulting in the demise of the kings and the capture of their cities.

∞

HOSHAMA. Hoshama, a figure of interest found within the genealogical records of the Old Testament, appears as one of the sons or descendants of Jeconiah, also known as Jehoiachin, the captive king of Judah. Jeconiah's reign coincided with a tumultuous period in the history of Judah, characterized by political upheaval and the subsequent Babylonian exile.

The biblical account, specifically 1 Chronicles 3:17-18,[231] provides a genealogical listing of the descendants of Jeconiah, which includes the presence of Hoshama. This genealogical record serves the purpose of tracing the lineage of the Davidic monarchy, emphasizing the continuity and significance of the royal line despite the exile and the subsequent historical challenges encountered by the descendants of Jeconiah.

∞

HOTHAM. Hotham, a notable figure mentioned in the Old Testament, appears in two distinct contexts:

First. Hotham is identified as a resident of Aroer and is recognized as the father of Shama and Jeiel, two of King David's renowned and

---

[231] Massachusetts Institute of Technology. The Holy Bible: New International Version. 1 Chronicles 3, https://web.mit.edu/jywang/www/cef/Bible/NIV/NIV_Bible/1CHRON+3.html

valiant warriors, commonly referred to as his "mighty men". These courageous individuals served within David's army and were celebrated for their exceptional martial prowess and valor. The specific account pertaining to Hotham and his sons can be found in 1 Chronicles 11:44.[232]

Second. Hotham is mentioned as an Asherite, the son of Heber, hailing from the lineage of Beriah. This reference is recorded in 1 Chronicles 7:32.[233] The book of Chronicles frequently provides genealogical details, meticulously tracing the ancestral lines of various tribes and families within the broader context of ancient Israel.

While the extant information concerning Hotham is somewhat limited, these references situate him within the historical and genealogical of ancient Israel. The mention of Hotham as the father of "mighty men" implies his distinguished position and likely denotes his own esteemed status within the society of the time. Furthermore, it suggests that his sons followed in his footsteps, inheriting not only his lineage but also his valorous qualities, as they served as esteemed warriors in the esteemed ranks of King David's forces.

∞

HUPHAM. Hupham, a figure of interest from the Old Testament, appears as a son of Benjamin, one of the twelve tribes of Israel. Hupham assumes prominence as the head of the family known as the Huphamites, an esteemed clan within the tribe of Benjamin.

The specific mention of Hupham can be found in the genealogical records documented in the book of Numbers. In Numbers 26:39,[234]

---

[232] Massachusetts Institute of Technology. The Holy Bible: New International Version. 1 Chronicles 11, https://web.mit.edu/jywang/www/cef/Bible/NIV/NIV_Bible/1CHRON+11.html

[233] Massachusetts Institute of Technology. The Holy Bible: New International Version. 1 Chronicles 7, https://web.mit.edu/jywang/www/cef/Bible/NIV/NIV_Bible/1CHRON+7.html

[234] Massachusetts Institute of Technology. The Holy Bible: New International Version. Numbers 26, https://web.mit.edu/jywang/www/cef/Bible/NIV/NIV_Bible/NUM+26.html

the descendants of Benjamin are meticulously listed, and Hupham is recognized as one of his sons. Furthermore, Numbers 26:38-41 provides an enumeration of the various clans and families within the tribe of Benjamin, with the Huphamites identified as one of these clans. It is plausible to infer that Hupham himself is the eponymous progenitor of this particular family group.

∞

HUSHAM. Husham, an intriguing figure within the biblical narrative, assumes prominence as an elective king of the Edomites, a neighboring kingdom to ancient Israel. The available information regarding Husham is primarily derived from the genealogical records presented in Genesis 36:34[235] and 1 Chronicles 1:45.[236] According to these passages, Husham held the distinguished position of kingship among the Edomites. Notably, the reference to "the land of Temani" in conjunction with Husham suggests a plausible association with the prominent Edomite clan known as Teman, thereby hinting at a possible lineage or tribal connection.

∞

ISHME-SHAMASH. The historical figure known as Ishme-Shamash, or Shamash-eriba, appears as a compelling persona within ancient Mesopotamia. The appellation "Ishme-Shamash" derives from the Akkadian language and signifies "Shamash has heard". Shamash, the solar deity of Mesopotamian religious belief, held a prominent position within the gods worshipped in the region.

Our understanding of Ishme-Shamash primarily stems from a corpus of legal and administrative tablets dating to the Old Babylo-

---

[235] Massachusetts Institute of Technology. The Holy Bible: New International Version. Genesis 36, https://web.mit.edu/jywang/www/cef/Bible/NIV/NIV_Bible/GEN+36.html

[236] Massachusetts Institute of Technology. The Holy Bible: New International Version. 1 Chronicles 1, https://web.mit.edu/jywang/www/cef/Bible/NIV/NIV_Bible/1CHRON+1.html

nian period, spanning approximately from 2000 to 1600 BCE. These cuneiform tablets, inscribed with wedged-shaped characters, proffer valuable insights into the legal and economic undertakings of Ishme-Shamash, who appears to have occupied a position of authority or influence within the administrative machinery of the era. These tablets, which comprise a diverse array of records, illuminate Ishme-Shamash's involvement in a range of legal transactions, including land sales, loans, and the resolution of disputes. His presence is frequently noted as a witness, scribe, or active participant in these transactions, signifying his integral role in the legal and economic affairs of the time.

∞

ITHAMAR. Ithamar, an individual of notable significance within the Old Testament narrative, appears prominently within the context of the priestly lineage of the Israelites. His distinctiveness primarily stems from his identification as one of the sons of Aaron, the brother of Moses, and his ancestral connection to the tribe of Levi (i.e. Lemba Tribe DNA relation to the Cohen Modal Haplotype). References to Ithamar's name are dispersed throughout various scriptural passages, including Exodus 6:23[237] and 1 Chronicles 24:1,[238] which meticulously document the genealogical records pertaining to the priestly lineage. These accounts establish Ithamar, alongside his brothers Nadab, Abihu, and Eleazar, as being consecrated and ordained as priests, thereby assuming active roles within the sacred duties and liturgical practices of the Israelite religious system. Significantly, the priestly lineage, including Ithamar and his descendants, played a pivotal function within the religious life of Israel, specifically in the administration of the Taberna-

---

[237] Massachusetts Institute of Technology. The Holy Bible: New International Version. Exodus 6, https://web.mit.edu/jywang/www/cef/Bible/NIV/NIV_Bible/EXOD+6.html

[238] Massachusetts Institute of Technology. The Holy Bible: New International Version. 1 Chronicles 24, https://web.mit.edu/jywang/www/cef/Bible/NIV/NIV_Bible/1CHRON+24.html

cle and subsequently the Temple. Exodus 28:1[239] specifically designates Ithamar as one of the entrusted individuals responsible for overseeing the labor of the priests and the sacred vestments associated with their sacred service. The lineage of Ithamar continued to contribute to the priestly tradition for multiple generations. The establishment of a division of priestly duties by King David, as outlined in 1 Chronicles 24, specifically designates distinct roles and responsibilities for the descendants of Ithamar.

∞

JEHOVAH-SHAMMAH. The term "Jehovah-shammah" holds theological significance within biblical theology, particularly in the book of Ezekiel in the Old Testament. Derived from the Hebrew language, it translates to "The Lord is there" or "The Lord is present". This phrase appears in Ezekiel 48:35,[240] where it depicts a future state of Jerusalem envisioned by the prophet Ezekiel, wherein the divine presence of the Lord would dwell among His people. The verse in question, Ezekiel 48:35, describes a restored and glorified city of Jerusalem, with its name forever changed to reflect the abiding presence of God. The term "Jehovah-shammah" encapsulates the theological vision of a renewed Jerusalem, serving as a symbol of divine blessing, security, and intimate fellowship between God and His people.

The concept of "Jehovah-shammah" carries significant eschatological implications, reflecting the Israelites' hope for a future state in which God's presence would be manifest in a tangible manner. It signifies the restoration of the covenantal relationship between God and His chosen people, representing the consummation of divine promises and the ultimate fulfillment of God's purposes.

---

[239] Massachusetts Institute of Technology. The Holy Bible: New International Version. Exodus 28, https://web.mit.edu/jywang/www/cef/Bible/NIV/NIV_Bible/EXOD+28.html

[240] Bible Gateway. King James Version. Ezekiel 48.35, https://www.biblegateway.com/passage/?search=Ezekiel+48%3A35&version=KJV

Beyond its historical and prophetic context, "Jehovah-shammah" holds broader spiritual and theological implications for believers. It underscores the enduring truth of God's immanence, emphasizing His perpetual nearness and active involvement in the lives of individuals and the community of faith. The term serves as a reminder of God's abiding presence, offering guidance, solace, and support in all aspects of life.

∞

JEROHAM. The biblical narrative references several individuals named Jeroham, each of whom occupies a distinct role within their respective historical and tribal contexts:

First. Jeroham appears as the father of Elkanah and the grandfather of the prophet Samuel, as recounted in the Book of Samuel (1 Samuel 1:1).[241] The narrative emphasizes the anguish experienced by Elkanah's wife, Hannah, who was initially barren. Divine intervention ultimately grants Hannah the ability to conceive, resulting in the birth of Samuel, who assumes a pivotal role in Israel's history and religious development.

Second. Jeroham is mentioned in 1 Chronicles 27:22[242] as the father of Azareel, who served as the "captain" of the tribe of Dan. This passage provides insight into the organizational and administrative structure of King David's military, with appointed leaders overseeing specific periods of service within each tribe.

Third. A Jeroham is identified as a Benjamite in 1 Chronicles 8:27.[243] However, the available information regarding this individu-

---

[241] Massachusetts Institute of Technology. The Holy Bible: New International Version. 1 Samuel 1, https://web.mit.edu/jywang/www/cef/Bible/NIV/NIV_Bible/1SAM+1.html

[242] Massachusetts Institute of Technology. The Holy Bible: New International Version. 1 Chronicles 27, https://web.mit.edu/jywang/www/cef/Bible/NIV/NIV_Bible/1CHRON+27.html

[243] Massachusetts Institute of Technology. The Holy Bible: New International Version. 1 Chronicles 8, https://web.mit.edu/jywang/www/cef/Bible/NIV/NIV_Bible/1CHRON+8.html

al's specific role or historical significance remains limited within the biblical accounts.

Fourth. In 2 Chronicles 23:1,[244] Jeroham is depicted as the father of Azariah, one of the commanders in Jehoiada's campaign. This campaign sought to restore Joash, the rightful heir to the throne of Judah, and overthrow the oppressive queen Athaliah. Azariah's role as a commander highlights the significance of Jeroham's lineage within the political and military landscape of the time.

Fifth. The mention of a Jeroham as a priest appears in 1 Chronicles 9:12.[245]

∞

JOTHAM. Jotham, a prominent figure in the biblical narrative, is depicted as a king of Judah who reigned during the 8th century BCE. Our understanding of Jotham's rule derives primarily from the accounts presented in the books of 2 Kings and 2 Chronicles, which offer valuable insights into his political achievements, religious reforms, and the broader historical context in which he operated. Upon assuming the throne, Jotham inherited the kingdom from his father, Uzziah (also known as Azariah), who was incapacitated by leprosy. The biblical record informs us that Jotham ascended to power at the age of twenty-five and governed Jerusalem for a period of sixteen years (2 Kings 15:32-33;[246] 2 Chronicles 27:1).[247]

---

[244] Massachusetts Institute of Technology. The Holy Bible: New International Version. 2 Chronicles 23, https://web.mit.edu/jywang/www/cef/Bible/NIV/NIV_Bible/2CHRON+23.html

[245] Massachusetts Institute of Technology. The Holy Bible: New International Version. 1 Chronicles 9, https://web.mit.edu/jywang/www/cef/Bible/NIV/NIV_Bible/1CHRON+9.html

[246] Massachusetts Institute of Technology. The Holy Bible: New International Version. 2 Kings 15, https://web.mit.edu/jywang/www/cef/Bible/NIV/NIV_Bible/2KGS+15.html

[247] Massachusetts Institute of Technology. The Holy Bible: New International Version. 2 Chronicles 27, https://web.mit.edu/jywang/www/cef/Bible/NIV/NIV_Bible/2CHRON+27.html

Jotham's reign was marked by a number of military campaigns aimed at strengthening and securing Judah. Notably, he engaged the Ammonites, a neighboring territory, in armed conflict. The biblical narrative attributes Jotham's success in subduing the Ammonites and extracting tribute from them (2 Kings 15:37; 2 Chronicles 27:5).

In addition to his military endeavors, Jotham prioritized infrastructure development within his kingdom. He initiated construction projects, particularly the expansion and fortification of cities situated in the hill country of Judah. Significantly, the city of Ophel in the southern region of Jerusalem is highlighted as having been fortified under Jotham's rule (2 Chronicles 27:3).

Jotham's commitment to upholding the religious traditions of Judah is also emphasized in the biblical accounts. He is portrayed as a ruler who adhered to the righteous ways of the Lord, following in the footsteps of his father Uzziah. However, it should be noted that despite his overall faithfulness, the narrative points out that the high places, which served as sites for non-Yahwistic worship, were not eliminated during Jotham's reign (2 Kings 15:34-35).

The demise of Jotham's rule occurred upon his death, after which he was succeeded by his son Ahaz. While the biblical records provide valuable insights into Jotham's accomplishments and religious disposition, they offer a limited portrayal of his character and the broader historical milieu in which he operated.

∞

LORUHAMAH. Loruhamah is a name introduced in the biblical book of Hosea, found specifically in Hosea 1:6.[248] Within the context of the narrative, Loruhamah represents the second child born to the prophet Hosea and his wife Gomer. The name Loruhamah assumes symbolic significance within the text, serving as a conduit for conveying a divine

---

[248] Massachusetts Institute of Technology. The Holy Bible: New International Version. Hosea 1, https://web.mit.edu/jywang/www/cef/Bible/NIV/NIV_Bible/HOSEA+1.html

message and reflecting the tumultuous relationship between God and the people of Israel.

The book of Hosea chronicles the prophet's divinely ordained marriage to an unfaithful woman, which allegorically symbolizes Israel's unfaithfulness to God. The children born to Hosea and Gomer are given names that carry symbolic weight, embodying the prophetic message being communicated. Loruhamah, meaning "not pitied" or "not shown mercy," conveys the notion that God will no longer extend compassion or mercy to the people of Israel due to their ongoing disobedience and unfaithfulness. The name Loruhamah operates as a metaphorical expression of divine judgment and the consequences that Israel will inevitably face as a result of their actions. It signifies the cessation of divine favor and protection, heralding the impending judgment and retribution that will befall the nation. While the name Loruhamah is intimately tied to the narrative presented in the book of Hosea, its symbolic import resonates with broader themes exhibited throughout the prophetic literature of the Hebrew Bible. It underscores the theological concept of divine judgment and the repercussions of human behavior, while also acknowledging the potential for repentance and restoration.

∞

MALCHAM. The name "Malcham" denotes two distinct individuals within the Hebrew Bible, as recorded in separate passages:

First. In 1 Chronicles 8:9,[249] Malcham is identified as the son of Shaharaim and Hodesh, both of whom hailed from the tribe of Benjamin. This mention of Malcham occurs within a genealogical account intended to establish a comprehensive record of ancestral lineage and familial connections among the Israelite tribes.

---

[249] Massachusetts Institute of Technology. The Holy Bible: New International Version. 1 Chronicles 8, https://web.mit.edu/jywang/www/cef/Bible/NIV/NIV_Bible/1CHRON+8.html

Second. An altogether separate figure named Malcham, also known by the names Milcom or Molech, appears within the biblical narrative as a deity associated with idolatrous practices and condemned rituals. This Malcham is cited in various passages, including Jeremiah 32:35,[250] in connection with pagan worship that encompassed abhorrent acts such as child sacrifices.

The first Malcham mentioned in 1 Chronicles 8:9 is documented as a descendant of Shaharaim and Hodesh, contributing to the genealogical lineage of the tribe of Benjamin. However, the second Malcham, referenced in relation to idolatrous worship, serves as an emblematic representation of the abominable practices prevalent in certain ancient cultures. While the Hebrew Bible furnishes limited information regarding the first Malcham, the genealogical framework establishes his familial connection within the tribe of Benjamin. Conversely, the second Malcham embodies a broader theological and societal context, symbolizing the religious deviations and condemnations pronounced by the biblical prophets.

∞

MISHAM. In the genealogical records of the Hebrew Bible, specifically in 1 Chronicles 8:16,[251] Misham is enumerated as a descendant of Shaharaim, a prominent figure within the tribe of Benjamin. This passage details Misham's lineage as the son of Elpaal, himself a member of the tribe of Benjamin. Elpaal's lineage can be traced back to Shaharaim, who is identified as his father. As a result, Misham is positioned as the grandson of Shaharaim and a descendant of the distinguished tribe of Benjamin.

---

[250] Massachusetts Institute of Technology. The Holy Bible: New International Version. Jeremiah 32, https://web.mit.edu/jywang/www/cef/Bible/NIV/NIV_Bible/JER+32.html

[251] Massachusetts Institute of Technology. The Holy Bible: New International Version. 1 Chronicles 8, https://web.mit.edu/jywang/www/cef/Bible/NIV/NIV_Bible/1CHRON+8.html

The genealogical accounts presented in 1 Chronicles serve to establish a comprehensive and meticulously documented record of ancestral lineage within the Israelite tribes. By tracing the lineage of various individuals and families, these genealogies shed light on familial connections, tribal affiliations, and wider ancestral heritage.

∞

NAHAMANI. In the Nehemiah narrative found within the Hebrew Bible, specifically Nehemiah 7:7,[252] we encounter the figure of Nahamani. Noted as one of the chiefs or leaders among the exiles who returned from Babylon alongside Zerubbabel, Nahamani assumes a position of significance within this historical context. The verse in question, Nehemiah 7:7, provides a concise account of the descendants of the province who emerged from the captivity of Nebuchadnezzar, the Babylonian king. These individuals returned to their respective towns in Jerusalem and Judah, thus contributing to the reestablishment of the Jewish community in their homeland.

While the passage does not furnish us with extensive information concerning Nahamani's specific role or contributions, it does underscore his status as a notable leader among the exiles who embarked upon the journey back to Jerusalem and Judah. As such, we may surmise that Nahamani played a significant part in the post-exilic community and the restoration of the Jewish people.

∞

PROPHET MUHAMMAD. Prophet Muhammad, a descendant of Prophet Abraham and Hagar through his son Ishmael, born in 570 CE in the city of Mecca, Saudi Arabia, stands as a central figure within the Islamic faith and is regarded as the last and final prophet. His life and teachings have had a profound impact on millions of individuals

---

[252] Massachusetts Institute of Technology. The Holy Bible: New International Version. Nehemiah 7, https://web.mit.edu/jywang/www/cef/Bible/NIV/NIV_Bible/NEH+7.html

worldwide, shaping the course of history and influencing the development of Islamic civilization. Muhammad's mission was to preach and confirm the monotheistic teachings of previous prophets, including Adam, Abraham, Moses, Christ, and others.

According to Islamic tradition, at the age of 40, Muhammad experienced a transformative event when he received the initial of a series of revelations from God, transmitted through the angel Gabriel. These revelations, spanning a period of 23 years, are believed by Muslims to constitute the Quran, the sacred scripture of Islam. The Quran encompasses a wide range of subjects, including matters of faith, morality, guidance for personal and communal conduct, and the establishment of a just and compassionate society.

Muhammad's teachings emphasized the unity and oneness of God, known as Tawhid, as well as the imperative of submitting to God's will, encapsulated in the concept of Islam. He championed the principles of monotheism, social justice, compassion, and ethical behavior. Muhammad's teachings encompassed various spheres of life, encompassing personal piety, familial relationships, communal dynamics, governance, and social interactions.

Throughout his lifetime, Muhammad encountered numerous challenges and faced opposition from the ruling elites of Mecca, who resisted his message. In 622 CE, he and his followers embarked on the momentous migration, known as the Hijra, to the city of Medina. This event marked a significant turning point and the genesis of the Islamic calendar. In Medina, Muhammad assumed a pivotal role in establishing an exemplary society predicated upon Islamic principles, unifying disparate tribes, and instituting principles of governance and social welfare.

Muhammad's leadership extended beyond the religious sphere, encompassing political and military dimensions. He led defensive battles to safeguard the nascent Muslim community and propagate the message of Islam throughout the Arabian Peninsula.

The example set forth by Muhammad, as well as his teachings, collectively referred to as the Sunnah, serve as a guiding light for Muslims, shaping their beliefs, practices, and conduct. Muslims strive to emulate his character, characterized by traits such as integrity, compassion, mercy, and unwavering devotion to God. Prophet Muhammad's enduring legacy as a prophet and leader has left an indelible imprint upon the lives of millions worldwide. Regarded as the final prophet, he represents the culmination and fulfillment of the prophetic tradition, with his teachings serving as the bedrock of the Islamic faith.

∞

RAHAM. Raham, a biblical figure mentioned in the Old Testament, appears in the genealogical records found in the book of 1 Chronicles. This text traces Raham's lineage back to the prominent figures Caleb and Hezron, within the broader context of the tribe of Judah. According to 1 Chronicles 2:44-48,[253] Raham is identified as the son of Shema and the father of Jorkeam. These genealogical records serve to establish connections between individuals and families, providing a historical framework for understanding the lineage of the Israelite people.

Raham's significance lies primarily in his position within the genealogical lineage of Caleb and Hezron, who hold key ancestral roles in the history of the Israelites. While the specific details of Raham's life and his contributions to biblical events are not extensively elaborated upon in the scriptures, his presence in the genealogical records contextualizes his place within the broader narrative of the Israelite tradition.

∞

SELA-HAMMAHLEKOTH. The term "Sela-hammahlekoth," derived from the Hebrew language and mentioned in Psalm 58:10[254] of the

---

[253] Massachusetts Institute of Technology. The Holy Bible: New International Version. 1 Chronicles 2, https://web.mit.edu/jywang/www/cef/Bible/NIV/NIV_Bible/1CHRON+2.html

[254] Massachusetts Institute of Technology. The Holy Bible: New International

Old Testament, carries metaphorical significance within the context of the psalm. It can be understood as a composite term consisting of "Sela," meaning "rock," and "hammahlekoth," which can be translated as "divisions" or "splits". In the poetic and metaphorical language of the psalm, "Sela-hammahlekoth" symbolically represents a divine intervention or judgment that results in divisions or splits among the wicked. The term encapsulates the notion that God, acting as a just judge, brings forth a separation or disruption among those who perpetrate wrongdoing or engage in acts of injustice.

∞

SHAMA. The Hebrew term "Shama" conveys a rich array of meanings related to the acts of hearing, listening, giving attention, understanding, submitting to, and obeying. Its multifaceted nature makes it a pivotal concept within the Hebrew Bible, carrying both theological and practical implications. At its core, "Shama" denotes the sensory perception of auditory stimuli However, its application extends beyond mere sensory reception. It encompasses attentiveness, comprehension, and a willingness to respond or take action based on what is heard. Within a religious and ethical framework, "Shama" assumes a more profound significance. It signifies an active and wholehearted response to God's word, commandments, or teachings. It entails not only grasping their meaning but also embracing them with a sense of submission and obedience. The concept of "Shama" holds a central place in Judaism, underscoring the importance of actively listening to and internalizing God's instructions while translating them into concrete actions. It reflects a commitment to a covenantal relationship with the divine, characterized by unwavering adherence to divine guidance and a readiness to align one's conduct with God's commandments. Furthermore, the resonance of "Shama" extends beyond the

---

Version. Psalm 58, https://web.mit.edu/jywang/www/cef/Bible/NIV/NIV_Bible/PS+58.html

individual level, encompassing communal life as well. It embodies a responsibility to heed and respond to the needs and voices of others within the community.

"Shama" encapsulates the multidimensional acts of hearing, listening, understanding, giving attention, submitting to, and obeying. Its theological and practical significance within the Hebrew Bible emphasizes active engagement with God's teachings and a steadfast dedication to living in harmony with divine will.

∞

SHAMASH. Shamash, a prominent deity in ancient Mesopotamian religion, assumes a dual role as the god of the sun and justice. In earlier Mesopotamian traditions, Shamash was known by the name Utu and was considered the son of Sin (e.g. Mount Sinai, Sinites, tribe, Sinolgoy, at. el.), the god associated with the moon. Notably, Shamash is recognized as the twin sibling of Ishtar, the revered Queen of Heaven and is acknowledged as the father of Kittum, who is alternatively identified as Niĝgina, Mamu, Sisig, Zaqar, Šumugan, and Ishum. Within the divine circle of Shamash, a sequence of individuals is mentioned, including Umu, Kittum, Mīšaru, and Dajjānu. The inclusion of these figures likely signifies their association with the deity and potentially indicates their respective roles or attributes within the broader religious and mythological framework.

Furthermore, the concept of an Astral Triad, consisting of Sin, Shamash, and Ishtar, becomes apparent. This triad represents a celestial hierarchy and symbolizes the interplay of cosmic forces. Sin symbolizes the moon, Shamash personifies the sun, and Ishtar embodies the heavens. Shamash, in particular, assumes the mantle of the sun god, representing light, warmth, and justice. His association with justice underscores his role as a divine judge and the enforcer of moral order. Analogous to the sun's illumination of the world, Shamash's radiance brings clarity and truth, thereby establishing him as an emblem of righteousness and truthfulness.

∞

SHAMASH CANDLE. The Shamash Candle, an integral component of the Jewish holiday of Hanukkah, holds a notable role within the context of this festive observance. Hanukkah, commonly referred to as the Festival of Lights, is an eight-day celebration commemorating the rededication of the Second Temple in Jerusalem and the miracle of the oil. During the observance of Hanukkah, a distinctive nine-branched candelabrum, known as a menorah or Hanukkiah, is prominently displayed and lit. The menorah typically consists of eight candles, symbolizing the eight days that the oil miraculously burned in the Temple. Positioned slightly higher or lower than the other candles, the central or ninth candle on the menorah is known as the Shamash Candle. In practical terms, the Shamash Candle serves a crucial purpose in the Hanukkah ritual. It is employed to kindle the other candles on the menorah. Each night of Hanukkah, an additional candle is lit, commencing with the Shamash Candle, which is then utilized to ignite the remaining candles. This ceremonial process symbolizes the dissemination of light and commemorates the miraculous event associated with the holiday.

Beyond its functional role, the Shamash Candle also carries symbolic significance. It embodies the concept of the "helper" or "attendant" - a luminous guide that facilitates the fulfillment of the mitzvah, or religious commandment, of kindling the Hanukkah candles. The distinctiveness of the Shamash Candle, set apart from the other candles, serves as a reminder to observers of its specific purpose in illuminating and assisting in the proper observance of the holiday. The lighting of the Shamash Candle, accompanied by the subsequent kindling of the other candles, is accompanied by the recitation of blessings, prayers, and traditional songs. This ritual act constitutes a central element of the Hanukkah celebration, fostering a sense of unity, joy, and commemoration among Jewish individuals and communities.

∞

SHAMAYIM. Shamayim, a Hebrew term frequently translated as "heaven" or "the heavens" in English, occupies a prominent place within Jewish religious and cultural contexts. Found throughout the Hebrew Bible (Tanakh), this term carries multifaceted meanings and connotations, reflecting its rich theological significance. Within Jewish belief, shamayim denotes the divine, serving as the abode of the Almighty and the spiritual dimension transcending the earthly plane. It encompasses the dwelling place of celestial beings, including angels and the souls of the righteous, constituting a locus of divine presence and cosmic harmony. Shamayim further embodies notions of transcendence, sacredness, and eschatological aspirations. It represents the dimension in which prayers ascend, resonating with the Jewish understanding of an afterlife wherein the righteous are rewarded in the World to Come.

∞

SHAMER. Shamer ("Shomer") is identified as the son of Heber, hailing from the tribe of Asher. This lineage is documented in the genealogical records found in 1 Chronicles 7:32.[255] These genealogies, constituting an integral aspect of ancient Israelite society, served to establish and delineate the ancestral lines and tribal affiliations of the Israelite people, thereby reinforcing their collective identity.

∞

SHAMGAR. The mention of Shamgar in the biblical narrative introduces an intriguing complexity, as it appears to refer to two distinct individuals:

The first Shamgar, known as the son of Anath, presents a fascinating connection to Canaanite mythology. Anath, the Canaanite goddess associated with both love and war, holds a prominent place within the

---

[255] Massachusetts Institute of Technology. The Holy Bible: New International Version. 1 Chronicles 7, https://web.mit.edu/jywang/www/cef/Bible/NIV/NIV_Bible/1CHRON+7.html

ancient religious pantheon. Shamgar's affiliation with Anath suggests a potential intertwining of Canaanite religious traditions with the narrative of the Israelite judges. This Shamgar, identified as a judge who succeeded Ehud, is briefly mentioned in Judges 3:31.[256] Regrettably, the biblical text provides minimal information regarding the specific exploits or duration of Shamgar's judgeship. Nevertheless, his inclusion within the list of judges in ancient Israel underscores his significance within the historical and religious framework of the period.

The second Shamgar, referenced in Judges 5:6[257] within the Song of Deborah, offers an additional layer of complexity. This poetic account describes the challenges faced by the Israelites, including the lack of secure travel on the highways during Shamgar's time. While the verse does not provide explicit details about Shamgar's lineage or role, it provides insights into the broader historical context characterized by instability and vulnerability.

∞

SHAMHUTH. The mention of Shamhuth in the biblical narrative, specifically in relation to King David's arrangement of his army, provides a glimpse into the organizational structure and leadership hierarchy that characterized the military establishment of ancient Israel during this period. While the biblical text offers limited details about Shamhuth or his specific contributions, his designation as the fifth captain for the fifth month highlights his position and role within the military framework.

∞

---

[256] Massachusetts Institute of Technology. The Holy Bible: New International Version. Judges 3, https://web.mit.edu/jywang/www/cef/Bible/NIV/NIV_Bible/JUDG+3.html

[257] Massachusetts Institute of Technology. The Holy Bible: New International Version. Judges 5, https://web.mit.edu/jywang/www/cef/Bible/NIV/NIV_Bible/JUDG+5.html

SHAMIR. The name "Shamir" holds multifaceted significance within a range of historical and biblical contexts, offering intriguing possibilities for interpretation and association:

First. Within the Book of Joshua, Shamir is referenced as one of the settlements apportioned to the tribe of Ephraim (Joshua 19:22).[258]

Second. The Book of Judges provides two distinct references to Shamir. In Judges 10:1,[259] we encounter a figure named Shamir, son of Anath, who appears as a judge in Israel. However, the biblical text provides scant details regarding Shamir's specific achievements or the duration of his judgeship. Additionally, Judges 10:12[260] mentions Shamir as a place associated with Jair, another judge, although the precise geographical location of this place remains uncertain.

Third. The Book of Jeremiah employs the name Shamir metaphorically in Jeremiah 17:1,[261] where it alludes to a tool employed for engraving or carving. The passage poetically describes the divine law being inscribed with a "pen of iron" and "point of a diamond" upon the tablets of the people's hearts, evoking a lasting and indelible impression.

Fourth. Within Jewish tradition, Shamir is linked to a mythical creature or substance possessing the extraordinary ability to cut through hard materials, including stone. This tradition, found in texts such as the Talmud and various ancient Jewish writings, portrays Shamir as a miraculous entity or stone that aided in the construction of the First Temple in Jerusalem.

---

[258] Massachusetts Institute of Technology. The Holy Bible: New International Version. Joshua 19, https://web.mit.edu/jywang/www/cef/Bible/NIV/NIV_Bible/JOSH+19.html

[259] Massachusetts Institute of Technology. The Holy Bible: New International Version. Judges 10, https://web.mit.edu/jywang/www/cef/Bible/NIV/NIV_Bible/JUDG+10.html

[260] Massachusetts Institute of Technology. The Holy Bible: New International Version. Judges 10, https://web.mit.edu/jywang/www/cef/Bible/NIV/NIV_Bible/JUDG+10.html

[261] Massachusetts Institute of Technology. The Holy Bible: New International Version. Jeremiah 17, https://web.mit.edu/jywang/www/cef/Bible/NIV/NIV_Bible/JER+17.html

∞

SHAMMAH. The name "Shammah" holds considerable significance within biblical narratives and ancient Israelite history. Its appearances in various contexts shed light on the multifaceted contributions of individuals associated with this name, enriching our understanding of the broader cultural and history of the time:

First. We encounter Shammah, the son of Agee, in the Second Book of Samuel (23:11-12),[262] where he is enlisted among King David's esteemed "mighty men". This passage recounts Shammah's remarkable feat of defending a field of lentils single-handedly against a Philistine assault, exemplifying exceptional bravery and valor. Shammah's unwavering commitment to safeguarding the land embodies the indomitable spirit and unwavering dedication epitomized by David's formidable warriors.

Second. The Book of Genesis (36:13, 17)[263] introduces us to Shammah, the son of Reuel, who traces his lineage back to Esau, the twin brother of Jacob. This genealogical reference illuminates Shammah's ancestral connection within the broader ancient Edomite history, affording insights into the social and political structures of the region during that era.

Third. The First Book of Chronicles (11:27)[264] introduces Shammah as the father of Elika, another illustrious member of David's renowned "thirty" warriors. Although the biblical narrative does not delve into specific details concerning Shammah's personal exploits, his

---

[262] Massachusetts Institute of Technology. The Holy Bible: New International Version. 2 Samuel 23, https://web.mit.edu/jywang/www/cef/Bible/NIV/NIV_Bible/2SAM+23.html

[263] Massachusetts Institute of Technology. The Holy Bible: New International Version. Genesis 36, https://web.mit.edu/jywang/www/cef/Bible/NIV/NIV_Bible/GEN+36.html

[264] Massachusetts Institute of Technology. The Holy Bible: New International Version. Chronicles 11, https://web.mit.edu/jywang/www/cef/Bible/NIV/NIV_Bible/1CHRON+11.html

inclusion among the warriors of King David underscores his esteemed status and the valor associated with his familial lineage.

∞

SHAMMAI. Shammai, a renowned Jewish scholar of the 1st century CE, occupies a significant position within the Judaism's foundational work of rabbinic literature, the Mishnah. As a prominent figure during a formative period of Jewish legal and ethical thought, Shammai exerted substantial influence on the development of Jewish law and religious practice.

Shammai's scholarly contributions primarily manifested through his active involvement in spirited debates and intellectual exchanges with Hillel the Elder, another distinguished sage of the time. These two prominent figures, along with their respective schools of thought, the House of Shammai and the House of Hillel, engaged in rigorous discourse on diverse matters pertaining to Jewish law, ethics, and interpretation. The discourses between Shammai and Hillel encompassed a wide range of topics, including matters of divorce, ritual purity, Sabbath observance, and scriptural interpretation. Shammai was particularly known for his adherence to a strict and meticulous approach to Jewish law, advocating for a literal understanding of the commandments found within the Torah. His teachings emphasized the importance of upholding the letter of the law and maintaining a disciplined religious practice. The influence of Shammai extended beyond his lifetime. His opinions and rulings continue to hold sway within the Mishnah, the authoritative compilation of rabbinic Jewish law. While the majority of the Mishnah tends to align with the more lenient positions of Hillel, Shammai's perspectives and those of his school are also represented, underscoring the lasting impact of his scholarship. It is worth noting that despite their divergent views, Shammai and Hillel engaged in their debates with a sense of mutual respect. The exchanges between these two sages epitomize the dynamic nature of Jewish legal and ethical discourse, showcasing the richness and diversity of perspectives within Judaism and the ongoing quest for elucidation and interpretation of religious principles. Shammai's enduring legacy as an influential Jewish scholar resides in his contributions to Jewish intellectual history. His teachings and debates with Hillel exemplify the intellectual vibrancy of Jewish legal thought during a pivotal period, embodying the ongoing pursuit of understanding and application of religious principles within the Jewish tradition.

∞

SHAMMUA. The name "Shammua" appears in various contexts within biblical narratives, denoting multiple individuals who played significant roles during different periods of Israelite history:

First. We encounter Shammua, the son of Zaccur, who is prominently mentioned as one of the twelve spies dispatched by Moses to explore the land of Canaan. Representing the tribe of Reuben, Shammua embarked on a reconnaissance mission that aimed to assess the land's inhabitants, resources, and challenges. The reports provided by Shammua and his fellow spies influenced subsequent events and decisions within the Israelite community during their wilderness sojourn.

Second. We encounter Shammua as the son of King David and Bathsheba, a figure mentioned within the genealogical records found in the Book of Chronicles. This Shammua, along with his brothers Shobab, Nathan, and King Solomon, signifies the restoration and blessing that followed a period of turmoil in the lives of David and Bathsheba. Their birth represents a significant narrative development, highlighting the familial lineage of King David and the subsequent establishment of the Davidic dynasty.

Third. We encounter another Shammua, a Levite, whose presence is recorded in the genealogies of postexilic Jerusalem inhabitants, specifically in the Book of Nehemiah. This Shammua is identified as the father of Abda, also known as Obadiah, who is listed as an inhabitant of Jerusalem during the restoration period. It is interesting to note that this Shammua is referred to as Shemaiah in alternative biblical passages, suggesting potential discrepancies or variations in naming conventions across different sources or traditions.

Fourth. We encounter Shammua as the head of the clan of Bilgah during the period of restoration, as documented in the Book of Ezra and Nehemiah. As a clan leader, Shammua played a pivotal role in the reestablishment and organizational efforts of the community following the Babylonian exile. His leadership within the Bilgah clan showcases his contribution to the broader restoration endeavors and the reconstitution of communal structures.

The diverse instances of "Shammua" within biblical texts provide valuable insights into the lives and contributions of individuals associated with this name across distinct historical periods. The multifaceted nature of their roles and the varied contexts in which they emerge contribute to our comprehensive understanding of the ancient Israelite milieu, shedding light on historical, cultural, and sociopolitical aspects of the period.

∞

SHAMSHI. The name "Shamshi" is found in various cultural and historical contexts, and its interpretation requires careful consideration of the specific cultural and linguistic milieu in which it appears. Allow us to explore a few possible interpretations of this name.

First. Within the ancient Near East, "Shamshi" may be regarded as a truncated form of names derived from the Akkadian language. For instance, "Shamshi-Adad" was a notable name borne by several rulers of the Assyrian Empire. Among them, Shamshi-Adad I, a prominent king during the early 18th century BCE, implemented substantial political and administrative reforms while expanding the Assyrian kingdom.

Second. It is worth noting that the Hebrew Bible does not explicitly mention an individual named "Shamshi". However, one can draw a connection to the Mesopotamian sun god "Shamash" and the Hebrew word for "sun," which is "Shemesh". The Bible often employs "Shemesh" metaphorically or symbolically, representing concepts such as light, warmth, and divine presence.

∞

SHAPHAM. 1 Chronicles 5:11-26[265] provides a genealogical account of the tribes of Gad, Reuben, and the half-tribe of Manasseh. The passage focuses on the Gadites and their settlements in the land of Bashan. The Gadites lived in the region across from their kinsmen from the tribes of Reuben and Manasseh, extending from Bashan to Salecah. The passage lists several prominent individuals from the tribe of Gad and provides insight into their genealogy and historical context. Among the Gadites, four individuals are specifically mentioned: Joel, Shapham, Janai, and Shaphat. Joel is identified as the chief of the Gadites, indicating his leadership role within the tribe. Shapham is mentioned as the second in rank, suggesting his prominence and high standing among the Gadite community. Janai and Shaphat are also listed, although their specific roles or positions are not elaborated upon in this passage.

∞

SHOHAM. Within the Hebrew Bible, the name "Shoham" is associated with a figure of the Merarite Levites, specifically identified as the son of Jaaziah. The Merarites, as one of the Levitical clans, held a significant role in the maintenance and transportation of the Tabernacle, the portable sacred sanctuary employed by the Israelites during their sojourn in the wilderness prior to the construction of the Temple in Jerusalem. The Levites, including the Merarites, were a designated class entrusted with sacred duties, serving as assistants to the priests in various religious rituals and ceremonies.

Shoham, as a member of the Merarite clan, would have played a crucial part in the logistical aspects of the Tabernacle. This would have

---

[265] Massachusetts Institute of Technology. The Holy Bible: New International Version. 1 Chronicles 5, https://web.mit.edu/jywang/www/cef/Bible/NIV/NIV_Bible/1CHRON+5.html

involved the disassembling and reassembling of the Tabernacle and its constituent elements whenever the Israelites relocated from one site to another during their wilderness wanderings.

∞

SHUHAM. Within the Hebrew Bible, Shuham is mentioned as an individual of significance, specifically identified as the son of Dan and an ancestor of the Shuhamites. Dan, one of the twelve sons of Jacob and a prominent figure in the formation of the tribes of Israel, holds a distinct place in the ancestral lineage of the Israelite community. Shuham is listed among the sons or descendants of Dan in the biblical genealogies, indicating his familial relationship within the tribe. The Shuhamites, as the descendants of Shuham, form a lineage within the broader tribe of Dan.

∞

SHUPHAM. Within the Hebrew Bible, Shupham is mentioned as an individual of significance, specifically identified as the son of Bela and the grandson of Benjamin. Benjamin, one of the twelve sons of Jacob, holds a notable place among the founding fathers of the twelve tribes of Israel. The ancestral lineage of Benjamin, as elucidated in the biblical text, reveals the existence of various descendants, including Bela and his son Shupham.

∞

SIN-IQISHAM. The historical figure known as Sin-iqisham, or Sîn-iqīšam, assumes a position of significance within ancient Mesopotamia. The name "Sin-iqisham" finds its roots in the Akkadian language, denoting "Sin (the moon god) has given a name". Sin, the celestial deity presiding over the lunar domain, held a prominent role within the multifaceted Mesopotamian gods.

∞

THAMAH. Within the Hebrew Bible, Thamah is mentioned as an individual of significance. Specifically, Thamah is identified as one of the Nethinim, a class of temple servants or non-Israelite laborers who provided assistance to the Levites in the service of the Tabernacle and later the Temple. The Nethinim were believed to be descendants of the Gibeonites, who were assigned to perform menial tasks in service to the sanctuary.

During the period of the Babylonian exile, a significant number of Israelites were displaced from their homeland. However, following the decree of King Cyrus of Persia, allowing the exiled Jews to return to Jerusalem, a wave of repatriation led by Zerubbabel took place. Among those who chose to return were members of the Nethinim community, including Thamah.

The biblical text does not provide extensive details regarding the specific role or activities of Thamah or the Nethinim upon their return. However, their presence among the returning exiles suggests their commitment to the restoration of Jerusalem and the Temple, as well as their contributions to the religious and communal life of the post-exilic community. The mention of Thamah and the Nethinim in the biblical narrative sheds light on the diverse range of individuals and groups involved in the restoration and reestablishment of Jewish religious and cultural practices in the aftermath of the Babylonian exile.

∞

ZETHAM. Zetham, as recorded in the Hebrew Bible, holds a notable place as the son of Laadan, a Gershonite Levite. This reference can be found in 1 Chronicles 23:8,[266] where the meticulous organization and responsibilities of the Levitical divisions are outlined. Within the passage, we encounter the meticulous appointment of certain Levites by King David to oversee various duties essential to the functioning

---

[266] Massachusetts Institute of Technology. The Holy Bible: New International Version. 1 Chronicles 23, https://web.mit.edu/jywang/www/cef/Bible/NIV/NIV_Bible/1CHRON+23.html

of the tabernacle. Zetham, specifically identified as one of the sons of Laadan, assumes a position of leadership among the Gershonite Levites.

While the scriptural account does not provide extensive individual details about Zetham himself, his inclusion serves to underscore the structure and administrative roles within the Levitical priesthood during the reign of King David. It is worth emphasizing the significance of the Levitical priesthood in ancient Israel, as they were entrusted with the sacred tasks associated with the tabernacle and worship rituals. Zetham, as a member of the Gershonite Levites, would have played a crucial role in maintaining the sanctity and functionality of the religious practices of the time.

SIMULATED RENDITION OF SIMPLE DUALITY AS TIME[267]

---

[267] Julius Orion Smith III. Complex Sinusoids as Circular Motion. Stanford University. 2024. https://ccrma.stanford.edu/~jos/fp/Plotting_Complex_Sinusoids_Circular.html

above.below

within.without

BIBLIOGRAPHY

1. Gaia, Timothy Hogan, and Scott Wolter. (2024, March 29). Atlantean Secrets revealed by the Knights Templar [Video]. YouTube. 27:27 https://www.youtube.com/watch?v=wLjdgOe-LpA

2. Whitford, David M. "Was Ham Black?" The Curse of Ham: Race and Slavery in Early Judaism, Christianity, and Islam. (Princeton University Press). p. 144. https://books.google.com/books?id=iTyJ3HiNOAsC&q=burnt+swarthy+black&pg=PA144#v=snippet&q=burnt%20swarthy%20black&f=false

3. Woolley, Leonard. 1931. "Shamash." The British Museum. 2000BC-1750BC. https://www.britishmuseum.org/collection/object/W_1931-1010-2

4. Jacobsen, Thorkild and The Oriental Institute of the University of Chicago. The Sumerian King List. Edited by John A. Wilson and Thomas George Allen. Uploaded by Misty and Lewis Gruber. Assyriological Studies. Fourth. 1939. Reprint, The University of Chicago Press, 1939, pp. 83."Be mindful of Shamash" https://isac.uchicago.edu/sites/default/files/uploads/shared/docs/as11.pdf

5. Encyclopaedia Judaica. (2007). Sun. Jewish Virtual Library. https://www.jewishvirtuallibrary.org/sun

6. Gebhard J. Selz, Piotr Michalowski, Paul John Frandsen, Irene J. Winter, Erica Ehrenberg, Clemens Reichel, Reinhard Bernbeck, Michelle Gilbert, David Freidel, Michael Puett, Bruce Lincoln, Greg Woolf, Jerrold S. Cooper, & Kathleen D. Morrison. (2008). Religion and Power: Divine Kingship in the ancient world and beyond. In N. Brisch (Ed.), The Oriental Institute Seminars:

Vol. Number 4. The Oriental Institute, Chicago. https://isac.uchicago.edu/sites/default/files/uploads/shared/docs/ois4.pdf

7   Zgusta, Ladislav. 2024. "The science of onomastics." Encyclopedia Britannica. March 12, 2024. https://www.britannica.com/topic/name/The-science-of-onomastics

8   Flow, Christian B., and Rachel B Nolan. 2006. "'Go Forth From Your Country': Negotiation expert plans multi-national retracing of Abraham's path." The Harvard Crimson. November 16, 2006. https://www.thecrimson.com/article/2006/11/16/go-forth-from-your-country-for/

9   Trimm, C. (2022, March 15). The Destruction of the Canaanites: God, Genocide, and Biblical Interpretation. Amazon. https://www.amazon.com/Destruction-Canaanites-Genocide-Biblical-Interpretation/dp/0802879624

10 Bible Gateway. John 8. NIV. https://web.mit.edu/jywang/www/cef/Bible/NIV/NIV_Bible/JOHN+8.html

11 Güterbock, Hans G. "The Composition of Hittite Prayers to the Sun. Journal of the American Oriental Society 78, no. 4 (1958): 237–45, pp. 241, "son of mankind" https://www.jstor.org/stable/595787

12 Gray, Clifton Daggett. The Šamaš Religious Texts Classified in the British Museum Catalogue as Hymns, Prayers, and Incantations, with Twenty Plates of Texts Hitherto Unpublished, and a Transliteration and Translation of K.3182. 1901. Internet Archive, pp. 13, "light of the world" https://archive.org/details/samasreligiouste00grayrich

13 Becher, M. (n.d.). The Laws of Chanukah. Ohr Somayach. "the shamash" https://ohr.edu/1304

14 Amit, Yairah. "Tamar, From Victim to Mother of a Dynasty." In Oxford University Press eBooks, 294–305, 2013. https://academic.oup.com/book/3782/chapter-abstract/145230184?redirectedFrom=fulltext

15 Paz, Reut Yael: The Stubborn Subversiveness of Judaism's Matrilineal Principle, VerfBlog, 2021/9/29, https://verfassungsblog.de/the-stubborn-subversiveness-of-judaisms-matrilineal-principle/

16 Bryan W. Van Norden. Foreword by Jay L. Garfield. "Taking Back Philosophy: A Multicultural Manifesto" February 22, 2017. https://cup.columbia.edu/book/taking-back-philosophy/9780231184373

17	Bible Gateway. John 1:1-5 (NIV). https://web.mit.edu/jywang/www/cef/Bible/NIV/NIV_Bible/JOHN+1.html

18	Bible Gateway. Genesis 1:1-3 (NIV). https://web.mit.edu/jywang/www/cef/Bible/NIV/NIV_Bible/GEN+1.html

19	United Nations. (n.d.). Ethnic Cleansing. United Nations Office on Genocide Prevention and the Responsibility to Protect. https://www.un.org/en/genocideprevention/ethnic-cleansing.shtml

20	United Nations. (1948). Convention on the Prevention and Punishment of the Crime of Genocide. In United Nations. https://www.un.org/en/genocideprevention/documents/atrocity-crimes/Doc.1_Convention%20on%20the%20Prevention%20and%20Punishment%20of%20the%20Crime%20of%20Genocide.pdf

21	Lieberman, Benjamin, 'Ethnic Cleansing' versus Genocide?, in Donald Bloxham, and A. Dirk Moses (eds), The Oxford Handbook of Genocide Studies (2010; online edn, Oxford Academic, 18 Sept. 2012), https://academic.oup.com/edited-volume/40215/chapter-abstract/344567514

22	M. Goldenberg, D. (2005, April 7). The Curse of Ham: Race and Slavery in Early Judaism, Christianity, and Islam. Princeton University Press. https://press.princeton.edu/books/paperback/9780691123707/the-curse-of-ham

23	Bergsma, J. S.; Hahn, S. W. (2005). Noah's Nakedness and the Curse on Canaan (Genesis 9:20–27) (PDF). Journal of Biblical Literature. 124 (1): 25–40. https://www.jstor.org/stable/30040989

24	The Editors of Encyclopaedia Britannica. (2010, January 13). Redaction criticism | Textual Analysis, Source Criticism, Synoptic Gospels. Encyclopedia Britannica. https://www.britannica.com/topic/redaction-criticism

25	L. McKenzie, S. (1998, January 1). The Hebrew Bible Today: An Introduction to Critical Issues. Google Books, pp. 9. https://books.google.com/books?id=owwhpmIVgSAC&q=fifth#v=snippet&q=fifth&f=false

26	Department of History. "The Abrahamic Religions: A Very Short Introduction," December 7, 2023. https://history.wisc.edu/publications/the-abrahamic-religions-a-very-short-introduction/

27   Christopher Eames. What is the correct time frame for the exodus and conquest of the promised land? Armstrong Institute of Biblical Archelogy. https://armstronginstitute.org/350-what-is-the-correct-time-frame-for-the-exodus-and-conquest-of-the-promised-land

28   curse. (2024). In Merriam-Webster Dictionary. https://www.merriam-webster.com/dictionary/curse

29   Bible Gateway. Proverbs 18. NIV. https://web.mit.edu/jywang/www/cef/Bible/NIV/NIV_Bible/PROV+18.html

30   Branch, Taylor. At Canaan's Edge: America in the King Years, 1965-68. https://www.google.com/books/edition/At_Canaan_s_Edge/BNuog1T4XnsC?hl=en&gbpv=1

31   Luther King, M., Jr. (1958, June 3). Paul's Letter to American Christians, Sermon delivered to the Commission on Ecumenical Missions and Relations, United Presbyterian Church, U.S.A. The Martin Luther King, Jr. Research and Education Institute. https://kinginstitute.stanford.edu/king-papers/documents/pauls-letter-american-christians-sermon-delivered-commission-ecumenical

32   "Church Commissioners for England warmly welcomes Oversight Group's report." 2024. The Church of England. April 3, 2024. https://www.churchofengland.org/media/press-releases/church-commissioners-england-warmly-welcomes-oversight-groups-report

33   StudyLight.org. "Coffman's Commentaries on the Bible.: Bible Commentaries. Genesis 9.," n.d. https://www.studylight.org/commentaries/eng/bcc/genesis-9.html#verses-25

34   We shall overcome. (n.d.). The Kennedy Center. https://www.kennedy-center.org/education/resources-for-educators/classroom-resources/media-and-interactives/media/music/story-behind-the-song/the-story-behind-the-song/we-shall-overcome/

35   McNeil, W. K. "Encyclopedia of American Gospel Music." Routledge & CRC Press, September 29, 2005. https://www.routledge.com/Encyclopedia-of-American-Gospel-Music/McNeil/p/book/9780415875691

36   NAACP. Lift Every Voice and Sing. February 17, 2023. https://naacp.org/find-resources/history-explained/lift-every-voice-and-sing

37 Dr. Martin Luther King, Jr. An Amazing Grace. WABC-TV (Television Station. New York, N.Y.). Internet Archive, 1978. https://archive.org/details/drmartinlutherkingjranamazinggrace/drmartinlutherkingjranamazinggrace.mov

38 Magazine, B. M. (2023, March 21). "Follow the drinking gourd" lyrics. Classical Music. https://www.classical-music.com/articles/follow-the-drinking-gourd-lyrics

39 Whitford, David M. "A Calvinist Heritage to the 'Curse of Ham': Assessing the Accuracy of a Claim About Racial Subordination." Church History and Religious Culture 90, no. 1 (January 1, 2010): 25–45. https://brill.com/view/journals/chrc/90/1/article-p25_2.xml?language=en

40 David M. Whitford. The Curse of Ham in the Early Modern Era: The Bible and the Justifications for Slavery. St Andrews Studies in Reformation History. Farnham: Ashgate Publishing Limited, 2009. Xiv + 211 Pp. Index. Illus. Bibl. $99.95. ISBN: 978-0-7546-6625-7. Renaissance Quarterly 63, no. 3 (January 1, 2010): 952–54. https://www.cambridge.org/core/journals/renaissance-quarterly/article/abs/david-m-whitford-the-curse-of-ham-in-the-early-modern-era-the-bible-and-the-justifications-for-slavery-st-andrews-studies-in-reformation-history-farnham-ashgate-publishing-limited-2009-xiv-211-pp-index-illus-bibl-9995-isbn-9780754666257/06F8E7DA8DF6A86D3CE685EE540E9931

41 M. Fredrickson, G. (2015, September 15). Racism: A Short History. Princeton University Press. https://press.princeton.edu/books/paperback/9780691167053/racism

42 Ham, Paul. 2014. "The 'Curse of Ham': How People of Faith Used a Story in Genesis to Justify Slavery." The Conversation. March 24, 2014. https://theconversation.com/the-curse-of-ham-how-people-of-faith-used-a-story-in-genesis-to-justify-slavery-225212

43 The Constitution: How Did it Happen? (2023, November 28). National Archives. https://www.archives.gov/founding-docs/constitution/how-did-it-happen#:~:text=The%20framers%20compromised%20by%20giving,threatened%20to%20derail%20the%20Union

44 Locke, Joseph L., and Ben Wright. 2019. "11. The Cotton Revolution." The American Yawp. January 22, 2019. https://www.americanyawp.com/text/11-the-cotton-revolution/

45 Locke, Joseph L., and Ben Wright. 2019. "2. Colliding Cultures." The American Yawp. January 22, 2019. https://www.americanyawp.com/text/02-colliding-cultures/

46 Locke, Joseph L., and Ben Wright. 2019. "The American Yawp Reader: A Documentary Companion to the American Yawp, Volume I." The American Yawp. https://www.americanyawp.com/reader/wp-content/uploads/The-American-Yawp-Reader-Vol-1-Fall-2020.pdf

47 The Civil Rights Movement | The Post War United States, 1945-1968 | U.S. History Primary Source Timeline | Classroom Materials at the Library of Congress | Library of Congress. (n.d.). The Library of Congress. https://www.loc.gov/classroom-materials/united-states-history-primary-source-timeline/post-war-united-states-1945-1968/civil-rights-movement/

48 Brown v. Board of Education (1954). (2024, March 18). National Archives. https://www.archives.gov/milestone-documents/brown-v-board-of-education

49 National Archives and Records Administration & National Committee on the March on Washington. (n.d.). The March, Part 3 of 3. In Archival Research Catalog (ARC) Identifier 2602934. https://www.archives.gov/files/social-media/transcripts/transcript-march-pt3-of-3-2602934.pdf

50 Voting Rights Act (1965). (2022, February 8). National Archives. https://www.archives.gov/milestone-documents/voting-rights-act

51 Prather, C., Fuller, T. R., Jeffries, W. L., Marshall, K. J., Howell, A. V., Belyue-Umole, A., & King, W. (2018). Racism, African American Women, and their Sexual and Reproductive Health: A Review of historical and contemporary evidence and Implications for Health Equity. Health Equity, 2(1), 249–259. https://twu.edu/media/documents/history-government/Autonomy-Revoked--The-Forced-Sterilization-of-Women-of-Color-in-20th-Century-America.pdf

52 Rosenberg, Y. (2023b, December 18). Why does America support Israel? The Atlantic. https://www.theatlantic.com/newsletters/archive/2022/07/biden-israel-lobby-america-walter-mead/676794/

53 John D. Rockefeller 3rd, statesman and founder of the Population Council. (2000, September 1). Population Reference Bureau. https://www.prb.org/resources/john-d-rockefeller-3rd-statesman-and-founder-of-the-population-council/

54   Daniels, C., Davis, C., Anunkor, I., & Parker, S. (2015). The Effects of Abortion on the Black Community. In Star Parker & Center for Urban Renewal and Education (Eds.), CURE Document 202.479.2873. https://www.congress.gov/115/meeting/house/106562/witnesses/HHRG-115-JU10-Wstate-ParkerS-20171101-SD001.pdf

55   Kaplan, Steven. "Coercion and Control: Ethiopian Israeli Women and Contraception." International Journal of Ethiopian Studies 10, no. 1 & 2 (2016): 35–50. https://www.jstor.org/stable/26554851

56   Carey, Jane. 2012. "The Racial Imperatives of Sex: Birth Control and Eugenics in Britain, the United States and Australia in the Interwar Years." Women's History Review 21 (5): 733–52. https://www.tandfonline.com/doi/abs/10.1080/09612025.2012.658180

57   King, M. L. (1963). Letter from Birmingham Jail. In California State University, Chico. https://www.csuchico.edu/iege/_assets/documents/susi-letter-from-birmingham-jail.pdf

58   Wishengrad, H. (1934, October 12). Christopher Columbus a Jew? New evidence supports theory. Jewish Telegraphic Agency. https://www.jta.org/archive/christopher-columbus-a-jew-new-evidence-supports-theory (not a secure site, scanned article: http://pdfs.jta.org/1934/1934-10-12_2970.pdf)

59   Vincent H. deP. Cassidy. "Columbus and 'The Negro.'" The Phylon Quarterly 20, no. 3 (1959): 294–96. https://www.jstor.org/stable/273057

60   Amanda Borschel-Dan. 2018. "Christopher Columbus — the hidden Jew?: With a murky past, theories abound for the origin story of the intrepid explorer — from pirate to crypto-Jew." The Times of Israel. October 8, 2018. https://www.timesofisrael.com/christopher-columbus-the-hidden-jew/

61   Garcia, Charles. 2012. "Was Columbus secretly a Jew?" CNN. May 24, 2012. https://www.cnn.com/2012/05/20/opinion/garcia-columbus-jewish/index.html

62   Wiener, Leo. 1928. "Africa and the Discovery of America." Internet Archive. pp. 34. https://archive.org/details/africadiscoveryo0001leow/page/34/mode/2up

63   Sharon, Jeremy. 2024. "PM's office says it's 'preposterous' to say his invoking Amalek was a genocide call." The Times of Israel. January 16, 2024. https://

www.timesofisrael.com/pms-office-says-its-preposterous-to-say-invoking-amalek-was-a-genocide-call/

64   Ellis, George Edward. The Red Man and the White Man in North America from Its Discovery to the Present Time. Internet Archive. 1882, pp. 63. https://archive.org/details/redmanwhitemanin00elliuoft/page/62/mode/2up?view=theater

65   Bible Gateway. Leviticus 16 (NIV), "scapegoat." https://web.mit.edu/jywang/www/cef/Bible/NIV/NIV_Bible/LEV+16.html

66   Rev. C.I. Scofield, D.D. The Scofield Reference Bible. The Holy Bible. 1917. https://archive.org/details/scofieldreferenc0000revc/page/16/mode/2up?view=theater

67   Seminole History. Florida Department of State. https://dos.fl.gov/florida-facts/florida-history/seminole-history/#:~:text=The%201770s%20is%20when%20Florida,found%20refuge%20among%20the%20Indians

68   McKusick, Marshall. "Canaanites in America: A New Scripture in Stone?" The Biblical Archaeologist 42, no. 3 (1979): 137–40. https://www.jstor.org/stable/3209381

69   Elizabeth Fenton. Old Canaan in a New World. Native Americans and the Lost Tribes of Israel. NYU Press. (2019, July 2). https://nyupress.org/9781479866366/old-canaan-in-a-new-world/

70   Jacobs, Joseph, and Schulim Ochser. n.d. "Rome." Jewish Encyclopedia. https://jewishencyclopedia.com/articles/12816-rome#1005

71   Duits, Simon, and Jost De Negker. "Holy Roman Empire." World History Encyclopedia, April 2, 2024. https://www.worldhistory.org/Holy_Roman_Empire/

72   The Hebrew University of Jerusalem Communications. (2022, November 30). Ancient DNA Provides New Insights into Ashkenazi Jewish History: Analysis reveals medieval genetic diversity, illuminates founder event. Harvard Medical School. https://hms.harvard.edu/news/ancient-dna-provides-new-insights-ashkenazi-jewish-history

73   The New Jewish Encyclopedia, Heritage: Civilization and the Jews, A History of the Jews, The Jewish Community in Rome, Encyclopedia Judaica, Jewish Communities of the World, Rome Tour.org, et al. n.d. "Virtual Jewish World: Rome, Italy." Jewish Virtual Library. https://www.jewishvirtuallibrary.org/rome-jewish-history-tour

74 Byline Times and The Citizens. "Up To £1.1 Billion in Government PPE Contracts Awarded to Firms Linked to Religious Sect." Byline Times, November 19, 2020. https://bylinetimes.com/2020/11/18/plymouth-exclusive-brethren-ppe-contracts-uk-government/

75 Marsden, George M. (1982). Fundamentalism and American Culture: The Shaping of Twentieth Century Evangelicalism, 1870-1925. Oxford University Press. p. 46. ISBN 978-0-19-503083-9 https://www.goodreads.com/book/show/911709

76 Mangum, R. Todd, and Mark S. Sweetnam. 2009. "The Scofield Bible: Its History and Impact on the Evangelical Church." Google Books. December 10, 2009. https://books.google.com/books/about/The_Scofield_Bible.html?id=oRKA1w6TPPcC

77 The Holy Scriptures, Tanakh 1917 Edition. The Jewish Publication Society, https://jps.org/books/holy-scriptures-tanakh-1917-edition/

78 KJV Old Scofield Study Bible - Classic Edition. The KJV Store. https://www.thekjvstore.com/kjv-old-scofield-study-bible-classic-edition/

79 "Cecil Rhodes and the Rhodes Trust. Saïd Business School," https://www.sbs.ox.ac.uk/about-us/support-us/impact-and-recognition/cecil-rhodes-and-rhodes-trust

80 Rhodes Trust. "Legacy, Equity & Inclusion." https://www.rhodeshouse.ox.ac.uk/impact-legacy/legacy-equity-inclusion/

81 Flowcomm. "Cecil Rhodes Distorted Politics in South Africa Long Before Apartheid." Africa at LSE, July 20, 2023. https://blogs.lse.ac.uk/africaatlse/2023/07/20/cecil-rhodes-distorted-politics-in-south-africa-long-before-apartheid/#:~:text=Cecil%20Rhodes'%20policy%20reforms%20disenfranchised,de%20Kadt%20and%20Joachim%20Wehner

82 "Nathaniel Mayer (Natty) de Rothschild (1840-1915)." n.d. The Rothschild Archive. https://family.rothschildarchive.org/people/61-nathaniel-mayer-natty-de-rothschild-1840-1915

83 Chapman, S. D. "Rhodes and the City of London: Another View of Imperialism." The Historical Journal 28, no. 3 (1985): 647–66. http://www.jstor.org/stable/2639143

84 Koss, A. "Zionism in Ukraine: How and why Ukraine was arguably the most important cradle for early Zionists." My Jewish Learning. May 12, 2022. https://www.myjewishlearning.com/article/zionism-in-ukraine/

85 The Zionist Masquerade: The Birth of the Anglo-Zionist Alliance, 1914-1918. 9780230547186. Renton, J., https://www.amazon.com/Zionist-Masquerade-Anglo-Zionist-Alliance-1914-1918/dp/0230547184

86 League of Arab States. 1948. "Jewish Atrocities in the Holy Land : Memorandum Presented by the Representative of the Arab Higher Commission for Palestine at U.N.O." The Library of Congress. 1948. https://www.loc.gov/item/2017498758/

87 Mosaic Magazine. "The Forgotten Truth About the Balfour Declaration & Raquo; Mosaic." Mosaic, April 29, 2019. https://mosaicmagazine.com/essay/israel-zionism/2017/06/the-forgotten-truth-about-the-balfour-declaration/

88 "Balfour Declaration." 1917. The Avalon Project. November 2, 1917. https://avalon.law.yale.edu/20th_century/balfour.asp

89 Abdullah, Daud Vicary. "A Century of Cultural Genocide in Palestine." In Routledge eBooks, 227–45, 2019. https://www.taylorfrancis.com/chapters/oa-edit/10.4324/9781351214100-10/century-cultural-genocide-palestine-daud-abdullah

90 UN Women – Headquarters. "'Scared, Exhausted, and Expecting the Worst' – Women in Gaza Describe Humanitarian Crisis. UN Women – Headquarters," January 19, 2024. https://www.unwomen.org/en/news-stories/feature-story/2024/01/scared-exhausted-and-expecting-the-worst-women-in-gaza-describe-humanitarian-crisis

91 "A Guide to the United States' History of Recognition, Diplomatic, and Consular Relations, by Country, since 1776: The Congo Free State." n.d. Office of the Historian. https://history.state.gov/countries/congo-free-state

92 Johnson, Steven. University of Central Florida. King Leopold II's Exploitation of the Congo From 1885 to 1908 and Its Consequences, https://stars.library.ucf.edu/cgi/viewcontent.cgi?article=2641&context=honorstheses1990-2015

93 Belgian Jews Greet King Leopold III. (1934, March 20). Jewish Telegraphic Agency. https://www.jta.org/archive/belgian-jews-greet-king-leopold-iii (not a secure site, scanned article: http://pdfs.jta.org/1934/1934-03-20_2796.pdf)

94 World Jewish Congress, International Jewish Cemetery Project, Southern Africa Jewish Genealogy, The Jewish Travelers' Resource Guide, & Encyclopedia Judaica. (n.d.). Democratic Republic of Congo (ZAIRE) Virtual Jewish History Tour. Jewish Virtual Library. https://www.jewishvirtuallibrary.org/democratic-republic-of-congo-zaire-virtual-jewish-history-tour

95 R. Biden, J., Jr. (2002, August 1). Hearings to examine threats, responses, and regional considerations surrounding Iraq. U.S. Government Publishing Office. https://www.govinfo.gov/content/pkg/CHRG-107shrg81697/html/CHRG-107shrg81697.htm

96 House, W., & R. Biden, J., Jr. (2023, October 18). Remarks by President Biden at Community Engagement to Meet with Israelis Impacted or Involved in the Response to the October 7th Terrorist Attacks | Tel Aviv, Israel. The White House. "You don't have to be a Jew to be a Zionist." https://www.whitehouse.gov/briefing-room/speeches-remarks/2023/10/18/remarks-by-president-biden-at-community-engagement-to-meet-with-israelis-impacted-or-involved-in-the-response-to-the-october-7th-terrorist-attacks-tel-aviv-israel/

97 Minayev, V. (1953). Zionist Agents of the American Secret Service. In Central Intelligence Agency. https://www.cia.gov/readingroom/docs/CIA-RDP78-03362A001600090007-6.pdf

98 The Book of Jubilees. https://www.ccel.org/ccel/c/charles/otpseudepig/files/jubilee/index.htm

99 Thomas, M. G., Parfitt, T., Weiss, D. A., Skorecki, K., Wilson, J. F., le Roux, M., Bradman, N., & Goldstein, D. B. (2000). Y chromosomes traveling south: the cohen modal haplotype and the origins of the Lemba--the "Black Jews of Southern Africa." American journal of human genetics, 66(2), 674–686. https://www.ncbi.nlm.nih.gov/pmc/articles/PMC1288118/pdf/AJHGv66p674.pdf

100 Architect of the Capitol. "Hammurabi, Relief Portrait." https://www.aoc.gov/explore-capitol-campus/art/hammurabi-relief-portrait

101 Bible Gateway. Genesis 46. NIV. https://web.mit.edu/jywang/www/cef/Bible/NIV/NIV_Bible/GEN+46.html

102 Book of Jubilees 8:10. https://www.sefaria.org/Book_of_Jubilees.8.10?lang=bi&with=all&lang2=en

103   Book of Jubilees 8:11. https://www.sefaria.org/Book_of_Jubilees.8.11?lang=bi&with=all&lang2=en

104   Lyman Coleman. An Historical Text Book and Atlas of Biblical Geography, pp. 13, https://caleb-cangelosi-437x.squarespace.com/s/Coleman-Lyman-An-Historical-Text-Book-and-Atlas-of-Biblical-Geography.pdf

105   Africa: Human Geography. "The origin of the name 'Africa' is greatly disputed by scholars" https://education.nationalgeographic.org/resource/africa-human-geography/

106   Wolff, H. Ekkehard. Afro-Asiatic languages. Encyclopedia Britannica, March 8, 2024. https://www.britannica.com/topic/Afro-Asiatic-languages

107   Leibovich-Dar, Sara. "The Hannibal Procedure - Haaretz Com." Haaretz.Com, May 20, 2003. https://www.haaretz.com/2003-05-21/ty-article/the-hannibal-procedure/0000017f-dbb8-db22-a17f-ffb9aba40000

108   Bible Gateway. Genesis 10 (NIV). "The Hamites" https://www.biblegateway.com/passage/?search=Genesis+10&version=NIV

109   Mellish, John. David Rumsey Historical Map Collection. "The Places Recorded in the Five Books of Moses," 1815. https://www.davidrumsey.com/luna/servlet/detail/RUMSEY~8~1~250605~5517137:The-Places-Recorded-in-the-Five-Boo?sort=pub_list_no_initialsort%2Cpub_date%2Cpub_list_no%2Cseries_no&qvq=q:author%3D%22Mellish%2C%2BJohn%22;sort:pub_list_no_initialsort%2Cpub_date%2Cpub_list_no%2Cseries_no;lc:RUMSEY~8~1&mi=9&trs=12

110   Bible Gateway. Genesis 17. NIV. https://web.mit.edu/jywang/www/cef/Bible/NIV/NIV_Bible/GEN+17.html

111   "Chart of the Genealogy of Abraham: Abraham's Family Tree." n.d. Conforming to Jesus. https://www.conformingtojesus.com/images/webpages/genealogy_of_abraham_1.jpg

112   Soloveichik, Meir and Azure. 2013. "Motherhood and Matrilineal Descent." The Tikvah Fund. December 11, 2013. https://tikvahfund.org/library/exploring-matrilineal-descent/

113   Halpern, Baruch, and דוב רפלה. "יציאת מצרים וההיסטוריונים המקראיים / The Exodus and the Israelite Historians." Eretz-Israel: Archaeological, Historical

and Geographical Studies / ארץ-ישראל: מחקרים בידיעת הארץ ועתיקותיה דכ (1993): 89*-96*. https://www.jstor.org/stable/23624618

114 Eames, Christopher. n.d. "The Amarna Letters: Proof of Israel's Invasion of Canaan?: The ancient Habiru battled their way through Canaan during the 14th century b.c.e. Who were these people?" Armstrong Institute of Biblical Archaeology. https://armstronginstitute.org/881-the-amarna-letters-proof-of-israels-invasion-of-canaan

115 Patterns Of Evidence. 2022. "Signs of Israelite Slavery in Egypt - the Exodus." https://www.youtube.com/watch?v=lfQdjdSm2AE

116 Junior, Nyasha. 2019. "Hagar." Oxford Bibliographies. August 28, 2019. https://www.oxfordbibliographies.com/display/document/obo-9780195393361/obo-9780195393361-0270.xml?rskey=ZRTExz&result=1&q=hagar#firstMatch

117 Halpern-Amaru, Betsy. "Bilhah and Naphtali in Jubilees: A Note on 4QT-Naphtali." Dead Sea Discoveries 6, no. 1 (1999): 1–10. https://www.jstor.org/stable/4193108

118 Bible Gateway. Genesis 10. NIV. https://web.mit.edu/jywang/www/cef/Bible/NIV/NIV_Bible/GEN+10.html

119 The Catholic Encyclopedia; an International Work of Reference on the Constitution, Doctrine, Discipline, and History of the Catholic Church. Herbermann, Charles George, 1840-1916. Internet Archive, 1907. "'Naphtali': 'buried in Egypt.'" https://archive.org/details/catholicencyclop10herbuoft/page/748/mode/2up?view=theater

120 Bible Gateway. Genesis 25. NIV. https://web.mit.edu/jywang/www/cef/Bible/NIV/NIV_Bible/GEN+25.html

121 Bible Gateway. Genesis 36. NIV. https://web.mit.edu/jywang/www/cef/Bible/NIV/NIV_Bible/GEN+36.html

122 Assis, Elie. Identity in Conflict: The Struggle between Esau and Jacob, Edom and Israel. Vol. 19. Penn State University Press, 2016. https://www.jstor.org/stable/10.5325/j.ctv1bxgwxb

123 Anderson, John E. Jacob and the Divine Trickster, 2011. https://www.jstor.org/stable/10.5325/j.ctv1bxgxcj

124 Bradford Ashworth Anderson. "Election, Brotherhood and Inheritance: A Canonical Reading of the Esau and Edom Traditions." Thesis. Durham Theses. Durham University, 2010. https://etheses.dur.ac.uk/315/1/Bradford_Anderson.thesis.pdf

125 Bowen, Emanuel. 1747. "A New & Accurate Map of Negroland and the Adjacent Countries..." The Library of Congress. 1747. https://www.loc.gov/resource/g8735.ct010406/?r=-0.457,-0.053,1.898,0.919,0

126 Eggert, By Nalina. 2018. "Tracing Sickle Cell Back to One Child, 7,300 Years Ago." British Broadcasting Corporation (BBC). March 13, 2018. https://www.bbc.com/news/world-africa-43373247

127 Bitoungui, Valentina J. Ngo, Gift D. Pule, Neil Hanchard, Jeanne Ngogang, and Ambroise Wonkam. 2015. "Beta-Globin Gene Haplotypes Among Cameroonians and Review of the Global Distribution: Is There a Case for a Single Sickle Mutation Origin in Africa?" Omics 19 (3): 171–79. https://www.ncbi.nlm.nih.gov/pmc/articles/PMC4356477/pdf/omi.2014.0134.pdf

128 Rund, Deborah, Naomi Kornhendler, Oded Shalev, and Ariella Oppenheim. 1990. "The Origin of Sickle Cell Alleles in Israel." Human Genetics 85 (5). https://link.springer.com/article/10.1007/BF00194229

129 Bible Gateway. Genesis 25. NIV. https://web.mit.edu/jywang/www/cef/Bible/NIV/NIV_Bible/GEN+25.html

130 Ighodaro, Peter and Elebute, Ayo. Hypothetical cases for cultural relation between Edo Benin (Nigeria) and Edo Tokyo (Japan). Institution, Smithsonian. https://www.si.edu/object/hypothetical-cases-cultural-relation-between-edo-benin-nigeria-and-edo-tokyo-japan-peter-ighodaro%3Asiris_sil_913792

131 Haber, Marc et al. "A Rare Deep-Rooting D0 African Y-Chromosomal Haplogroup and Its Implications for the Expansion of Modern Humans Out of Africa." Genetics vol. 212,4 (2019): 1421-1428. https://www.ncbi.nlm.nih.gov/pmc/articles/PMC6707464/pdf/1421.pdf

132 Britannica, T. Editors of Encyclopaedia. Ten Lost Tribes of Israel. Encyclopedia Britannica, January 2, 2024. https://www.britannica.com/topic/Ten-Lost-Tribes-of-Israel

133 Lost Tribes and Promised Lands: The Origins of American Racism: Sanders, Dr Ronald. https://www.amazon.com/Lost-Tribes-Promised-Lands-American/dp/1626542767

134 Steinmeyer, Nathan. "Oldest Canaanite Sentence Found." Biblical Archaeology Society, June 26, 2023. https://www.biblicalarchaeology.org/daily/biblical-artifacts/inscriptions/oldest_written_canaanite_sentence/

135 William H. Shea. The 'Izbet Sartah Ostracon. The Biblical Research Institute. Andrews University Seminary Studies, Spring 1990, Vol. 28, No. 1, 59-86 https://digitalcommons.andrews.edu/cgi/viewcontent.cgi?referer=&httpsredir=1&article=1938&context=auss

136 Carlpage. "How the First Biblical Writing Links to the Alphabet." Patterns of Evidence, March 28, 2024. https://www.patternsofevidence.com/2019/03/02/first-biblical-writing/

137 King, L. W. n.d. "Code of Hammurabi." The Avalon Project. https://avalon.law.yale.edu/ancient/hamframe.asp

138 Musée Du Louvre. "Code De Hammurabi," https://collections.louvre.fr/en/ark:/53355/cl010174436#

139 Lawhon, Taylor. "Shamash: The Sun God – Ancient Art," March 12, 2015. https://ancientart.as.ua.edu/shamash-the-sun-god/

140 Hemingway, Seán, and Colette Hemingway. Africans in Ancient Greek Art. The Met's Heilbrunn Timeline of Art History, January 1, 1AD. https://www.metmuseum.org/toah/hd/afrg/hd_afrg.htm

141 Musée Du Louvre. "Girsu Vase." https://collections.louvre.fr/en/ark:/53355/cl010140094

142 Campbell, John. "Macron Leads Renewed Calls for Return of Looted African Artifacts." Council on Foreign Relations, November 28, 2018. https://www.cfr.org/blog/macron-leads-renewed-calls-return-looted-african-artifacts

143 Gbadamosi, Nosmot. "Stealing Africa: How Britain Looted the Continent's Art." Al Jazeera, October 26, 2021. https://www.aljazeera.com/features/2021/10/12/stealing-africa-how-britain-looted-the-continents-art#:~:text=During%20war%20and%20colonisation%2C%20Western,campaign%20to%20get%20them%20returned

144 Institute of Ethiopian Studies Collection of Ethiopian Manuscripts [14th Century-21st Century]. Endangered Archives Programme. https://eap.bl.uk/collection/EAP286-1

145 Isis and Horus. Late Period–Ptolemaic Period. The Metropolitan Museum of Art. https://www.metmuseum.org/art/collection/search/545969

146 Michael P. Duricy. Montserrat Black Madonna. University of Dayton, Ohio. (2024, May 17). https://udayton.edu/imri/mary/m/montserrat-black-madonna.php

147 Cuneiform Digital Library Initiative. "Shamash Religious Texts Pl. 10 Sm 0728 (P425559)" https://cdli.mpiwg-berlin.mpg.de/artifacts/425559

148 Gray, Clifton Daggett. The Šamaš Religious Texts Classified in the British Museum Catalogue as Hymns, Prayers, and Incantations, with Twenty Plates of Texts Hitherto Unpublished, and a Transliteration and Translation of K.3182. 1901. Internet Archive. https://archive.org/details/samasreligiouste00grayrich

149 Mullo-Weir, Cecil J. "Restoration of a Hymn to Shamash." Journal of the Royal Asiatic Society of Great Britain & Ireland 62, no. 1 (1930): 41–42. https://www.cambridge.org/core/journals/journal-of-the-royal-asiatic-society/article/abs/restoration-of-a-hymn-to-shamash/99248AF65E267C80B5C5397F3DB84EEC

150 Prince, J. Dyneley. "A Political Hymn to Shamash." Journal of the American Oriental Society 33 (1913): 10–15. https://www.jstor.org/stable/592812?-searchText=Hymn+to+Shamash&searchUri=%2Faction%2FdoBasicSearch%3FQuery%3DHymn%2Bto%2BShamash%26so%3Drel&ab_segments=0%2Fbasic_search_gsv2%2Fcontrol&refreqid=fastly-default%3Ae-2baf7e333c8e4a7b2cde9f18022e056

151 Ebeling, Erich; Weidner, Ernst F.: Reallexikon der Assyriologie. Berlin ; [München] [2019]. Reallexikon der Assyriologie und vorderasiatischen Archäologie, https://publikationen.badw.de/en/rla/index#8407

152 Adam Stone, 'Nanna/Suen/Sin (god)', Ancient Mesopotamian Gods and Goddesses, Oracc and the UK Higher Education Academy, 2019, https://oracc.museum.upenn.edu/amgg/listofdeities/nannasuen/

153 Kramer, Samuel Noah. "The Sumerians." The University of Chicago Press, 1963. pp. 137, "Ningal" https://isac.uchicago.edu/sites/default/files/uploads/shared/docs/sumerians.pdf

154 Yağmur Heffron, 'Inana/Ištar (goddess)', Ancient Mesopotamian Gods and Goddesses, Oracc and the UK Higher Education Academy, 2019, https://oracc.museum.upenn.edu/amgg/listofdeities/inanaitar/

155 Britannica, T. Editors of Encyclopaedia. "Shamash." Encyclopedia Britannica, November 9, 2023. https://www.britannica.com/topic/Shamash

156 Ruth Horry, 'Šerida/Aya (goddess)', Ancient Mesopotamian Gods and Goddesses, Oracc and the UK Higher Education Academy, 2019, https://oracc.museum.upenn.edu/amgg/listofdeities/aya/

157 Sinite. The Institute for Creation Research. https://www.icr.org/books/defenders/276

158 Schwemer, Daniel. "8 Religion and Power" In Handbook Hittite Empire: Power Structures edited by Stefano de Martino, 355-418. Berlin, Boston: De Gruyter Oldenbourg, 2022. https://www.degruyter.com/document/doi/10.1515/9783110661781-009/html?lang=en

159 Bible Gateway. Genesis 10 (NIV). "Sinites" https://www.biblegateway.com/passage/?search=Genesis+10&version=NIV

160 Karel van der Toorn and Pieter Willem van der Horst. Dictionary of Deities and Demons in the Bible. pp. 357, "Kengir." https://books.google.com/books?id=yCkRz5pfxz0C&pg=PA32#v=onepage&q=kengir&f=false

161 Fletcher Fund. The Metropolitan Museum of Art. Neo-Sumerian. The Metropolitan Museum of Art, 1949. "Mesopotamia, probably from Girsu." https://www.metmuseum.org/art/collection/search/324061

162 Bible Gateway. Genesis 10 (NIV). "Girgashites" https://www.biblegateway.com/passage/?search=Genesis+10&version=NIV

163 Statue of Gudea, named "Gudea, the man who built the temple, may his life be long." Neo-Sumerian. The Metropolitan Museum of Art. https://www.metmuseum.org/art/collection/search/329072

164 Judea. Abarim Publications. The amazing name Judea: meaning and etymology. https://www.abarim-publications.com/Meaning/Judea.html

165 Niels Peter Lemche. The A to Z of Ancient Israel. Jebus, Jebusites, pp. 161, https://books.google.com/books?id=qzGtpvH_BAwC&q=Siege+of+Jebus+lemche&pg=PA161#v=onepage&q&f=false

166 Ogunkoya, T. O. "The Early History of Ijebu." Journal of the Historical Society of Nigeria 1, no. 1 (1956): 48–58. http://www.jstor.org/stable/41856613

167 Minority Rights Group. "Amazigh in Morocco - Minority Rights Group," January 30, 2024. https://minorityrights.org/communities/berber/

168 Institut Royal de la Culture Amazighe (IRCAM). "Moroccan Tamazight Vernacular Romanization." https://www.loc.gov/catdir/cpso/romanization/tamazight.pdf

169 Massachusetts Institute of Technology. The Holy Bible: New International Version. 2 Samuel 19, https://web.mit.edu/jywang/www/cef/Bible/NIV/NIV_Bible/2SAM+19.html

170 King James Bible Dictionary. "King James Bible Dictionary - Reference List - Chimham." https://kingjamesbibledictionary.com/Dictionary/Chimham

171 Britannica, T. Editors of Encyclopaedia. "Chimú." Encyclopedia Britannica, August 30, 2021. https://www.britannica.com/topic/Chimu

172 Daniel Schwemer. The Storm-Gods of the Ancient Near East: Summary, Synthesis, Recent Studies: Part I., pp. 146, "Mīšaru." https://eprints.soas.ac.uk/7075/1/JANER7%3A2offprint.pdf

173 Burkhart Kienast. The Oriental Institute of the University of Chicago. Assyriological Studies. Igigui und Anunnakku Nach den Akkadischen Quellen, no. 16, pp. 141, "Dajjānu, 'the judge gods'" https://isac.uchicago.edu/sites/default/files/uploads/shared/docs/as16.pdf

174 Bible Gateway. Genesis 10 (NIV). "Calah" https://www.biblegateway.com/passage/?search=Genesis+10&version=NIV

175 Putnam, Ruth. California: The Name. 1917, pp. 306 https://archive.org/details/cu31924008278347/page/n23/mode/2up?view=theater

176 Bible Gateway. Genesis 10 (NIV). "Arkites" https://www.biblegateway.com/passage/?search=Genesis+10&version=NIV

177 Florida State Parks. "The Rare Florida Torreya Tree." https://www.floridastateparks.org/learn/rare-florida-torreya-tree

178 Restall, Matthew. The Black Middle: Africans, Mayas, and Spaniards in Colonial Yucatan. Stanford University Press. https://www.sup.org/books/title/?id=6995

179 Batmaz, Atilla. "A New Ceremonial Practice at Ayanis Fortress: The Urartian Sacred Tree Ritual on the Eastern Shore of Lake Van." Journal of Near Eastern Studies 72, no. 1 (April 1, 2013): 65–83. https://www.journals.uchicago.edu/doi/abs/10.1086/669099

180 Chandra Chronicles. Sirius Matters: Alien Contact. November 28, 2000, "Dogon." https://chandra.harvard.edu/chronicle/0400/sirius_part2.html

181 Ali, Mohamed Nuuh. "A Linguistic Outline of Early Somali History." Ufahamu 12, no. 3, pp. 237-238 (January 1, 1983). https://escholarship.org/uc/item/450167x3

182 Mali Empire and Djenne Figures. https://africa.si.edu/exhibits/resources/mali/index.htm

183 Kramer, Samuel Noah. "The Sumerians." The University of Chicago Press, 1963. pp. 114, "dingir" https://isac.uchicago.edu/sites/default/files/uploads/shared/docs/sumerians.pdf

184 The Editors of Encyclopaedia Britannica. (2009, June 18). Shangdi. Supreme God, Ancient China, Creator. Encyclopedia Britannica. https://www.britannica.com/topic/Shangdi

185 Bible Gateway. Acts 13. NIV. https://web.mit.edu/jywang/www/cef/Bible/NIV/NIV_Bible/ACTS+13.html

186 Janz, and Janz. 2024. "Territories Allotted to the Twelve Tribes of Israel." World History Encyclopedia. June 19, 2024. https://www.worldhistory.org/image/14576/territories-allotted-to-the-twelve-tribes-of-israe/

187 All The People in the Bible. All the People in the Bible: An A-Z Guide to the Saints, Scoundrels, and Other Characters in Scriptures. "Simeon Niger" https://books.google.com/books?id=j9db9kGwG3MC&pg=PA403#v=onepage&q&f=false

188 Exhibition Tour—Africa & Byzantium. Met Exhibitions. The Met. December 1, 2023. https://www.youtube.com/watch?v=NHIT9vq6mJU

189 Department of Arts of Africa, Oceania, and the Americas and Authors: Department of Arts of Africa, Oceania, and the Americas. "Trade and the Spread of Islam in Africa." The Met's Heilbrunn Timeline of Art History, January 1, 1AD. https://www.metmuseum.org/toah/hd/tsis/hd_tsis.htm

190 The Met. Large Print Exhibition Text Africa and Byzantium, "Christian religious and artistic traditions nevertheless flourished in African kingdoms" https://cdn.sanity.io/files/cctd4ker/production/3753a4bdd69811380de-95a2c209581c8f45958a4.pdf

191 Uruk: First City of the Ancient World: Crusemann, Nicola, Van Ess, Margarete, Hilgert, Markus, Salje, Beate, Potts, Timothy, pp. 325 https://books.google.com/books?id=muCvDwAAQBAJ&pg=PT327#v=onepage&q&f=false

192 Kathryn Stevens, 'An/Anu (god)', Ancient Mesopotamian Gods and Goddesses, Oracc and the UK Higher Education Academy, 2019 http://oracc.museum.upenn.edu/amgg/listofdeities/an/

193 J. Mark, J. (2011, February 25). The Mesopotamian Pantheon. World History Encyclopedia. https://www.worldhistory.org/article/221/the-mesopotamian-pantheon/

194 The Great Ziggurat Was Built as a Place of Worship, Dedicated to the Moon God Nanna in the Sumerian City of Ur in Ancient Mesopotamia. Today, After More Than 4,000 Years, the Ziggurat Is Still Well Preserved in Large Parts as the Only Major Remainder of Ur in Present-day Southern Iraq, https://www.defense.gov/Multimedia/Photos/igphoto/2001116584/

195 Bible Gateway. John 8. NIV. https://web.mit.edu/jywang/www/cef/Bible/NIV/NIV_Bible/JOHN+8.html

196 Güterbock, Hans G. "The Composition of Hittite Prayers to the Sun. Journal of the American Oriental Society 78, no. 4 (1958): 237–45, pp. 241, "son of mankind" https://www.jstor.org/stable/595787

197　Gray, Clifton Daggett. The Šamaš Religious Texts Classified in the British Museum Catalogue as Hymns, Prayers, and Incantations, with Twenty Plates of Texts Hitherto Unpublished, and a Transliteration and Translation of K.3182. 1901. Internet Archive, pp. 13, "light of the world" https://archive.org/details/samasreligiouste00grayrich

198　Dominique Collon. The British Museum. Statue. "suggestions include Sargon, Naram-Sin and Manishtushu." https://www.britishmuseum.org/collection/object/W_C-281

199　Dalley, S. Mary. "Sargon." Encyclopedia Britannica, April 5, 2024. https://www.britannica.com/biography/Sargon

200　The Akkadians. Embassy of the Republic of Iraq in Washington, D.C. https://www.iraqiembassy.us/page/the-akkadians

201　Swanson, Mark. The Babylonian Number System. Educational, 2021. https://www.nku.edu/~longa/classes/2014fall/mat115/mat115-006/images/babylonian/BabylonianNumbers.pdf

202　Hodgkin, Luke. A History of Mathematics. Oxford University Press, 2005. https://uruk-warka.dk/news/2020-MATH/A_History_of_Mathematics_From_Mesopotamia_to_Modernity_by_Luke_Hodgkin.pdf

203　Hayes, Adam. "Sine Wave: Definition, What It's Used for, Example, and Causes." Investopedia, January 4, 2022. https://www.investopedia.com/terms/s/sinewave.asp

204　The Wabash Center. A Common Cosmology of the Ancient World also known as the Three-Story Universe. https://www.wabashcenter.wabash.edu/syllabi/g/gier/306/commoncosmos.htm

205　Chinese Philosophy of Change (Yijing) (Stanford Encyclopedia of Philosophy), September 18, 2023. https://plato.stanford.edu/entries/chinese-change/

206　Bible Gateway. Revelation 12. NIV. https://web.mit.edu/jywang/www/cef/Bible/NIV/NIV_Bible/REV+12.html

207　September 11th, the Day Jesus Christ Was Born: Ray, Tony. https://www.amazon.com/September-11th-Jesus-Christ-Born/dp/1466232382

208 Keevan Lavell Crawford. Astro-chart. Natal Chart. Patterns, September 22, 1982, Paramount, CA, 15:17. https://astro-charts.com/chart/7a944f1cf/

209 Bitoungui, Valentina J. Ngo, Gift D. Pule, Neil Hanchard, Jeanne Ngogang, and Ambroise Wonkam. 2015. "Beta-Globin Gene Haplotypes Among Cameroonians and Review of the Global Distribution: Is There a Case for a Single Sickle Mutation Origin in Africa?" Omics 19 (3): 171–79. https://www.ncbi.nlm.nih.gov/pmc/articles/PMC4356477/pdf/omi.2014.0134.pdf

210 Rund, Deborah, Naomi Kornhendler, Oded Shalev, and Ariella Oppenheim. 1990. "The Origin of Sickle Cell Alleles in Israel." Human Genetics 85 (5). https://www.researchgate.net/profile/Ariella-Oppenheim/publication/21177689_The_origin_of_sickle_cell_gene_in_Israel/links/5eecb4cd458515814a6ad500/The-origin-of-sickle-cell-gene-in-Israel.pdf

211 Jasim, Sabah Abboud and Oriental Institute Publications. 2021. "Tell Abada: Ubaid Village in Central Mesopotamia." The University of Chicago. 2021. 6,000 to 5,000 BCE. https://isac.uchicago.edu/sites/default/files/uploads/shared/docs/Publications/OIP/oip147.pdf

212 Carter, Robert A. and Philip, Graham. 2010. Beyond the Ubaid. The Oriental Institute, Chicago. https://isac.uchicago.edu/sites/default/files/uploads/shared/docs/saoc63.pdf

213 Zusammenfassung Abkommen Zwischen Der Bundesrepublik Deutschland Und Dem Staate Israel [Wiedergutmachungsabkommen], 10. September 1952 / Bayerische Staatsbibliothek (BSB, München). Bayerische Staatsbibliothek 1997-2009. https://www.1000dokumente.de/index.html?c=dokument_de&dokument=0016_lux&object=abstract&st=&l=de

214 Gilder Lehrman Institute of American History. Historical Context. Facts About the Slave Trade and Slavery. https://www.gilderlehrman.org/history-resources/teacher-resources/historical-context-facts-about-slave-trade-and-slavery

215 Senator Sheldon Whitehouse. 2024. "Kerry, Corker, Whitehouse Announce Nelson Mandela Will Be Removed From Terror Watch Lists - Senator Sheldon Whitehouse." February 20, 2024. https://www.whitehouse.senate.gov/news/release/kerry-corker-whitehouse-announce-nelson-mandela-will-be-removed-from-terror-watch-lists/

216 Jeremy Scahill. "Blacklisted Academic Norman Finkelstein on Gaza, "The World's Largest Concentration Camp"" The Intercept, May 21, 2018. https://

theintercept.com/2018/05/20/norman-finkelstein-gaza-iran-israel-jerusalem-embassy/

217 "Onomastics | EPFL Graph Search," n.d. https://graphsearch.epfl.ch/en/concept/145171

218 Turfa, Jean Macintosh. "Fragments of Carthage Rediscovered." Expedition Magazine 63, no. 1 (February, 2021): -. Accessed April 26, 2024. https://www.penn.museum/sites/expedition/fragments-of-carthage-rediscovered/

219 Kennedy, Maev. "Carthaginians Sacrificed Own Children, Archaeologists Say." The Guardian, February 14, 2018. https://www.theguardian.com/science/2014/jan/21/carthaginians-sacrificed-own-children-study

220 Massachusetts Institute of Technology. The Holy Bible: New International Version. Jeremiah 41, https://web.mit.edu/jywang/www/cef/Bible/NIV/NIV_Bible/JER+41.html

221 Massachusetts Institute of Technology. The Holy Bible: New International Version. Numbers 1, https://web.mit.edu/jywang/www/cef/Bible/NIV/NIV_Bible/NUM+1.html

222 Massachusetts Institute of Technology. The Holy Bible: New International Version. Genesis 22, https://web.mit.edu/jywang/www/cef/Bible/NIV/NIV_Bible/GEN+22.html

223 Massachusetts Institute of Technology. The Holy Bible: New International Version. 2 Samuel 8, https://web.mit.edu/jywang/www/cef/Bible/NIV/NIV_Bible/2SAM+8.html

224 Massachusetts Institute of Technology. The Holy Bible: New International Version. Joshua 19, https://web.mit.edu/jywang/www/cef/Bible/NIV/NIV_Bible/JOSH+19.html

225 Massachusetts Institute of Technology. The Holy Bible: New International Version. Esther 3, https://web.mit.edu/jywang/www/cef/Bible/NIV/NIV_Bible/ESTH+3.html

226 Massachusetts Institute of Technology. The Holy Bible: New International Version. 1 Chronicles 7, https://web.mit.edu/jywang/www/cef/Bible/NIV/NIV_Bible/1CHRON+7.html

227   Massachusetts Institute of Technology. The Holy Bible: New International Version. Ezekiel 39, https://web.mit.edu/jywang/www/cef/Bible/NIV/NIV_Bible/EZEK+39.html

228   Massachusetts Institute of Technology. The Holy Bible: New International Version. Genesis 34, https://web.mit.edu/jywang/www/cef/Bible/NIV/NIV_Bible/GEN+34.html

229   Massachusetts Institute of Technology. The Holy Bible: New International Version. Genesis 46, https://web.mit.edu/jywang/www/cef/Bible/NIV/NIV_Bible/GEN+46.html

230   Massachusetts Institute of Technology. The Holy Bible: New International Version. Joshua 10, https://web.mit.edu/jywang/www/cef/Bible/NIV/NIV_Bible/JOSH+10.html

231   Massachusetts Institute of Technology. The Holy Bible: New International Version. 1 Chronicles 3, https://web.mit.edu/jywang/www/cef/Bible/NIV/NIV_Bible/1CHRON+3.html

232   Massachusetts Institute of Technology. The Holy Bible: New International Version. 1 Chronicles 11, https://web.mit.edu/jywang/www/cef/Bible/NIV/NIV_Bible/1CHRON+11.html

233   Massachusetts Institute of Technology. The Holy Bible: New International Version. 1 Chronicles 7, https://web.mit.edu/jywang/www/cef/Bible/NIV/NIV_Bible/1CHRON+7.html

234   Massachusetts Institute of Technology. The Holy Bible: New International Version. Numbers 26, https://web.mit.edu/jywang/www/cef/Bible/NIV/NIV_Bible/NUM+26.html

235   Massachusetts Institute of Technology. The Holy Bible: New International Version. Genesis 36, https://web.mit.edu/jywang/www/cef/Bible/NIV/NIV_Bible/GEN+36.html

236   Massachusetts Institute of Technology. The Holy Bible: New International Version. 1 Chronicles 1, https://web.mit.edu/jywang/www/cef/Bible/NIV/NIV_Bible/1CHRON+1.html

237   Massachusetts Institute of Technology. The Holy Bible: New International Version. Exodus 6, https://web.mit.edu/jywang/www/cef/Bible/NIV/NIV_Bible/EXOD+6.html

238 Massachusetts Institute of Technology. The Holy Bible: New International Version. 1 Chronicles 24, https://web.mit.edu/jywang/www/cef/Bible/NIV/NIV_Bible/1CHRON+24.html

239 Massachusetts Institute of Technology. The Holy Bible: New International Version. Exodus 28, https://web.mit.edu/jywang/www/cef/Bible/NIV/NIV_Bible/EXOD+28.html

240 Bible Gateway. King James Version. Ezekiel 48.35, https://www.biblegateway.com/passage/?search=Ezekiel+48%3A35&version=KJV

241 Massachusetts Institute of Technology. The Holy Bible: New International Version. 1 Samuel 1, https://web.mit.edu/jywang/www/cef/Bible/NIV/NIV_Bible/1SAM+1.html

242 Massachusetts Institute of Technology. The Holy Bible: New International Version. 1 Chronicles 27, https://web.mit.edu/jywang/www/cef/Bible/NIV/NIV_Bible/1CHRON+27.html

243 Massachusetts Institute of Technology. The Holy Bible: New International Version. 1 Chronicles 8, https://web.mit.edu/jywang/www/cef/Bible/NIV/NIV_Bible/1CHRON+8.html

244 Massachusetts Institute of Technology. The Holy Bible: New International Version. 2 Chronicles 23, https://web.mit.edu/jywang/www/cef/Bible/NIV/NIV_Bible/2CHRON+23.html

245 Massachusetts Institute of Technology. The Holy Bible: New International Version. 1 Chronicles 9, https://web.mit.edu/jywang/www/cef/Bible/NIV/NIV_Bible/1CHRON+9.html

246 Massachusetts Institute of Technology. The Holy Bible: New International Version. 2 Kings 15, https://web.mit.edu/jywang/www/cef/Bible/NIV/NIV_Bible/2KGS+15.html

247 Massachusetts Institute of Technology. The Holy Bible: New International Version. 2 Chronicles 27, https://web.mit.edu/jywang/www/cef/Bible/NIV/NIV_Bible/2CHRON+27.html

248 Massachusetts Institute of Technology. The Holy Bible: New International Version. Hosea 1, https://web.mit.edu/jywang/www/cef/Bible/NIV/NIV_Bible/HOSEA+1.html

249 Massachusetts Institute of Technology. The Holy Bible: New International Version. 1 Chronicles 8, https://web.mit.edu/jywang/www/cef/Bible/NIV/NIV_Bible/1CHRON+8.html

250 Massachusetts Institute of Technology. The Holy Bible: New International Version. Jeremiah 32, https://web.mit.edu/jywang/www/cef/Bible/NIV/NIV_Bible/JER+32.html

251 Massachusetts Institute of Technology. The Holy Bible: New International Version. 1 Chronicles 8, https://web.mit.edu/jywang/www/cef/Bible/NIV/NIV_Bible/1CHRON+8.html

252 Massachusetts Institute of Technology. The Holy Bible: New International Version. Nehemiah 7, https://web.mit.edu/jywang/www/cef/Bible/NIV/NIV_Bible/NEH+7.html

253 Massachusetts Institute of Technology. The Holy Bible: New International Version. 1 Chronicles 2, https://web.mit.edu/jywang/www/cef/Bible/NIV/NIV_Bible/1CHRON+2.html

254 Massachusetts Institute of Technology. The Holy Bible: New International Version. Psalm 58, https://web.mit.edu/jywang/www/cef/Bible/NIV/NIV_Bible/PS+58.html

255 Massachusetts Institute of Technology. The Holy Bible: New International Version. 1 Chronicles 7, https://web.mit.edu/jywang/www/cef/Bible/NIV/NIV_Bible/1CHRON+7.html

256 Massachusetts Institute of Technology. The Holy Bible: New International Version. Judges 3, https://web.mit.edu/jywang/www/cef/Bible/NIV/NIV_Bible/JUDG+3.html

257 Massachusetts Institute of Technology. The Holy Bible: New International Version. Judges 5, https://web.mit.edu/jywang/www/cef/Bible/NIV/NIV_Bible/JUDG+5.html

258 Massachusetts Institute of Technology. The Holy Bible: New International Version. Joshua 19, https://web.mit.edu/jywang/www/cef/Bible/NIV/NIV_Bible/JOSH+19.html

259 Massachusetts Institute of Technology. The Holy Bible: New International Version. Judges 10, https://web.mit.edu/jywang/www/cef/Bible/NIV/NIV_Bible/JUDG+10.html

260   Massachusetts Institute of Technology. The Holy Bible: New International Version. Judges 10, https://web.mit.edu/jywang/www/cef/Bible/NIV/NIV_Bible/JUDG+10.html

261   Massachusetts Institute of Technology. The Holy Bible: New International Version. Jeremiah 17, https://web.mit.edu/jywang/www/cef/Bible/NIV/NIV_Bible/JER+17.html

262   Massachusetts Institute of Technology. The Holy Bible: New International Version. 2 Samuel 23, https://web.mit.edu/jywang/www/cef/Bible/NIV/NIV_Bible/2SAM+23.html

263   Massachusetts Institute of Technology. The Holy Bible: New International Version. Genesis 36, https://web.mit.edu/jywang/www/cef/Bible/NIV/NIV_Bible/GEN+36.html

264   Massachusetts Institute of Technology. The Holy Bible: New International Version. Chronicles 11, https://web.mit.edu/jywang/www/cef/Bible/NIV/NIV_Bible/1CHRON+11.html

265   Massachusetts Institute of Technology. The Holy Bible: New International Version. 1 Chronicles 5, https://web.mit.edu/jywang/www/cef/Bible/NIV/NIV_Bible/1CHRON+5.html

266   Massachusetts Institute of Technology. The Holy Bible: New International Version. 1 Chronicles 23, https://web.mit.edu/jywang/www/cef/Bible/NIV/NIV_Bible/1CHRON+23.html

267   Julius Orion Smith III. Complex Sinusoids as Circular Motion. Stanford University. 2024. https://ccrma.stanford.edu/~jos/fp/Plotting_Complex_Sinusoids_Circular.html

MAPS & IMAGES

Page 20   The Metropolitan Museum of Art. "Head of Gudea. Neo-Sumerian. Neo-Sumerian. The Metropolitan Museum of Art," https://www.metmuseum.org/art/collection/search/324061. Wikimedia Commons contributors, "File:Head of Gudea (Metropolitan Museum of Art).jpg," Wikimedia Commons, https://commons.wikimedia.org/w/index.php?title=File:Head_of_Gudea_(Metropolitan_Museum_of_Art).jpg&oldid=737492455 (accessed June 20, 2024).

Page 28   Osama Shukir Muhammed Amin FRCP (Glasg), CC BY-SA 4.0, via Wikimedia Commons. https://commons.wikimedia.org/w/index.php?title=File:Fired_clay_statue_of_a_seated_god,_probably_Shamash._From_Ur,_Iraq._Old-Babylonian_period,_2000-1750_BCE.jpg&oldid=760203389

Page 60   Wikimedia Commons contributors, "File:Ksenophontov noah.jpg," Wikimedia Commons, https://commons.wikimedia.org/w/index.php?title=File:Ksenophontov_noah.jpg&oldid=811917966 (accessed June 6, 2024)

Page 84   Lyman Coleman. An Historical Text Book and Atlas of Biblical Geography, pp. 13, https://caleb-cangelosi-437x.squarespace.com/s/Coleman-Lyman-An-Historical-Text-Book-and-Atlas-of-Biblical-Geography.pdf

Page 90   Wikimedia Commons contributors, "File:Egypt NK edit.svg," Wikimedia Commons, https://commons.wikimedia.org/w/index.php?title=File:Egypt_NK_edit.svg&oldid=850305393 (accessed June 9, 2024)

243

Page 91   Mellish, John. David Rumsey Historical Map Collection. "The Places Recorded in the Five Books of Moses," 1815. https://www.davidrumsey.com/luna/servlet/detail/RUMSEY~8~1~250605~5517137:The-Places-Recorded-in-the-Five-Boo?sort=pub_list_no_initialsort%2Cpub_date%2Cpub_list_no%2Cseries_no&qvq=q:author%3D%22Mellish%2C%2BJohn%22;sort:pub_list_no_initialsort%2Cpub_date%2Cpub_list_no%2Cseries_no;lc:RUMSEY~8~1&mi=9&trs=12

Page 100   Abraham's Family Tree. Chart of the Genealogy of Abraham. Conforming to Jesus. https://www.conformingtojesus.com/images/webpages/genealogy_of_abraham_1.jpg

Page 109   The Library of Congress. "A New & Accurate Map of Negroland and the Adjacent Countries : Also Upper Guinea, Showing the Principle European Settlements & Distinguishing Wch. Belong to England, Denmark, Holland & C : The Sea of the Rivers Being Drawn From Surveys & the Best Modern Maps and Charts, & Regulated by Astron. Observns," https://www.loc.gov/resource/g8735.ct010406/?r=-0.457,-0.053,1.898,0.919,0

Page 110   Wikimedia Commons contributors, "File:Terracotta statue of Baal-Hammon on a throne AvL.JPG," Wikimedia Commons, https://commons.wikimedia.org/w/index.php?title=File:Terracotta_statue_of_Baal-Hammon_on_a_throne_AvL.JPG&oldid=607961579 (accessed June 6, 2024)

Page 136   Güterbock, Hans G. "The Composition of Hittite Prayers to the Sun. Journal of the American Oriental Society 78, no. 4 (1958): 237–45, pp. 241, https://www.jstor.org/stable/595787

Page 137   Rev. C.I. Scofield, D.D. The Scofield Reference Bible. The Holy Bible. 1917. pp. 1126, https://archive.org/details/scofieldreferenc0000revc/page/1126/mode/2up?view=theater

Page 138   Gray, Clifton Daggett. The Šamaš Religious Texts Classified in the British Museum Catalogue as Hymns, Prayers, and Incantations, with Twenty Plates of Texts Hitherto Unpublished, and a Transliteration and Translation of K.3182. 1901. Internet Archive, pp. 13, https://archive.org/details/samasreligiouste00grayrich

Page 139   Dictionary of Deities and Demons in the Bible. pp. 357, https://books.google.com/books?id=yCkRz5pfxz0C&pg=PA32#v=onepage&q=kengir&f=false

Page 140 Ebeling, Erich; Weidner, Ernst F.: Reallexikon der Assyriologie. Berlin ; [München] [2019]. Reallexikon der Assyriologie und vorderasiatischen Archäologie, pp. 312, https://publikationen.badw.de/en/rla/index#8407

Page 157 Hemingway, Seán, and Colette Hemingway. 1AD. "Africans in Ancient Greek Art." The Met's Heilbrunn Timeline of Art History. January 1, 1AD. https://www.metmuseum.org/toah/hd/afrg/hd_afrg.htm

Page 158 Wikimedia Commons contributors, "File:Kazimierz Zagórski - Mangbetu woman.jpg," Wikimedia Commons, https://commons.wikimedia.org/w/index.php?title=File:Kazimierz_Zag%C3%B3rski_-_Mangbetu_woman.jpg&oldid=741716227 (accessed June 21, 2024).

Page 155 Rund, Deborah, Naomi Kornhendler, Oded Shalev, and Ariella Oppenheim. 1990. "The Origin of Sickle Cell Alleles in Israel." Human Genetics 85 (5). https://www.researchgate.net/profile/Ariella-Oppenheim/publication/21177689_The_origin_of_sickle_cell_gene_in_Israel/links/5eecb4cd458515814a6ad500/The-origin-of-sickle-cell-gene-in-Israel.pdf

www.ingramcontent.com/pod-product-compliance
Lightning Source LLC
Chambersburg PA
CBHW071112160426
43196CB00013B/2551